14-120-527

FENOLLOSA AND HIS CIRCLE

With Other Essays in Biography

VAN WYCK BROOKS *has written*

MAKERS AND FINDERS: A History of
the Writer in America, 1800-1915
I. THE WORLD OF WASHINGTON IRVING
II. THE FLOWERING OF NEW ENGLAND
III. THE TIMES OF MELVILLE AND WHITMAN
IV. NEW ENGLAND: INDIAN SUMMER
V. THE CONFIDENT YEARS: 1885-1915

OPINIONS OF OLIVER ALLSTON
THE LIFE OF EMERSON
THE ORDEAL OF MARK TWAIN
THE PILGRIMAGE OF HENRY JAMES
EMERSON AND OTHERS
THREE ESSAYS ON AMERICA: America's Coming-of-Age,
Letters and Leadership, The Literary Life in America
SKETCHES IN CRITICISM
A CHILMARK MISCELLANY
THE WRITER IN AMERICA
SCENES AND PORTRAITS
JOHN SLOAN: A Painter's Life
HELEN KELLER: Sketch for a Portrait
DAYS OF THE PHOENIX
FROM A WRITER'S NOTEBOOK
THE DREAM OF ARCADIA
HOWELLS: HIS LIFE AND WORLD
FROM THE SHADOW OF THE MOUNTAIN
FENOLLOSA AND HIS CIRCLE: With Other
Essays in Biography

FENOLLOSA

AND

HIS CIRCLE

With Other Essays in Biography

By Van Wyck Brooks

E. P. DUTTON & CO., INC.

NEW YORK, 1962

ACKNOWLEDGMENTS

In order to write my essay, "Fenollosa and His Circle," I searched for material far and wide, and I have to thank a number of persons for their kindness in assisting me. Mr. Owen Biddle of Philadelphia, Fenollosa's grandson, who showed me photographs and newspaper clippings, gave me permission to quote from letters that Fenollosa wrote to Mr. Biddle's mother, Brenda Fenollosa Biddle. The nephew of Fenollosa, Mr. Manuel Fenollosa, lent me other letters, and I read the letters of Fenollosa in the New York Public Library. Mr. Usher P. Coolidge of the Fogg Museum described for me the memorials to Fenollosa and Dr. Sturgis Bigelow, beautifully cared for, at Miidera in Japan. Mr. Norris Carter, formerly curator of Fenway Court in Boston, gave me anecdotes of Mrs. Jack Gardner and her friendship with Fenollosa, and I must thank Mr. W. H. Bond of the Houghton Library at Harvard for permission to quote from the conversations of Dr. and Mrs. Frederick Winslow with Dr. Sturgis Bigelow. Mrs. Winslow Suttle of Boston had kindly told me where I could find the manuscript of these conversations. I am indebted also to Mr. Kojiro Tomita, curator of Far Eastern art at the Boston Museum of Fine Arts, who enabled me to read Dr. Sturgis Bigelow's notes on the Buddhist religion; and my dear friend, Mr. Chiang Yee, helped me greatly by reading and correcting the essay I had written. For my treatment of Edward S. Morse, Percival Lowell, Henry Adams, John La Farge and Lafcadio Hearn, I drew from well-known printed sources. As for the central figure of the "circle," whom I have seen referred to as the "shadowy" Fenollosa,—a "European scholar,"—I have long been surprised that no effort had been made to rediscover this extraordinary fellow-countryman.

Two or three years ago, on a ship to Rotterdam, I met the well-known Mrs. Cecilia Payne Gaposhkin. The English-born wife of a Russian astronomer and herself the chairman of the Department of Astronomy at Harvard, Mrs. Gaposhkin told me much about Fanny Wright of whom I had vaguely heard in connection with Walt Whitman. She had inherited a collection of letters about Fanny Wright which she permitted me later to examine. The letters had lain undisturbed for two or three generations under the bed of Mrs. Gaposhkin's great-aunt in England, and they largely concerned her forbears, Fanny Wright's friends, the daughters of John Garnett of New Brunswick, New Jersey. After their father's death, the Garnett daughters and their mother went to Paris, where they became friends of Stendhal and Prosper Mérimée, and Fanny Wright, visiting them there again, became a protégée of Lafayette and returned with him to America to establish Nashoba in Tennessee. This first attempt to liberate the Southern slaves attracted the attention of Jefferson, who was an admirer of Fanny Wright, of the Swiss historian Sismondi, a cousin by marriage of the Garnetts, and of the mother of Anthony Trollope, who came to America to live at Nashoba. The widow of the poet, Mary Shelley, was also drawn to Fanny Wright, and there were letters of hers in the collection, with many letters from Sismondi and Mrs. Trollope and many copies of letters of Lafayette. Jeremy Bentham and Robert Owen of Lanark and New Harmony, Indiana, actively figured in the story. In short, Mrs. Gaposhkin's letters were a literary treasure-trove, although their possessor was far from being unknown.

The anecdotes of Maurice Prendergast were written for the catalogue of the Prendergast exhibition in the Addison Gallery at Andover. They were related to me in 1938 by my friend Charles Prendergast, Maurice's brother. My older friend Randolph Bourne is, I find, clearly remembered forty-four years after his death. I am indebted to several persons, especially Bourne's niece, Mrs. James Sayen of Princeton, for the essay I have written about him. There have been three unpublished biographies of Randolph Bourne, aside from the published book by Louis Filler, and I have examined all these three and have to thank the authors of them. In addition, I must thank Miss Alyse Gregory, Miss Elizabeth Shepley Sergeant, Mrs. Agnes de Lima and Mr. Carl Zigrosser for permission to quote from their letters, and I am also indebted to Mr. Stephen Siteman who gave me a collection of Bourne's letters that he had assembled for one of the unpublished biographies. I found most illuminating Miss Alyse Gregory's fine novel, *Hester Craddock,* in which Bourne appears under another name. Randolph Bourne's letters brought back most poignantly to me the feeling of the years before the first world war. Those were the years when, as John Butler Yeats said, "the fiddles were tuning all over America."

V. W. B.

CONTENTS

CONTENTS

FENOLLOSA AND HIS CIRCLE

With Other Essays in Biography

FENOLLOSA AND HIS CIRCLE

I

THE Far East seemed closer to Salem than to any other American town when Ernest Fenollosa was born there in 1853. While the great East India trade had long since vanished, a considerable stream of commerce still flowed on, and even as late as the eighteen-eighties two hundred and fifty letters a month left the Salem post-office for India, China and Japan. In Singapore a visitor found that people knew much about Salem who had never heard of Boston. The name was familiar because of the sea-captains and the brigs, barques and clipper-ships hailing from there.

Fenollosa, born in the year in which Commodore Perry opened Japan,—with his "black ships" in the Bay of Tokyo,—was the son of a Spanish musician who had settled in Salem and married one of his pupils, Mary Silsbee. This young girl was the daughter of an old East India shipowner in the days when the Chinese merchants exchanged for boiled sea-slugs their silks, lacquers and teas. Fenollosa's father had been a member of a Spanish band that had been brought over in an American frigate and that had given concerts for several years during the thirties in Washington, New York, Boston and Portland, Maine. The young man had come from Malaga;

he had led the choir in the cathedral there, and, as a musical prodigy on both the piano and the violin, he had played in public from the age of ten. He had qualified for the military band that was sailing for the United States by practising all night on the French horn, and, as a teacher of music in Salem, he played in Boston orchestras, often missing the late returning train. He sometimes walked home after the concert fifteen miles through the snow, with his violin slung across his back. A Roman Catholic, he became, in Salem, an Episcopalian, and he was a protégé of George Peabody, who had a collection of musical instruments and was a player himself on the violoncello. Manuel Fenollosa spent many evenings in his patron's studio where the two made music together. George Peabody had founded in 1867 the Essex Institute of which Edward Sylvester Morse was curator and director. Morse had visited Japan in order to study brachiopods, and the younger Fenollosa was later summoned to the University of Tokyo mainly through the influence of this Salem worthy.

Ernest Fenollosa's mother well remembered as a child the arrival of her father's ships from the Far East and the long lines of stevedores carrying up through the garden paths the treasures of the Orient that had been brought back. There were boxes of tea and silks, lacquers and porcelain and curious objects from the Polynesian islands. Ernest Fenollosa's own first memory was of lying on the floor, as an infant, in the sun near a window while his mother at the piano and his father, with a violin, played what he later knew as a Beethoven sonata. A sensitive young man in the Harvard class of 1874, he sang in the chorus of the Handel and Haydn Society, and, presently studying philosophy as a disciple of Hegel, he was active in forming the Herbert Spencer Club. That was the moment when John Fiske was expounding the theory of Evo-

lution, as Herbert Spencer presented it, in popular lectures, a
new conception of the unity of nature in which all its phenomena were parts of an unbroken chain of cause and effect.
Man was involved in this cosmic drama in which sun, stars,
animals and plants followed one law of development from a
common source, all the various forms of nature evolving from
previous forms through the vast sweep of time from the pri-
meval vapour. But Fenollosa, a brilliant student who was also
the class poet, was already interested in art as well as in philosophy. He began a course in drawing and painting at the Art
School of the Boston Museum. He was a student also of
Charles Eliot Norton, the recently appointed professor of the
history of art.

It was Norton who, presently, recommended Fenollosa to
Edward S. Morse, and Morse arranged to send him to Japan
at a time when the University of Tokyo opened its doors to
foreign instruction, obliging all the students to learn English
in advance. It was true that Norton had no sympathy for
Japanese art, and he protested vigorously later when Bernard
Berenson ranked Carlo Crivelli with it rather than with European painting. Berenson said that Crivelli's forms had the
strength of line and the metallic lustre of old Satsuma and
lacquer, and Norton was outraged that anyone should give
naturalization papers, as it were, to this supposedly inferior
Oriental art. But, after all, Fenollosa's appointment had nothing, at first, to do with art; he was expected to teach political
economy and philosophy, and he lectured on the history of philosophy from Descartes to Hegel. His discourses, "lacking in
subtlety and exactness, gave an impression," said Yujiro Miyoké,
"akin to that produced by scratching one's feet outside one's
shoes, yet his eloquence had no small influence upon students."
At the same time he continued to preach Herbert Spencer,

"the world's greatest thinker," as Lafcadio Hearn called him a few years later. In Spencer, Hearn discovered the doctrines of Eastern philosophy on which he based so many imaginative visions,—the ideas of Nirvana, metempsychosis, Karma,—remarking that Shinto, Buddhism and the thinking of Spencer did not merely "mix well" but "rushed together." At this time of transition in Japan, the young men were eager for Spencer; they wished to forget altogether their ancestral religion, and they looked to Fenollosa to transplant a Western wisdom useful to Japan. He taught the most brilliant boys chosen by the Daimios of the great old feudal clans, many of whom became the statesmen of the future, and he was reappointed every two years from 1878 to 1886. But, largely influenced by Morse, who had brought him to Japan and who was collecting Japanese pottery himself, he gradually abandoned philosophy for the study of art. He had felt an instant sympathy with the Japanese spirit.

This was a moment in the history of Japan when everything was at sixes and sevens, following the break-up of the old feudal system after the fall of the Shoguns and the restoration of the Emperor in the revolution of 1868. One of the statesmen had declared that feudalism "stood on thoroughly worm-eaten, though externally lacquered and gilded pillars." The castles or fortified mansions where the feudal nobles or Daimios had dwelt were turned into schools or abandoned and ruined, their broken walls mantled with ivy and lichen, although only a dozen years before they had stood in all the pride of the Middle Ages. The great collections of most of the Daimios, who were often reduced to poverty, were broken up and scattered, or they were sold by their sons for means to live on, and the "night of Asia" that had stifled the country for centuries under the Shoguns had given place to a riot of

Western ideas. Japan, the hermit empire, that had thought itself the mightiest of nations, felt only a sudden humiliation as it confronted the wonders of the West; it went in for waltzing, mesmerism, planchette and cock-fighting, while everything Japanese seemed on the point of being swept away. As foreign teachers and missionaries flocked into the country, the Japanese ceased to cherish their traditions and heirlooms. Monasteries were forced to part with their treasures; bronze statues were sold for the old metal they contained; the ancient Noh stages were destroyed, the court troupes of actors were dispersed, and Japanese students were sent abroad in hundreds to study the miracles of Western civilization. New buildings rose in stucco and brick with crimson carpets and French clocks, European costumes came to be adopted, and French milliners appeared selling Occidental head-gear; but the ancient art of the tea-ceremony was virtually forgotten while young Japan was getting on its feet. The Samurai gave up wearing their traditional badge of two swords in the girdle and yielded up their revenues to the crown. What had taken centuries to bring about in Europe had been accomplished in a few months in Japan. Meanwhile, the old native arts were regarded as barbaric and French and Italian professors taught Japanese artists the technique of European painting and sculpture. Art students were trained in crayon drawing from Greek casts and marble madonnas, Japanese drawing was no longer taught in the schools, and stiff graphite pencils making lines that were hard and sharp replaced the soft pliant Japanese brushes of old.

To Fenollosa, for whom at first Japan was a fairyland in which he felt only the rapturous surprise of others like Lafcadio Hearn and T. S. Perry, all this seemed curiously topsy-turvy as he experienced, more and more, the shock and the enchantment of Japanese art. To him, as to Perry, the grand-nephew of the Commodore, who was later a professor in Japan, the whole Western world was simply another East Boston in comparison with this magical Oriental country, in which for twenty years the most precious works were treated as rubbish. Where else did people hang verses on trees in honour of their beauty, and where did families travel a long way before the dawn to see the first light touch the newly formed buds? Where else did the newspapers announce the spring opening of the blossoms? Fenollosa's interest in the art of Japan was aroused during his first days there by some kakemonos in the window of a curio shop. He had studied at Harvard the history of the fine arts,—he knew a good deal about European painting,—and now he was attracted by these not very good wall-hangings which he was scarcely yet in a position to judge. He bought then his first pieces of Japanese art. John La Farge had written a chapter on the subject in *Across America and Asia,* his friend Raphael Pumpelly's book of travels, and James Jackson Jarves had also written *A Glimpse at the Art of Japan* two years before Fenollosa arrived there. This was, Jarves said, a "new world to explore," but as yet no one had explored it, and Jarves's little volume was apparently the first that any Westerner had written on Japanese art. He had seen Japanese art objects at the Paris exposition of 1867, and Russell Sturgis had a collection of them as early as 1869, the year of La Farge's essay in Pumpelly's book. Jarves had studied the subject with an Italian in Florence who had learned in Paris to speak Japanese, and, like John La Farge, he had written mainly about Hokusai and the coloured prints that were virtually all the West knew of Japanese art. For the rest, neither of these writers had visited the country. As for Fenollosa, he said to Viscount Kaneko, who observed that his pictures were not the best, "I cannot see the best. There is no museum here." Thereupon

Kaneko introduced him to the Marquis Kuroda, who had kept his wealth and his collection and who said, "An American cannot judge. This art is beyond him." Nevertheless, he permitted Fenollosa to see his pictures, and Fenollosa knelt down in front of the kakemonos and remained in the room for an hour looking at them. He returned a second and a third time, remarking, "Now I have seen the work, where is a book that will tell me about its sources?" But no book that he could read existed in Japan.

Then Fenollosa set to work studying the history of Japan and China, examining all the schools of Chinese and Japanese art and reading the lives of the artists. His teacher in Tosa and Buddhist painting was Hirotaka, the last Sumiyoshi, who died in 1885, and his teacher in the Chinese and Kano painting was the third Kano Yeitoku. From Hirotaka he derived the traditional views of a thousand years, while Kano Tomonobu, another of his teachers, was the blood descendant of a school that had learned its art before 1868 in the Shogun's great academy. Kano Yeitoku was the present head of the Kano house, and Fenollosa was adopted into the Kano family and authorized to use the name Kano Yei. He called himself Kano Yeitan, "Endless Seeking." It was quite a thing, he wrote to Morse, to have the greatest critics in Japan admitting him to equality in this fashion. But, while the second-rate workmen were employed in cheap production for the foreign market,— for the craze for Japanese bric-a-brac had begun in the West,— the masters, the great artists, were driven to the wall. Hereditary artists were reduced to straits, for their traditional art was no longer cared for; and, while many artists changed their profession, only a few persevered. The grand old man of the Kano school, Kano Hogai, had been obliged to throw away his brushes. He supported himself by selling brooms and baskets while his wife helped the household by weaving at night, and Fenollosa was able to set Kano Hogai to work again by taking lessons from him at twelve yen a month. This "priestly painter with soul a-fire" of Fenollosa's *East and West,* a poem that he wrote a few years later, was, he said, "the greatest Japanese painter of recent times . . . my most valued teacher" and "one of my dearest friends."

> O sweet dead artist and seer, O tender prophetic priest,
> Draw me aside the curtain that veils the heart of your East,

So, in his poem, he invoked the painter, after his death in 1888, as the re-incarnate spirit of Oriental art; and Kano was the real hero of *The Dragon Painter,* the novel by the second Mrs. Fenollosa. Old Kano, the last of his mighty line, is looking for an apprentice who will carry on his work, and a wild young artist, a foundling, who paints only dragons, marries with tragic results his only daughter. For the rest, Fenollosa found that many upper-class people regarded all old Buddhist art as vulgar, not only Kano art but old Tosa art, Ashikaga art and Koyetsu art. They used to say, he remembered, that "nothing but ink rocks and black bamboos are refined enough for a gentleman to paint."

Fenollosa was twenty-five when he arrived in Japan, and, returning to the United States for a brief visit the following year, he married a Miss Millett, also of Salem. Together in Tokyo they lived in a large low wooden house, a European or American house that was very simple, though the woodwork had been constructed with great care. This house became in time a centre for Japanese and American artists and scholars. In summer the Fenollosas moved to Nikko where it was high and cool, an ancient city surrounded by mountains with a group of famous temples on their slopes. It was wild and rugged

there, and the stone foundations of the temples were clothed
with lichen and moss and beautiful ferns sprang from the
crevices of the rock. At intervals the clang of a temple bell
came down from the forest, as Morse wrote, like the note of a
gigantic, deep-throated bird. But to Morse the temples themselves meant nothing, at least in these early years. He was
interested mainly in the shells that he found in the mountains.

II

Morse was the magnet that attracted to Japan not only
Fenollosa but Percival Lowell,—who had heard him lecturing
in Boston,—and, especially Dr. William Sturgis Bigelow, who
accompanied him on his return for a third visit. Morse had
exposed the shortcomings of the *soi-disant* authorities in the
new universities and schools of Japan, often sea-captains and
merchants with little preparation; and the president of the
University of Tokyo had asked him to name desirable candidates for vacant positions. As one of the new professors himself who was also teaching Darwinism,—which, he said, went
well with Shintoism,—he was doing for science in Japan, for
biology, botany and archæology, what Fenollosa was to do
for art. An assistant of Agassiz in conchology, he had been lecturing in San Francisco when he heard of the great green
Japanese brachiopods, and he resolved to go and find them if
it obliged him, as he wrote, to "come down to one meal a day."
He had no interest in Japanese history, religion, philosophy
or government, but, arriving in Japan, he saw from the window
of the train a shell lying beside the railway track. It was near
Omori, and he knew that this weather-beaten shell, like others
he saw on the embankment, was at least five thousand years
old. He recognized as a kitchen midden a pile of bleached

shells near by, and this discovery of the ancient shell mounds of Omori was the beginning of archæology in Japan. In a country that had been isolated for three hundred years, archæology, like zoology and marine biology, had been totally unknown. It was said later that Japanese progress in virtually all the sciences had sprung from Morse's ninety most promising students. He had been invited to organize a department of zoology at the university and to found a museum of natural history. He had begun to teach there in 1877, the year before Fenollosa's arrival.

At Enoshima, Morse built a little laboratory in a fisherman's hut rented for him by the university, and there he dredged all day, finding the sea-bottom rich in starfish, shells, sea-urchins and other marine life. He rowed to a cave that was dedicated to the goddess protector of sea-farers, but he ignored the rock carvings and only scanned the walls closely to see if he could find twilight insects there. To his delight he discovered two little spiders, two very small sow-bugs and two cave crickets. He was too busy to enquire into the history of the red lacquer shrines on the hilltop above, dedicated to Shinto goddesses; and he soon moved his marine collection in a fifty-mile trip by jinricksha to unload them in Tokyo for the new museum. He and his assistant each carried in his lap a basket of coral, shells and glass sponges, all found in this little fisherman's village where, alone for weeks, thrown only with poor fisherfolk, he had seen the reality of Hokusai's pictures. The people were all polite, from the poorest to the richest: good manners, he discovered, were universal in Japan. He accustomed himself to eating for supper a well-filled plate of marine worms, like our own angleworms but slightly larger; and, devouring them raw, he found the taste precisely like the odour of sea-weed at low tide. He also ate things that he did not know, nor could he guess what they were, writing in his diary, "I am keeping body and its animating principle together, but long for a cup of coffee and a slice of bread and butter."

During three visits to Japan, Morse, a born collector, had developed a sudden interest in Japanese pottery, and he was to become the supreme authority in this field, consulted by experts in Europe, America and Asia. His American friends were surprised by this, for Morse had had no aesthetic training: his favourite painter was Rosa Bonheur and his favourite musical composition was the "Pilgrims' Chorus," played by a brass band. But his Tokyo doctor advised him to find some hobby, some interest to follow during his walks in the city, and he discovered in a china shop a small saucer that might almost have been a pecten shell. This was the lid of the bowl that he found, years later, in London, recognizing it at once as the missing part. At any rate, thereafter, on his daily walks, passing shops, he looked for other pieces that were modelled on shells, and he began to note, and memorize, the idiographs, the marks of the various potters on the bottoms of the pieces. He carried in his memory hundreds of these signatures. He began to study pottery with Noritano Minigawa, a student of ceramics who came to his house and knelt on his heels examining the pottery Morse had purchased during the walks of a week. Minigawa taught Morse the secrets of this art, instructing him in the feeling of clays from the various provinces, along with the methods of firing the glazes. His enthusiasm for their pottery charmed the Japanese. Count Kanaka from a far-away province presented him with a collection of Takatori ware, and Count Okuma was struck by Morse's appreciation of every piece when he showed Morse his collection. He sent the whole collection as a gift to Morse's house. A few years later, Viscount Tanaka, who was collecting pottery himself, said, "That rascal Morse has carried away every decent bit of old pottery in Japan and put it behind glass in the Boston Museum."

While Morse had come to Japan with his dredges and his microscopes to study the various brachiopods in Japanese waters, he was soon travelling to distant provinces as much in search of pottery as for this more strictly professional interest. As an advisor to the government in science, he had official freedom to travel in all parts of the Japanese empire, and he went through sections of the country where no foreigner had ever been before. He rode on horseback over densely forested mountain ranges inhabited only by bears and hairy Ainus, walking many miles in search of ancient shell-heaps as well as of pots, jars, cups and bowls. Adaptable, adventurous and ready for any chance event, he dined once at the governor's house in a far-away province. He had been told that there was a cave in the side of a hill in which were a few pottery vessels. Knowing the peculiar form of cave-pottery further north, he asked the governor for a brush and paper and ventured to draw the outlines of the vessels in the cave, aware that caves were burial-places and that the vessels were placed there for offerings of rice and wine to the departed spirits. Then, approaching the cave, he entered by a hole in the roof and dropped into water nearly up to his waist. There was a momentary silence, he wrote, and then shouts of horror came echoing down from the openings in the roof. His assistant told him that great poisonous centipedes were crawling out through this aperture, and, having on his wide-brimmed hat, and a slippery rubber coat, he noted that huge centipedes were dropping on him. He had supposed that they were crumbs of earth and pebbles tumbling from the sides of the ragged hole. He stood in a cascade of the venomous creatures that scampered around the walls of the cave, dropping from the ceiling as so many frightened spiders would have done. Growing accustomed to the dim light, he saw them by hundreds floating in the water, and, waiting till the current drained them off, he groped around for pottery in the sand at the bottom. There was a deposit on the floor of two feet or more of sand and mud, and luckily the centipedes could not retain a hold on his slippery overcoat and tumbled into the water as fast as they struck him. He got three specimens of the creatures for his museum, made a rapid sketch of the wall of the cave facing the opening and then had a rope lowered to pull him up. He induced two jinricksha men to go down and scratch about in the sand, and they discovered four specimens of pottery, one perfect, another slightly broken and large fragments of two others. Then the governor of the province drew out his sketch, and he spoke to the natives in wonder that a foreigner could describe in advance the shapes of the vessels to be found there, none of which they themselves had ever seen. The governor presented Morse with the Satsuma bottle from which he had been drinking.

By this time, the all-curious Morse knew Japanese pottery better than any Westerner had ever known it, aware of the delicate distinctions in methods of glazing and the subtle qualities of the colour-tones. He had travelled through all the provinces from the extreme North to the Southwest, visiting the famous potters of Kyoto where he gathered a mass of notes about the generations of families there. One old potter represented the twelfth generation of his family who had made for three hundred years a pottery called Raku. He showed Morse a complete set of Raku bowls, exemplifying all the generations. Morse made outlines and rubbings of the marks, and he finally packed up twenty-nine hundred pots to carry back to Salem with him. He even made a brief visit to China, stopping at Shanghai and Hong Kong and going up to Canton on the Pearl river. He engaged a boat and a crew of six hands to call at a pottery village not far from Canton, putting a pistol in his pocket, for he was surrounded by a hostile crowd, and he watched a pot in process of being made there. Meanwhile, he had studied in Japan the intricate tea-ceremony and had even taken lessons in Japanese singing. To master the tea-ceremony he joined a class of Japanese, and the teacher told him that he was the first foreigner ever to take lessons in the art. The famous teacher of Noh singing and acting, Minoru Umewaka, seemed pleased that a foreigner should wish to take lessons in this other art. He had, adjoining his house, a stage for Noh plays, and Morse read slowly in Umewaka's singing-book the words that he was expected to learn, writing the words down as well as he could. Umewaka placed before him a little music-stand and gave him a fan which he held resting on his leg, while the master sang a line and Morse sang it after him, then another till he reached the eleventh line of the composition. After trying it twice that way, the two sang together; and Morse realized how rich and sonorous Umewaka's voice was. At the end Umewaka told him, perhaps to encourage him, that probably in a month's time he could sing in a Noh play. Morse felt that by taking lessons in the tea-ceremony and Japanese singing he might learn many things from the Japanese standpoint.

Morse kept a daily journal in Japan, and he published this many years later under the title *Japan Day by Day*. His friend Dr. Sturgis Bigelow had urged him to do this. Bigelow had written, "You are still frittering away your valuable time on the lower forms of animal life, which anybody can attend to, instead of devoting it to the highest, about the manners and customs of which no one is so well qualified to speak as

you. Honestly, now, isn't a Japanese a higher organism than
a worm? Drop your damned Brachiopods. They'll always be
there . . . Remember that the Japanese organisms which you
and I knew familiarly forty years ago are vanishing types,
many of which have disappeared completely from the face of
the earth, and that men of our age are literally the last people
who have seen these organisms alive. For the next generation
the Japanese we knew will be as extinct as belemnites." In
fact, so little had the country changed that most of his notes
and sketches might have been records of a thousand years
before: there were the wandering story-tellers and various
habits of the Japanese as they were before the Revolution.
Many of the men still wore their hair in a waxed queue at the
back of the head, and little by little Morse understood why
the Japanese had always described as barbarians the foreigners
they encountered. House-breaking and pocket-picking were
unknown in this pagan country,—you could leave your umbrella on a bench in a crowd and find it there an hour later;
and at any hour of day or night a man was safer in the wilder
regions than he would be in the quiet streets of Salem. Their
houses had no locks or bolts or keys, and in their methods of
house-adornment they showed greater refinement than the
people of the West, for their tastes were normally artistic.
Precepts from the classics decorated the walls of even country
inns, and one looked out on a garden with a tank full of turtles, perhaps, aquatic ferns, a bronze crab and a rock. There
were as yet few railroads, there were no automobiles, and the
jinrickshas spun noiselessly over earthen roads in all but absolute silence, the barelegged runners moving with a long
swinging lope. There was little that Morse omitted in his
diary of the late seventies, with his accounts of flower-
arrangement, types and type-setting, women's hair-dressing,

thatched roofs, falconry, games and outdoor fairs. His hundreds of pen-and-ink sketches were made under trying circumstances, often in bumping jinrickshas or in jostling crowds, but years before Lafcadio Hearn he gave one a detailed account of Japan that could never have been equalled or replaced.

III

There were many entries in Morse's diary referring to Ernest Fenollosa, one of four western professors who sang with spirit on a certain occasion "Old Hundred" and "All Honour to the Soldier Be." Fenollosa wrote for Morse a boatman's song, showing that, although he was a lover of the beautiful, he was yet simple in his tastes. He might have said, like the Greeks of whom Thucydides wrote, "We cultivate the mind without loss of manliness." But it was only in the summer months that he could study Japanese art and find the time to travel and visit the temples, in some of the remote provinces, that were full of treasures, though by 1882 he had abandoned philosophy and gone into what became his permanent study. Before long he received an official appointment, and the government paid his expenses and even made him, within a few years, Commissioner of Fine Arts for the empire. With Morse he travelled hither and thither, Morse looking for pots and he for sculpture and pictures. His fellow-commissioner was Okakura Kakuzo, the author of the well-known *Book of Tea*. It was Okakura who organized the Imperial Art School in Tokyo. He too was opposed to the wholesale introduction of Western art and manners, and he was all for preserving the old life of Japan.

Fenollosa found a condition that was much like Italy's, as

Ruskin described this in *The Stones of Venice*. In 1846, Ruskin saw buckets set on the floor of the Scuola di San Rocco to catch the rain that came through the pictures of Tintoretto on the ceiling. In the Doges' Palace, Paulo Veronese's pictures were laid on the floor to be repaired, and Ruskin saw the breast of a white horse reillumined with a brush, at the end of a stick five feet long, dipped in a common house-painter's vessel of paint. More ancient masters were treated with neglect and contempt; and gold-background pictures were brought out of suppressed convents and churches and burned for the sake of the gold that was found in the ashes. In 1845, Ruskin said, even the most learned tourists had never heard Ghirlandajo's name. This was the time when James Jackson Jarves made the famous collection of primitives that nobody wanted. A tattered Correggio was found in the hands of an old-clothes dealer, a Michelangelo was sold by a rag-and-bone man, and Jarves discovered a great piece of sculpture in an ash-can. The "Muse of Cortona," when first disinterred, painted on slate, was used by a peasant to stop a hole in an oven. Just so, in 1884, Fenollosa found in an ash-barrel a fine ceramic head of Buddha, one of the earliest relics of the Tendai sculpture. It was probably part of a complete statue destroyed in the twelfth century by a fire, and the priests were tired of keeping the fragment and threw it away. In 1880, at Shodaiji, amid a mass of broken statues, he found a life-sized piece that seemed to have been one of the original Greco-Buddhist models, or at least experiments. It was like a huge wooden doll, apparently surfaced with over-layers of modelled clay. That same year he discovered a Bodhisattva with a beautiful plastic play of drapery over the shoulder, so like a Roman emperor's portrait-statue that he affectionately called it "Cæsar." In 1879, a year after he arrived in Japan, he had acquired a work from a picture-dealer who had never heard the name of Ganku and knew not how to place him. It was Ganku's masterpiece, a picture of two Japanese sacred deer, and Fenollosa believed this to be one of the finest animal paintings of the whole world.

But, for works of art, the temples were the chief treasure-houses, and they were usually placed in the most picturesque spots, at the head of a ravine, in a grove of trees or on top of a mountain. There was, for instance, the famous temple of Horiuji with its many buildings and many treasures of Korean art which had already, as models, found their way to Japan. On the immense altar of Kondo stood a solid block of masonry, about eighty feet long and thirty feet wide, and there one found the Tamamushi shrine, the tall wooden Kwannon and various smaller pieces. Other buildings were crowded with paintings, statues and sacred utensils brought to this central monastery, making Horiuji a natural and national museum. There, in the summer of 1884, Fenollosa and Okakura found the most important existing monument of Korean art, the standing Buddha in the Yumedono pavilion. This most beautiful statue was a little larger than life, and the priests of Horiuji said the central shrine in the octagonal pavilion had not been opened for more than two hundred years; but Fenollosa had credentials from the government which enabled him to requisition the opening of all godowns and shrines. The priests resisted for a long while, alleging that in punishment for the sacrilege an earthquake might well destroy the temple. Finally, Fenollosa prevailed, on fire as he was with the prospect of such a treasure, and "I shall never forget," he wrote, "our feelings as the long disused key rattled in the rusty lock. Within the shrine appeared a tall mass closely wrapped about in swathing bands of cotton cloth upon which the dust of ages had gathered." There were five hundred yards of cloth, and "our eyes and nostrils were in danger of being choked with the pungent dust. But at last the final folds of the covering fell away, and this marvellous statue, unique in the world, came forth to human sight for the first time in centuries. It was a little taller than life, but hollow at the back, carved most carefully from some hard wood which had been covered with gilding, now stained to the yellow brown of bronze. The head was ornamented with a wonderful crown of Korean openwork gilt bronze, from which hung long streamers of the same material set with jewels. We saw at once that it was the supreme masterpiece of Korean creation."

Horiuji was the first great monastery in Japan,—it remained the first great art museum,—and this, the finest known specimen of Korean art, had been made probably at the end of the sixth century. It was the first large work of sculpture brought to Japan when the spark of civilization leaped to the island empire from the neighbouring peninsula of Korea, and from this figure of Buddha the first Japanese sculptors derived their finest inspiration. There, too, was the first great original Japanese statue, a figure of the Bodhisattva Kwannon cut out of wood by Prince Shotoku. In the great monastery of Daitokuji, in the fields north of Kyoto, Fenollosa spent many a long series of days examining the wonderful Chinese paintings and questioning the friendly abbot concerning the principles of Zen; and he first saw Tofokuji in 1880, when it was an enormous monastery that was still intact. At the south it had a massive gateway, and there were two colossal halls between this and the famous hanging causeway over the valley. These halls were faced externally with gigantic pillars, made of single trunks of Chinese cedars, about fifty feet in height, that were supposed to have been floated from the head-waters of the

Yangtse and across the China Sea. The central halls were destroyed by fire in 1882, but Fenollosa lived for weeks at a time with the kindly Zen priests, and his artists were privileged to copy for months many of the wonderful relics. But "no visit," he wrote, "can give a tithe of the solemn-sweet impression—particularly at night and morning—of cool sanded courts crossed irregularly with granite steps, and banked with Sung compositions of ancient shrub and mossy stone and trickling stream . . . In those sweet days of the early eighties . . . I felt like an unworthy degenerate Noami privileged to revisit the very treasures that had delighted his eyes four hundred and fifty years before."

On three separate occasions in the eighteen-eighties, Fenollosa studied, as imperial commissioner, the treasures of the famous Shosoin of Nara, erected in the year 749. This great museum was opened only once a year, for drying, and at that time an imperial rescript was necessary for each visitor admitted. There were preserved, from the early T'ang period, writing-paper in rolls, garments from the imperial wardrobe, furs and slippers of the Empress, jewels, pans, bowls, knives, spoons and forks. There were bedsteads and couches, vases and boxes, silks for embroidery, banners and screens, manuscripts, mirrors and weapons, mostly deposited there in 749. In 1882, Fenollosa photographed the rubbish heaps at the back of the Chukondo altar of Kofukuji, where masses of remains and the broken "bones" of composition statues mingled with splendid contours of Buddhist torsos and the armour of knights. Then, in 1884, he saw a motley collection of deities in a chapel at Udzumasa, since destroyed, the whole pantheon, seated or standing, gilded or in colour, and before them the small square lacquered altar, with a silver mirror and a gilded apex. There were four candlesticks that burned lights of four colours, and the small square mat where you might sit and make yourself a purged circle immune against the devil. Among the works of art he found were the little bronze Kwannon of Contemplation, later owned by the Fine Arts Academy in Kyoto. He discovered this during one of his early explorations and bought it as a nucleus for treasures which he hoped that a museum attached to the coming school would eventually collect. He had bought in 1882 a great painting of Monotonobu which turned up in the emporium of Yamanaka in Osaka. This had been given away to a retainer by the Marquis Hashisake, as so many Daimio treasures were given in the sad parting of the years before. Then families of faithful retainers, loyal at times through seven centuries, were absolved from their feudal vows and became citizens of a new democratic Japan. Treasures like this soon found their way into pawnshops, and so, at a time when the revived taste of a new aristocracy had not yet formed, into the general market. Thus Fenollosa purchased for twenty-five yen what would be worth thousands were it sold in the Japan of twenty years later. When he first arrived, he said, but for the Kano Academy and the Shogun's passive patronage of Buddhist temples, all the Godoshis, Ririomins, Kakeis, Bayens and Mokkeis in Japan would have been swept away and burnt up as old lumber.

For instance, the name of Okio was hardly known in 1878 by Japanese dealers or collectors, though later he was held to be one of the great national geniuses and works by him were to be found in all the principal collections of the world. Fenollosa had known Wunkin, one of the last masters of Japanese flower painting, during the year in which he died, 1880, and he bought from the last artist of his line Kano Tanyu's copy of Mesanobu's great portrait of Confucius in the Ashikaga university, based upon an important Sung statue. One of Takan-

obu's finest pieces was the elaborate set of large paintings
narrating, in separate dramatic scenes, the whole romantic
life of Shotoku Taishi. This was the most interesting heir-
loom of the Sumiyoshi family at the death of its last patriarch,
Fenollosa's teacher, Hirotaka, in 1885. It was regarded by
generations of Tosas and Sumiyoshis as the typical example of
Takanobu in Japan, and Hirotaka sold it on his deathbed to
Fenollosa to save it from the possible wrangling of heirs and to
leave money to his widow. When Fenollosa had arrived in
Japan, no artist of the school of Yeitoku was clearly differenti-
ated from the founder, and through several years it was his
absorbing labour to identify the various styles of some fifteen
or twenty of his followers. The last professional Busshi was a
young man whose workshop, stacked with ancient and modern
portraits, Buddhas and carved works, he visited in Kyoto in
1882. This artist died a few years later, and the tradition was
lost, except in sporadic amateur work among a few Shingon
and Tendai priests.

In Japan, Fenollosa was known as an antiquarian, and he
was especially interested in the old aristocratic art of the Kano
and Tosa schools depicting the ancient court life. This was the
art that was favoured by the grandees, the three hundred
Daimios and the four hundred thousand Samurai, the sworded
gentry of the past, a mediæval art involved with Buddhism as
the art of mediæval Europe was involved with Christianity.
It was equally hieratic and idealistic. The upper classes despised
the Ukiyoye school of Japanese painting and print-designing
that for the last three centuries had expressed the common
people and their life. Its artists, sprung mostly from the ranks
of the people, confined themselves to the recreation and occupa-
tions of their class, and they reflected every phase and change
of fashion in the life of the capital. They mirrored Japanese

everyday life with the scenes and activities of women of the middle and lower classes. Among them were Utamaro, Hiroshige and Hokusai, who died at the age of ninety and with whom the history of Ukiyoye practically closed. In touch with the people, rendering modern low life, as the Tosa school had never done, they were the only school that Europeans and Americans knew as yet much about, for many Japanese prints were exported to London and Paris as soon as Japan was opened in the eighteen-fifties. John La Farge and Whistler studied them, especially the work of Hokusai, the great vulgarizer, the "Dickens of Japan," who was regarded in Europe as the greatest Japanese artist of all time. By the upper classes in Japan, Hokusai was condemned, Fenollosa said, as coarse and uninspired, although Fenollosa was not at first aware of his most important work, a painting on a large eight-panelled screen. He came to think this challenged comparison with the finest mural painting of the West, as "one of the world's transcendent masterpieces."

Fenollosa was to publish in 1896 *The Masters of Ukiyoye,* a glorified catalogue of the "popular school of Japanese artists," exhibited in New York in January of that year. This plebeian genre art, unknown to the Samurai, had developed side by side with the legitimate theatre under the first great actor of Japan, Danjuro, a histrionic art, also shunned by the upper classes, that became an organ of self-expression of the common people. The pit of the theatre was fragrant with the odours of raw fish and saki. Both this and the single-sheet print were regarded as hopelessly vulgar by the aristocratic admirers of Noh plays and Tosa art. Fenollosa pursued and finally captured the most important date at which hand-colouring went out and block-printing came in,—the application of colour by impression from flat wooden blocks. The two methods of colouring overlapped by a few years. The making of the last cheap hand-coloured prints stopped about 1742-1743.

"Of course it is natural," Fenollosa wrote to Edward S. Morse, "that some of the old fogy Japanese are suspicious and unwilling to trust me. I am proving that some of their supposed treasures are relatively worthless and bringing forth the real gems from unknown holes . . . I [have] bought several pictures dating from 700 and 900 A.D. Already people here [in Tokyo] are saying that my collection must be kept here in Japan for the Japanese. I have bought a number of the very greatest treasures secretly. The Japanese as yet don't know that I have them. I wish I could see them all safely housed forever in the Boston Art Museum; and yet, if the Emperor or the Mombusho should wish to buy my collection, wouldn't it be my duty to humanity, all things considered, to let them have it? What do you think?" Morse had already raised this question. Travelling, in 1882, with Fenollosa and Okakura, who sat listening while the others discussed the treasures found during the day, Morse remarked, "Many fine things of Japanese art are now on the market, like those we are buying. It is like the life-blood of Japan seeping from a hidden wound. They do not know how sad it is to let their beautiful treasures leave the country." Okakura had a sudden thought, and on their return to Tokyo he went to the officials and begged them to realize the situation. This resulted in the law of Koko Ho (national treasures), in 1884, that required all the remaining objects of ancient art to be registered and restricted from export. In return, this resulted in the great museums of Tokyo, Nara and Kyoto. But Fenollosa had already sold his collection of a thousand or more paintings to Dr. G. C. Weld of Boston to remain as the Weld-Fenollosa collection in the Boston Museum.

Again Fenollosa wrote to Morse, "I cannot see why my work this summer [1884] was not just as important at bottom as much of that which the world's archæologists are doing in Greece and Turkey. Of course people don't see the practical importance of Eastern civilization for the world with the same vividness as they do that of Greek culture . . . But from the point of view of human history as a whole it is absolutely indispensable. I expect the time will come when it will be considered as necessary for a liberally educated man to know the names and deeds of man's great benefactors in the East, and the steps in advance in their culture, as it is now to know Greek and Latin dates and the flavour of their production." Meanwhile, he founded, in 1881, a club of Japanese painters that was called Kangwakwai, assembling representations of the various schools, meeting once a month and exchanging opinions with various masters. The chief inspirer of this was Kano Hogai, last of the really great artists of old Japan, descendant of a long line of Kano painters; and the club arranged, in chronological order, old and new pictures and advised young painters to produce new works. A loan collection of Daimio treasures was exhibited annually at the club.

By 1882, a reaction had begun in the upper classes, and Fenollosa joined with others in starting the Art Club of Nobles. Three artists, including, with himself, the heads of the Kano and Tosa schools, composed the committee for criticism, and they undertook to criticize any paintings that were brought and give certificates if these were desired. Fenollosa denounced in a fervent speech a race that permitted its birthright to slip through its fingers, making no effort to retain it, and he deplored the tendency to teach American drawing in the schools and to study sculpture under Italian artists. At the end of the speech there was great excitement, and a rebirth followed of national pride and interest in Japanese art. In 1885 the use of Japanese ink, brushes and paper was reintroduced into the schools. Fenollosa was entrusted with the task of registering the art treasures of the country. He knew all the well-known connoisseurs, he had visited all the important temples, and he had been thrown with all the dealers and collectors as well as the remaining artists. In fact, Fenollosa, who persuaded the government to preserve the old worthy temples and shrines, had led the Japanese to respect their ancient tradition and keep it intact. "An American, Fenollosa, taught us how to admire the unique beauty of our art," said Professor Yaichi Haga; and when, in 1886, Fenollosa was about to return for a while to America, the Emperor said to him, "You have taught my people to know their own art; in going back to your great country, I charge you, teach them also."

IV

That was still some years in the future when Dr. Sturgis Bigelow arrived in Japan in 1882, in the company of Edward S. Morse, now director of the Peabody Museum of Salem, who was homesick, after his earliest visits, for Japan. The two had met at Tuckernuck island, off Nantucket, and Morse, convincing himself that his notes needed amplification, persuaded Dr. Bigelow to return with him. "Well, for good or ill," Bigelow wrote to Morse years later, "the cruise to Japan was the turning point of my life." There, in fact, he was to remain for seven years after Morse sailed back to Europe and America.

Now, Morse's Lowell lectures of 1881 had engrossed many of his friends in Boston. They actually started a movement, for there the world seemed to be moving too fast and the Bostonians found too much that was ugly in their civilization.

The "cloistered loveliness of old Japan," as Lafcadio Hearn was to call it, seemed gentler and kinder than the Western world, slower in its motions, always smiling, and, above all, endowed with an exquisite taste. Sturgis Bigelow was soon followed by the young Percival Lowell, and presently by Henry Adams and John La Farge, while in 1883 came Mrs. Jack Gardner, the "gloom-dispeller, corpse-reviver and general chirker-up," as Dr. Bigelow called her. Bigelow himself was rather like Dr. Peter Alden in Santayana's novel *The Last Puritan*, the doctor who never practised medicine and only put to the proof the adage, "Physician, heal thyself," who sailed in his yacht, the "Black Swan," with two Buddhas decorating the poop with their golden shrines. In his dream of Oriental loveliness, Dr. Peter Alden collected ivory carvings in China and Japan, intending to present them to the Boston Museum of Fine Arts. Dr. Bigelow had studied in Paris under Pasteur. In Japan he became immersed in Buddhist philosophy before he returned to lecture on Buddhism at Harvard.

Fenollosa joined Bigelow and Morse when they arrived in Tokyo for a journey to the great cities of Japanese art and antiquities, inaccessible to most foreigners hitherto; and, staying at native inns, they travelled by boat and jinricksha, for the railways had not yet been extended through the empire. This was a trip through the southern provinces; they went overland to Kyoto and then by steamer through the Inland Sea; and "We shall see," Morse wrote, "a little of the life of old Japan. I shall add a great many specimens to my collection of pottery. Dr. Bigelow will secure many forms of swords, guards and lacquers, and Mr. Fenollosa will increase his remarkable collection of pictures, so that we shall have in the vicinity of Boston by far the greatest collection of Japanese art in the world." Hunting for screens, pots and painted scrolls, they stopped at Nagoya and Nara, and in the evening, by candlelight, sprawling on soft straw mats, they showed one another the treasures found during the day, old swords, kakemonos, tea-jars and bowls. Arriving at Nagoya after dark, they spent four days there, Morse ransacking the city for pottery and the others for lacquers and paintings, and, visiting the curio-shops in every town, they rode across the plains of Osaka to the mountains beyond. At Osaka, Dr. Bigelow discovered an interesting temple pond in which were hundreds of turtles of various sizes, and he became very fond of raw fish at dinner. Meanwhile, he made a specialty of collecting Nishiyama Hoyens, of which he gave sixty or seventy to the Boston Museum. Morse came up from Kobe on a steamer that conveyed to Tokyo a number of ambassadors from Korea, all genial men with whom he became quickly acquainted. He made surreptitiously a few sketches of them, and he managed to ask them many questions, as they spoke Japanese, and to understand their answers. Two of them wore large goggles with coloured glasses, and they allowed him to examine them when, to his surprise, he found they were made of clear smoky-quartz crystals in tortoise-shell frames.

The following year Dr. Bigelow wrote to Morse, who had left Japan, "Everything the same, even Fenollosa stretched out flat on his back reading Emerson. Everything is just as it was a year ago. But we miss the old Woolly [Morse]. We want to see the look that he used to wear when he came in from a raid round a new town, accompanied by two or three grinning, astonished and obsequious dealers bearing a pile of boxes and loose pots. And then the triumph of the O.W. when he displayed his treasures,—got them all out on the floor, finally producing from his pocket as a thing too precious to let the other men bring home, some particularly demoralized-looking old coprolite. 'A Koyashi, by God! 650 years old; a genuine Unko Koyashi with a stamp! Never saw but two others, and one of those Ninagawa asked 30 yen for, and I got this for 15 sen!' "

Still a year later, 1884, Fenollosa wrote to Morse, "Been off two months and a half with the doctor [Bigelow] and an officer of Mombusho, who was sent on a special commission to travel with me and study art. We have been through all the principal temples in Yamashiro and Yamato armed with government letters and orders, have ransacked godowns, and brought to light pieces of statues from the lowest stratum of debris in the top stories of pagodas 1300 years old. We may say in brief that we have made the first accurate list of the great art treasures kept in the central temples of Japan . . . The doctor has taken 200 photographs and I innumerable sketches of art objects (paintings and statues); and, more than all, I have recovered the history of Japanese art from the sixth to the ninth centuries A.D., which has been completely lost. I have done it by a chain of close reasonings, based on a comparative study of all the specimens, many of which have never been shown to anyone before . . . I have found Chinese things called Japanese, and vice versa, many Japanese called Korean, new things called old, and even some old things called new; the names of individual artists hopelessly mixed up. Yet this is the result of native criticism for centuries."

Dr. Bigelow himself took up the study of Japanese gardens; then, falling in with a learned old abbot, a priest of the Shingon sect, he became an ardent Buddhist, taking spiritual exercises under the abbot's direction. Received into Buddhism, he "emanated a peaceful radiance," one of his later friends said, "mingled with a faint fragrance of toilet water," but this was after he returned to Boston, full of Buddhist lore, believing he had been aware of his former incarnations. He preferred, this friend said, an Asiatic religion while wearing beautiful Charvet neckties and handsome English clothes, and, a bearded mystic and epicure, he lived, in fastidious luxury, with the rarest wines and exquisite food and every kind of exotic delicacy. He was surrounded in Boston with Oriental porcelains, bronzes and tapestries; but, meanwhile, he was still in Japan when Percival Lowell arrived there, on the first of four visits, in 1883. A young man of fashion, Lowell hired a house in Tokyo and set up a luxurious establishment there, writing, first or last, three books about Japan and studying the language and the people. Fenollosa saw much of him and Morse became his lifelong friend, largely responsible for his appointment as advisor to the government of Korea. Lowell was given complete charge of the embassy to the United States, the first diplomatic mission from the Hermit Kingdom to any foreign power. He wrote a book, *Chosŏn*, about Korea, portraying the life of the upper classes that were soon swept away, never to reappear. Only two other Westerners at that time could speak the Korean language.

Lowell wrote a light-hearted account, rather in the manner of Robert Louis Stevenson, of a wild journey to the province of Noto, a peninsula that stood out from the Western coast of Japan with bold headlands and deep-bosomed bays. It was virtually unknown to foreigners, though one of them was resting at an inn with Lowell who said, "The passing of royalty or even a circus would have been tame news in comparison with this." Lowell passed a Daimio's castle turned into a public school, and he saw an old crone squatting on the bank of a river, contemplating what looked like the remains of a hoop-skirt, dangling from a pole half in and half out of the water. A similar bit of still life, bordering the brink like a meditative frog, sat on the other side of the river, and, recognizing them as the identical fisherfolk sitting in the paintings of Tomonobu, he almost looked for the master's seal somewhere in the corner of the landscape. Before *Noto,* he had written *The Soul of the Far East,* a "colossal, splendid, godlike book," Lafcadio Hearn exclaimed when he first read it in a New York bookshop. "Incomparably the greatest of all books on Japan," Hearn continued. "I have just finished it" and "feel like John of Patmos. I am not vain enough to think I can ever write anything so beautiful." It was, in fact, this book that largely suggested Lafcadio Hearn's going to Japan.

After his third visit in 1891, Lowell wrote *Occult Japan,* a study of the psychic phenomena connected with the Shinto faith, a book that was largely influenced by William James. In Shintoism, peaks were peculiarly sacred spots, and Lowell climbed Ontake, or the Honourable Peak, which ten thousand pilgrims ascended every summer. He watched three young men, clad in pilgrim white, lost in prayer before a shrine on this slumbering volcano. One pilgrim fell into a trance, another asked the name of the god who had thus deigned to descend and a third entered a similar possession. "I am Hokkai," a voice replied to the question. Mountains were especially good points for entering another world. Ontake was the mountain of trance and to its summit pilgrims ascended not simply to adore but to be there actually incarnate by the gods. Divine possession took place on it daily through the six weeks in which the gods received men. There were pilgrim clubs that took the road from the middle of July to the first of September, crowds wending their way to some shrine or other, peripatetic picnic parties faintly flavoured with piety, some to sacred summits, some to lowland shrines. The great shrines of Ise were especially favoured by pilgrimesses, bands of fifty to a hundred maidens of Osaka and Kyoto, at the time when the cherries

were in bloom. Sometimes little girls of eleven or twelve surreptitiously clubbed together and tramped to a shrine. Ise was
a province of what was still old Japan, and one could take it
for fairyland when it was all aglow with cloud-like masses of
pink-white blossoms. Carnival crowds of men, women and
children journeyed along the country roads chanting as they
moved beneath the canopy of flowers. Three hundred thousand pilgrims walked every spring to the shrines of Ise.

Percival Lowell gazed into the caves that had once been
inhabited by hermits. There were still a few hermits in the
hills, seeing no man during the three years they spent there,
and he fell in with some of them after their return to society.
Then he witnessed the Shinto miracles,—sometimes at seances
in his own house,—climbing the ladder of sword-blades, walking over live coals and the ordeal by boiling water. The priest
walked round a boiling kettle, repeating the scalding douche
with growing self-abandonment, lashing the water until he
collapsed upon the ground. These miracles belonged to the
esoteric side of Shinto, the way of the gods, the old native
faith, the ancient belief of the Japanese people the sentiment
of which throbbed as strongly as ever in the nation's heart. It
was an adoration of family wraiths, regarding the dead as
spiritually living, the antithesis of the Buddhist Nirvana that
regarded the living as spiritually dead.

Percival Lowell left Japan in 1893, and, never coming back,
he gave himself up to astronomy, his earliest interest. Morse,
who visited Flagstaff later, was heart and soul with Lowell in
his study of what he took for canals on Mars. Meanwhile,
Lowell wrote from Japan to his little sister Amy Lowell, who
grew up knowing all about the fox-sprites and spider-demons
of which he had told her in his long letters. Her poems were

to abound in time with the two-sworded nobles and the Japanese pixies of which she had first heard from Percival Lowell.

v

Fenollosa became interested, in 1882, in Noh plays. He fell in with Minoru Umewaka, who had taught Morse Noh singing, and he was struck at once by the analogy between the Noh plays and the early morality plays of Europe. The Noh theatre had been established at the close of the fourteenth century, absorbing dances performed at Shinto shrines in honour of spirits or the gods, and the Noh plays had been enjoyed exclusively by the military class; they were the principal entertainment of the Samurai. As they relied on a certain knowledge of past story or legend, the common people could not participate in them, and at first they had been performed only by Shinto priests in shrines to propitiate the gods. There had been performances of Noh lasting five days at marriages and initiations of the Shoguns, and in the Tokagawa days every rich Daimio had his own stage and his complete collection of properties. Noh was a necessary part of official ceremonies at Kyoto. Young nobles and princes, forbidden to attend the popular naturalistic theatre, were encouraged to perform in spectacles where music, speech, song and dance created an image of nobility and beauty. To Minoru Umewaka was due the fact that Noh did not wholly vanish with the overthrow of the Shoguns in 1868, for, at the restoration of the Mikado, people were convinced that an art so closely connected with the Shogunate ought to disappear with it.

Minoru Umewaka was one of the actors in the Shogun's main troupe, and he was acting in the Shogun's garden when the news of Perry's arrival stopped the play. For three years, performances ceased entirely and the troupes of actors were dispersed. Then, in 1871, Umewaka bought for a song an ex-Daimio's stage, set it up on the bank of the Sumida river at Tokyo and began to train his two sons. He bought masks and robes at sales of impoverished nobles, selling his own clothes to pay for them, and, while old actors returned and joined him, he lived in a mean house on a mean street. Possessing texts and stage directions, he guarded the old tradition, giving at first private performances like those that had once been given in noblemen's palaces and houses.

Fenollosa first called upon old Mr. Umewaka, presenting him with a large box of eggs, and asking him to accept fifteen yen as a gift, in consideration of his kindness to Professor Morse. Umewaka asked Fenollosa to sing for him, and, when Fenollosa sang "Hansakaba," he said he was already advanced enough to sing in a Japanese company. Fenollosa noted that "Morse and I are the only foreigners who have ever been taught Noh, and I am the only foreigner now practising it." For twenty years thenceforward he studied under Umewaka and his sons this art of posture, dancing, chanting and acting that was not mimetic, a drama of masks on a symbolic stage; for there was always in Japan a distinction between serious drama and the mimetic drama of the common people. At the same time he took down the oral traditions of the stage before the revolution of 1868, and he prepared translations of about fifty of the texts.

Thus the Noh drama was saved from the ashes of the Revolution. It had in it elements that had disappeared from the Western stage, resembling not only the morality play but religious mysteries and dances like those of the mediæval mass. The word "Noh" signified exhibition of talent, or accomplishment, and it had developed into a kind of opera in which the

performers alternately recited and danced. There were sometimes as many as nine players, all men, and it was quite usual
for an old actor, wearing a mask, to take the part of a young
woman. For the music, there were a flute-player, two hand-
drummers and sometimes also a big drum beaten with a stick.
A ship was represented by skeletons of willows or osiers
painted green, a fruit-tree by a bush in a pot, and a house,
palace or cottage was represented by four posts covered with
a roof. An actor usually carried a fan that was used to represent a knife or a brush; and, while dances were performed
with solemn gestures and slow steps, the text was partly in
prose, partly in verse. The Noh stage was a platform surrounded by the audience on three sides and reached by a
bridge from the green-room; it sloped slightly forward and
there was always a pine-tree in the background, a symbol of
unchanging green and strength. The form of the Noh plays
had been perfected in Kyoto in the fifteenth century, and the
same plays were enacted in the same manner as at first. The
players themselves passed on from father to son their elaborate
art, and most of the actors today shared the blood of the men
who created this drama five centuries before. It was intended
only for cultivated people who were able to understand the
allusions referred to in the ancient lyrics.

The Noh plays abounded in ghosts and spirits, who often
appeared in homely guise, and many began with a traveller,
sometimes a priest, asking his way with various questions. In
one play the hero and heroine were the ghosts of two lovers
who had died unmarried. Their spirits are united a hundred
years after their death near a hillside grave where their bodies
had lain together. In *Kakitsuhata*, a wandering priest stops at
an iris marsh, and, as he admires the flowers, a spirit appears
who has identified herself with the iris. In this iris marsh,

centuries before, the sage Nirihira had passed thinking of the damsel who had become the spirit and who, disguised as a simple girl, is suddenly transfigured into the splendidly dressed great lady whom Nirihira had loved of old. Some of the plays represented scenes from the lives of saints or the intervention of Buddha in human affairs, and among the dramatic types were elementals, animal spirits or hungry spirits, cunning or malicious. There were spirits of the moonlight, dragon kings from the water world, the souls of flowers or trees and angry devils. Fenollosa remembered the saying of Kobori Enshu, "Dancing is especially known, by its circulation of the blood, to keep off the disease of old age," and this form of drama seemed to him as intense and primitive and almost as beautiful as the ancient Greek drama at Athens. It, too, had risen out of religious rites, beginning as a sacred dance with a sacred chorus added, sung by priests. A full range of epic incident had sprung out of the Shinto god-dance.

Thirty years later, Ezra Pound, taking Fenollosa's pencil script, made his own revision of some of the translations, transferring a refrain, perhaps, or adding occasional words that seemed to him to belong to the particular emotion. For Pound had become, at the second Mrs. Fenollosa's request, a literary executor of Fenollosa, and he published a selection of the plays of this unemphatic drama and made them known to the Anglo-Saxon world. Fenollosa, Ezra Pound said, had unearthed treasures that "no Japanese had heard of," and presently William Butler Yeats invented a form of drama that was based on Ezra Pound's re-translation of the Noh plays. Yeats, who was tired of theatre work, was interested only in experiments now that seemed to belong to his own art, and he found himself "thinking of players," he said, "who needed perhaps but to unroll a mat in some Eastern garden." Reacting against the naturalistic European theatre, he felt it "should be again possible for a few poets to write as all once did, not for the printed page but to be sung," and he saw a possibility for the Irish dramatic movement in a kind of play that was distant from real life. He hoped to write a play for forty or fifty persons in a room, with masks, no scenery, three musicians, "with the music, the beauty of form and voice all coming to a climax in a pantomimic dance . . . In the studio or the drawing-room, we can found a true theatre of beauty," he said, and he looked to Japan "for a stage-convention, for more formal faces . . . and perhaps for those movements of the body copied from the marionette shows of the fourteenth century . . . Realism is created for the common people . . . and it is the delight today of all those whose minds, educated alone by schoolmasters and newspapers, are without the memory of beauty and emotional subtlety . . . All imaginative art keeps at a distance and this distance once chosen must be firmly held against a pushing world. Verse, ritual, music and dance in association with action require that gesture, costume, facial expression, stage arrangement must help in keeping the door." The form Yeats invented in *At the Hawk's Well* was symbolic and indirect, and for the pleasure of his friends and a few score people of good taste, he hoped to complete a dramatic celebration of the life of Cuchulain, planned long before.

Yeats had heard from Ezra Pound of the Japanese Noh plays, and he saw in some of them elements in common with Irish legend. The ghost lovers in one play reminded him of the story of the Arran island boy and girl, related by Lady Gregory, who come to the priest after their death to be married. Then he saw a Japanese dancer, Ito, dancing in a studio, or a drawing-room, on a very small stage lit by an excellent stage-light. *At the Hawk's Well* was the first of his "plays for dancers," which substituted for the rising of a curtain the folding and unfolding of a cloth, and it was intended to be played to the accompaniment of drum, flute and zither. Ito had attracted attention at the Regents' Park Zoo by prancing about outside the cages of the birds of prey, so that people thought that he was either mad or a follower of some Oriental religion that worshipped birds. "Ito was presently ready to evolve a dance based on the movements of the hawks as they hopped about and stretched their wings, and Yeats was often seen beside him at the Zoo, all attention . . . When completed, *At the Hawk's Well* admirably brought together the mythologies of Ireland and of Japan." So wrote Joseph Hone in his life of Yeats. A second performance of the play was given in a London drawing room for a war charity. Queen Alexandra, who was present, wearied of Yeats's preliminary explanation of Noh drama and sent a message by her lady-in-waiting to ask for it to be cut short. Joseph Hone also related this incident in his life of Yeats. It took place thirty years after Fenollosa first began to study the Noh plays.

VI

Henry Adams and John La Farge, who arrived in Japan in 1886, had both long been interested in Japanese art, which had come into vogue in America with the Centennial Exhibition in Philadelphia in 1876. Adams was a friend, in Washington, of the Japanese minister, Yoshida, and he had known the Oriental art dealers in Paris and New York. He had the collector's instinct, and in his house in Washington there were many Japanese and Chinese vases, bronzes, porcelains and other Far Eastern objects. He had gone to Japan, he said, "to

buy kakemonos for my gaunt walls." La Farge, who had written on Japanese art in 1869, had been well in advance of his
time in America and even in France, where the market had
been flooded with Japanese curios since the opening of Japan,
and various artists collected prints of Utamaro and Hokusai.
A Japanese print appeared in the background of Manet's portrait of Zola in 1868. While Ruskin warned European artists
against this heathen source, and Norton followed him in the
United States, there were Japanese museums in Holland and
in Dresden and there had been much importation of Japanese
porcelain into Holland since the seventeeth century. La Farge
said that Japanese prints "endangered with amateurs the reputation of the painter who publicly admired them," but he had
owned prints himself since 1863; and he noted that the Japanese excelled in energy, grandeur of style, refinement and an
enchanting harmony of colours.

Henry Adams had suggested their summer visit to Japan,
and they had undertaken not to read any books about it but
to "come as innocently as we could." On their way to San
Francisco, where they were to take the ship, an Omaha reporter asked them why they were going, and, when La Farge
said they were in search of Nirvana, the reporter said, "Are
you not rather late in the season?" Just the same, Henry
Adams studied Buddhism on the way, with the Four Noble
Truths and the Noble Eightfold Path by which Nirvana was
to be attained. He "hungered," he said, "for annihilation"
after his wife's death; he felt, with his Mrs. Lightfoot Lee,
"What rest it would be to live in the Great Pyramid and look
out forever at the polar star." He had been "living with not a
thought but from minute to minute." La Farge had undertaken
to paint his great picture for the Church of the Ascension in
New York, and he had, he said, a vague belief that he might

find in Japan certain conditions of line in the mountains which would help him. Actually, one day there, he saw before him a space of mountain and cloud and flat land which seemed to him what he needed. He made a rapid but careful study, so complete that the big picture was "only a part of the amount of work put into the study of that afternoon." His first impression of Japan was of the "splendour of light . . . as if the sky, in its variations, were the great subject of the drama we were looking at, or at least its great chorus." Again, he spoke, in *An Artist's Letters from Japan,* of the silvery milkiness and whiteness of the light.

Now Dr. Sturgis Bigelow was a cousin of Mrs. Henry Adams. He had visited the Adamses in Washington, and in Yokohama and Tokyo he took charge of the arriving friends as what Henry Adams called a "courier and master of ceremonies." He was full of the details of manners in Japan, now as familiar to him as those of Europe, and he took La Farge and Adams to his club to see and listen to some Noh plays. The plays were given in a theatre built at the club for this purpose. The men took off their shoes, so as not to injure the mats, and presently they heard wailings and the piercing notes of stringed instruments and flutes against a background of high, distinct declamation. La Farge described the Noh plays at Tokyo as often a pantomime with an actor making gestures to the accompaniment of music or the declamation of the choragus who told the poetic story. For the rest, there were many short plays, mostly based on legendary subjects, distinguished by gorgeous dresses, and occasionally some comic scenes of domestic life. It was all very different from the more or less disreputable theatre, but La Farge said, "I only vaguely understood what it was all about."

At Tokyo, Adams and La Farge met Fenollosa, "to be de-

lighted and instructed by the great authority on Japanese art."
"Fenollosa," said Henry Adams, "is a kind of St. Dominic and
holds himself responsible for the dissemination of useless
knowledge by others. My historical indifference to everything
but facts, and my delight at studying what is hopelessly de-
based and degraded, shock his moral sense . . . He has joined
a Buddhist sect. I was myself a Buddhist when I left America,
but he has converted me to Calvinism with leanings towards
the Methodists." Then he said, "Fenollosa and Bigelow are
stern with us. Fenollosa is a tyrant who says we shall not like
any work done under the Tokagawa Shoguns. As these gentlemen lived 250 years, or thereabouts, to 1860, and as there
is nothing at Tokyo except their work, La Farge and I are
at a loss to understand why we came; but it seems we are to
be taken to Nikko shortly, and permitted to admire some temples there." On looking up the question, he found presently
that these temples were the work of Tokagawa Shoguns, but
about this inconsistency he did not dare to ask.

Nikko, about ninety miles north of Tokyo, lay high and
cool, Henry Adams wrote, and this centre of beautiful scenery
had been chosen as a summer residence by Dr. Sturgis Bigelow. There he lived with his friends, Mr. and Mrs. Fenollosa,
and he hired for Adams and La Farge a little Japanese toy-
house near by. "Tokyo is amusing," said Adams, "but with
the thermometer above 90°, a somewhat cloying joy. For
smells it has no known rival . . . Ten days of Japanese or
hotel food made us curious to learn how clean Mrs. Fenollosa's
table might be; for a pervasive sense of oily nastiness charac-
terize every article of ordinary consumption." The little house
stood by a waterfall on the slope of a mountain with an enclosed garden facing the great temple groves. The enormous
mountains stood behind them, together with a high wall of

rock over which the torrent rolled, breaking three times. "In the sand of our little garden," wrote La Farge, "we set clumps of flowers, chrysanthemums mostly, and occasionally iris and azalea . . . A little fountain in the middle . . . In the early morning I sit in the bath-room and paint this little picture, while Adams, upstairs in the verandah, is reading in Dante's *Paradiso*, and can see, when he looks up, the great temple roof of the Buddhist Mangwanji."

The world-famous temples of Nikko were the greatest temples now standing in the empire, and Adams took photographs of them in their twenty acres on the mountain flank. In Nikko, he and La Farge spent a month near the Fenollosas, and "Mrs. Fenollosa," Adams wrote, "has rescued us from our trials. I cannot imagine what we should have done without her." One day, when Fenollosa was unwell and La Farge hard at work, he set out with Bigelow and Mrs. Fenollosa to visit Yumato, the Saratoga or White Sulphur of Japan that lay fourteen miles above them among the mountains. Mrs. Fenollosa summoned five pack-horses, one for herself, one for Sturgis Bigelow and a third for Henry Adams. A servant and baggage followed on a fourth, and the fifth carried beds, blankets, linen, silver, eatables and drinks. There were a dozen inns but no village at Yumato. Henry Adams said they had their little joke about all they saw and did, always ending in the conviction that they were playing baby and were living in doll-land. They were established in their doll-house with paper windows and matted floors, and the temples were evidently a toy, for everything was lacquer, gilding or green, red and blue paint. Meanwhile, they examined curios that were sent to them from Tokyo, Osaka and heaven knew where. Adams said that Fenollosa and Bigelow "are the highest authorities on lacquers and kakemonos; but they can only pick up a good thing now and then."

Bigelow and Fenollosa employed two men to hunt curios for Adams and La Farge, and bales of merchandise arrived and were unloaded at their door. Patient pack-horses stood in the enclosure of the yards and big parcels and piles of boxes and bundles encumbered the verandah, but they found almost nothing among the things brought them that could rank as works of high art. One day a large lot of kakemonos arrived, sent up by the great curio-dealer Yamanaka. Adams gleaned about two dozen out of the lot, and, though they were cheap enough, he feared that Fenollosa, who was in Tokyo, would say they were Tokagawa rot and would bully him into letting them go. He was even now trying to prevent Adams from having a collection of Hokusai's books; and Adams added, writing to John Hay, "I wish you were here to help us trample on him . . . I have still to report," he continued to John Hay, "that purchases for you are going on, but more and more slowly, for I believe we have burst up all the pawn-brokers' shops in Japan . . . Bigelow and Fenollosa cling like misers to their miserable hoards. Not a kakemono is to be found, though plenty are bought. Every day new bales of rubbish come up from Tokyo or elsewhere, mounds of books, tons of bad bronze, holocausts of lacquer. I buy literally everything that is merely possible, and yet I have got not a hundred dollars' worth of things I want for myself . . . I am trying to spend your money. It is hard work, but I will do it, or succumb . . . I want to bring back a dozen big bronze vases to put on the grass before our houses in summer, for palms or big plants, so as to give our houses the look of a cross between curio shops and florists. A man at Osaka has sent up some 250 dollars' worth of lacquers, sword-hilts, inlaid work and such stuff. As he has the best shop in Japan, we took the whole lot and have sent for more." To Elizabeth Cameron he wrote, "I have bought curios enough to fill a house, but nothing I like or want for myself . . . If I knew what would please you, I would load the steamer with it." Henry Adams collected porcelains and kakemonos, Hokusai drawings and gowns of silk for his friends and their wives at home.

John La Farge felt every day disgusted and ashamed looking at curios as an occupation, returning to it as a gambler might, he said, hoping to make it right with his conscience by some run of luck. He spent a whole day at Osaka examining bric-a-brac, arriving early at the big shop where tea was offered him in the merchant's little back room. Pieces of porcelain were brought from the warehouse, then there was more tea, followed by the inspection of many rooms full of odds and ends, again more tea, and more pieces were slowly and reluctantly drawn from the warehouse. Followed lunch and tea, then a visit to the upper rooms where hundreds of kakemonos were unrolled "to a crescendo of exasperation," all this to the unexpressed contempt of Dr. Bigelow, the great collector of precious lacquers. La Farge remembered in New York seeing one of the great dealers marking on his samples the colours that pleased most of his buyers: all other colours were tabooed in his instructions to the makers in Japan. But he felt, in the presence of the ancient paintings of the Buddhist divinities, what he had once felt at the first sight of old Italian art, and Fenollosa later recalled how he had taken La Farge to see the great white Kwannon by Mokkei at Daitokuji. La Farge, devout Roman Catholic that he was, could hardly restrain a bending of the head as he murmured "Raphael." There was one painting that La Farge felt was "directly meant" for him, a painting by the legendary artist of Japan, the Cimabue of a thousand years ago, Kose-no-Kanawoka, the inheritor and student of an even older Chinese art. It was still in fair condition, and it was a delight to him to recognize the lotus motives he had used himself, working at such a distance of time and place, when he "tried to render the tones and the transparency of our own fairy water-lily." La Farge painted a few for a Japanese friend, and he was pleased when he was shown his own early drawing "The Wolf Charmer." This was in the studio of a well-known Japanese artist who saluted him as "the wolf man" and said, "You must have painted that with a Japanese brush," which he had actually done.

At Kyoto, in the early morning, La Farge sat out on the wide verandah drawing or painting from the great panorama before him, the distant mountains making a wall lighted up clearly, with patches of burning yellow, white and green, against the Western sky. Though Adams was not so well pleased by their drifting existence, La Farge enjoyed it, letting himself be guided by the light of Lao Tzu. "After many years of wilful energy, of forced battle that I have not shunned, I like to try," La Farge wrote, "the freshness of the springs, to see if new impressions come as they once did in childhood"; and he liked "the old roads between *yashiki* walls, broken up with torrents and bridges; and the small shrines and sacred trees, stones and rocks that are sacred, why and wherefore no one actually knowing . . . The great Pan might still be living here, in a state of the world which has sanctified trees and groves and associated the spirit-world with every form of the earthly dwelling-place." Here were "the soul-informed rocks of the Greeks," for Buddhism joined with the faith of Shinto in attaching religious value to solitary places and mountain heights. There were stories everywhere of ascensions and disappearances, "all of which talk mingles," wrote La Farge, "with the vague interest of my painting. For I had proposed to make my studies serve for the picture of the 'Ascension', to use the clouds and the wilderness for my background, and to be, at least for moments, in some relation to what I have to represent—that is to say, in an atmosphere not inimical, as ours is, to what we call the miraculous. Here at least I am not forced to consider external nature as separate and opposed, and I can fall into moods of thought—or, if you prefer, feeling, —in which the edges of all things blend, and man and the outside world would pass into each other." The image that touched both La Farge and Adams most, partly because of the Eternal Feminine, was that of the incarnation called Kwannon, shown absorbed in the meditation of Nirvana. It brought back the Buddhist idea of compassion, for her name today was that of the Compassionate One.

During that summer Okakura spent much of his time with John La Farge. They discussed spiritual manifestations and all the Buddhist wonderland in which spiritual bodies take form and disappear again and the edges of the real and the imaginary melt into one another. Okakura chose for him Japanese and Chinese prints, of great purity and long tradition, that were to be a consolation to him in his last years. Such a "Kano" blue! The exact Chinese vermilion of the extremest best! Thinking of the colours of A.D. 812 or A.D. 1340 made him feel that for a moment luck sailed through the clouds. He felt the "vague recall of the antique that is dear to artists in the distinctly rigid muscles of the legs and thighs" of men seen in the streets, "the rippling swellings of the back—a godsend to a painter"; and he hoped soon, Henry Adams said, "to be a fluent talker of Daimio Japanese. As for me, I admire." La Farge was especially charmed by the civilized emptiness of Japanese houses beside the accumulations he had known at home: "the do-

mestic architecture is as simple, as transitory, as if it symbol-
ized the life of man . . . All framework and moving screens
instead of walls. No accumulations, no bric-a-brac . . . All the
same from the Emperor's palace to little tradesmen's cottages
. . . The set look of insisting on an idea, the idea of doing
with little, a noble one, certainly." He discovered in the temples
more details of beauty than all our architects could dream of
accomplishing. Their "wood and plaster had more of the
dignity of art than all we have at home, if melted together,
would result in." But then La Farge agreed with Stanford
White about our native American "Hottentot" style.

Edward S. Morse had discussed his own sketches of Japanese
architecture with the Boston architect Henry Greenough, who
was travelling in the Orient at the same time, a generation
before Ralph Adams Cram wrote his book about Japanese
architecture. Henry Adams grasped this theme in a "clear
and dispassionate and masterly way," talking about it, said La
Farge, with a natural reference to the past, for "Adams's historic sense amounts to poetry . . . His deductions and remarks
always set my mind sailing into new channels." Together
Adams and La Farge travelled to Nara, the ancient capital,—
thirty miles by ricksha,—where, in this summer of 1886, Fenollosa spent many weeks in delightful study with Kano Hogai.
The old city gloried in a grove of huge pines and cedars, sweep-
ing for a mile to the eastern mountains, sheltering the buildings
of the Shinto temple, Kasuga. Ancient Buddhist monasteries
flanked this on the north, and wild streams tore beds through
the trees. Archæologically, Fenollosa said, Nara was the treas-
ure-house of Japan.

Later, in Ceylon, Adams visited Kandy and the great Buddhist temple there, "the last remaining watchfire of our church,
except for Boston where Bill Bigelow and Fenollosa fan faint

embers." He went to the sacred Bo-tree and sat under it for half an hour, hoping to attain Nirvana; but he left the spot without reaching Buddhaship, for Buddhism made a poetic appeal but not a religious appeal to Adams. Meanwhile, the Fenollosas sailed back to America with him, and Mrs. Fenollosa brought her Japanese nurse. Fenollosa was now a Japanese official, travelling under Japanese orders and credentials. Adams had "some tons of curios," he said, most of which he sent by a tramp steamer around to New York. At home again, he began to study Chinese, two hours every day after six hours of history-writing; and his house, as the British ambassador said, was full of strange trophies from Japan. The idea of the Rock Creek monument over his wife's grave, representing silence and repose, had taken shape in his conversations with La Farge in Japan. La Farge had "reluctantly crawled away towards New York to resume the grinding routine of studio-work at a time when life runs low." So Adams wrote in his *Education*. He would rather himself have "gone back to the East, if it were only to sleep forever in the trade winds under the Southern stars, wandering over the dark purple ocean, with its purple sense of solitude and void."

VII

Fenollosa had gone home,—and to Europe,—for a year, on a commission from the Japanese government to study European methods of art education. With two Japanese colleagues, he visited for this purpose all the great cities of Europe. The excesses of Western custom introduced into Japanese schools were now rapidly on the wane. The era of confusion was melting away into that of reconstruction; and, thanks largely to Fenollosa's insistence, Japanese painting and drawing had been reinstated in the schools. Later, discussing his own theories, he said, "I do not like the word 'decoration.' It seems to imply too much artificiality, a superficial prettiness. The word we ought to use is 'structural.' The lines, the spaces, the proportions lie in the structure of the thing itself." Again, "Representation is not art, it is literature. That a picture represents a man does not interest us . . . It is a question of spacing, of how the pattern is worked out, that interests us . . . not the representational element but the structural element . . . not the realistic motive but the desire to find finer and finer space relations and line relations." In his lectures he referred equally to Japanese, Greek, Arabic, Polynesian and Egyptian art. He said that the most instructive works come just before the best in any school: "In the stage preceding the highest we have all the elements, not worked out to their best. There is the greatest individuality at this stage. Studying colour, going to the Venetian school, we must not go to Titian or Veronese. No, Bellini was solving the problem. We will learn from him, and not from Titian or Veronese, who had solved it."

After this, Fenollosa thought and spoke more and more of "the coming fusion of East and West." He was a prophet of the idea of "one world." At Nikko, in 1879, he had talked with General Grant, who was on his tour around the world, and General Grant said that the East was the theatre of coming events in which the union of Japan and China would be the only barrier to European spoliation. Japan wished for this union, but the Chinese could not believe in Japanese disinterestedness, and the Sino-Japanese war inevitably followed. Fenollosa's doctrine was union all round. The strength of Western civilization tended to lie in a knowledge of means, while that of the East lay in a knowledge of ends, and "means without ends are blind," he said, while "ends without means are para-

lysed." Eastern culture had held to ideals whose refinement
seemed markedly feminine, while the West had held to ideals
whose strength seemed markedly masculine, and the East had
the privilege of supplying what the West lacked, he remarked
in the preface to his long poem. This was the Phi Beta Kappa
poem, *East and West*, which he delivered at Harvard in 1892,
prophesying the synthesis of the two halves of the world,
brought together "for the final creation of man." Elsewhere he
said, "We cannot escape a stronger and stronger modification
of our standards by the pungent subtlety of Oriental thought,"
and, dreaming of a new world type, he welcomed the inflow-
ing of the Oriental stream in Western art.

Meanwhile, in this Phi Beta Kappa poem, addressing old
Kano, the "priestly painter," Fenollosa wrote,—

> I've flown from my West
> Like a desolate bird from a broken nest
> To learn thy secret of joy and rest.

He had become, in the eighties, a Buddhist, with Dr. Sturgis
Bigelow, who wrote of Nirvana in *Buddhism and Immortality*,
"There alone is peace, that peace which the material world
cannot give, the peace which passeth understanding trained
on material things,—infinite and eternal peace, the peace of
limitless consciousness unified with limitless will. That peace
is Nirvana." Fenollosa and Dr. Bigelow had studied with Archbishop Keitoku of the Tendai sect at Miidera temple on Lake
Biwa. The archbishop believed that the Western spirit was
nearly ripe to receive the lofty doctrine which Eastern guardians
had preserved, and Fenollosa looked up to him as his most
inspired and devoutly liberal teacher in matters religious. The
archbishop died in 1889, and precious were the days and nights
Fenollosa had had the privilege of spending with him in the

vicinity of Kyoto, Nara and Nikko. As for Dr. Bigelow, he jotted down notes* on the conversations that he and Fenollosa had with Archbishop Keitoku. A few of these notes follow:

> E. F. F. (Fenollosa) asked in the 18th year of Meiji at Kommei whether the task of a Buddhist priest is confined to this world, and the A. said no. But the A. did not answer F's question from actual experience.

> The "Law" of Buddha is a great truth which must be read by the eye of the mind. It is not written in books.

> From the religious point of view it is impossible for a priest to have a wife.

> Buddhism is like an emperor. If you set him on common things he can't do them as well as a petty officer. So Buddhism. This is why priests withdraw from the world.

> Everyone wishes to develop his wisdom, and to help such folks Shaka [Buddha] first teaches that he must leave the world. As his wisdom gradually increases he comes to know that true wisdom does not lie elsewhere than in the world which he left.

> One who sees the coarse dust about himself becomes a Rakan. One who gets rid of the fine dust becomes a Bosatsu.

> The reason Shaka could do his work in eighty years (a very short time) is because he spent so many years in preparing for it.

> I ask about time. There is time in Shaka's state. But he had finished his plan of rescuing all people, and in his eyes they are all rescued.

> Shaka honoured those who abused him as a father who knows that he intends to transfer all his property to his son, though the son does not know it, and that he must become inferior or dependent himself.

* Preserved in a notebook now kept in the Oriental division of the Boston Museum of Fine Arts.

Shaka's appearing in so many countries seems strange till we remember that a Bosatsu can make his appearance in as many places as he wishes at the same time, and can see with his eyes what is going on in the different countries.

I ask whether they are appearing as men, or only as Notoke, etc. He answers, as men or animals or anything. Even as a dog, to save the dogs.

The real object of life is to acquire freedom from the ties that limit consciousness by connecting it with the material world (to the law of which it habitually conforms). The real object of religion is to facilitate the acquisition of such freedom.

(25 years later, 1914. Should change wording to this: "To expand consciousness beyond the limitations which the material world would impose on it.")

Many years later still,—in Boston, in 1922,—Dr. Bigelow discussed Buddhism with Dr. and Mrs. Frederick Winslow. In these conversations* the name of Fenollosa also appeared, in connection with wayside shrines and holy places. Dr. Winslow asked, "Do the Japanese feel that any special spirit inhabits Fuji?" and Dr. Bigelow replied, "Not only Fuji, but every mountain in Japan, almost. Much as it is in India. You go out to walk; you are apt to pass a wayside shrine; or in a clump of trees where the dæmon of that particular place is worshipped, you are likely to find one or two little offerings there, flowers or food or something of that kind. People are very simple-minded about it. I remember one night at a place near Kyoto where Fenollosa and I used to go to get a swim in the evening. There was a little ten or twelve-year-old girl who was employed as a servant about the house, and, one night as I walked down the length of the piazza, I found her putting a little china plate

* Notes on these conversations are preserved in the Houghton Library at Harvard.

of beans on top of the corner post of the piazza railing. I said, 'Hello! What are you doing that for?' She said, 'The moon.' There was a little new moon off in the sunset. A little grove hardly more than fifty yards on a side. There was a little stone shrine there, not ornamented but cut in the regular shape of a temple, and in front was a straight stone with two circular hollows, one at each end, just to hold water, and somebody was in the habit of putting in fresh water and fresh flowers." *Mrs. Winslow:* "That accounts for the way the Japanese feel about flowers and trees, etc. Anesaki spoke of the way people here pull at trees and shrubs as they go by, often pulling off leaves or twigs. He said you did not see that in Japan. Perhaps the recognition of the indwelling deity is the reason." *Dr. Bigelow:* "Yes. When a deity gets accustomed to a certain combination of form, a certain group of trees, the intimacy gets strengthened by repetition."

In these conversations, Dr. Bigelow spoke of Kano Hogai, the great friend of Fenollosa and Okakura, as "simple to the last degree." He painted, the very last thing he did,—he didn't quite finish it,—a picture of the goddess Kwannon holding a baby. The early Roman Catholic missionaries who came to the Far East pitched on Kwannon as embodying characteristics of the Virgin. "So they took her," Dr. Bigelow said, "and put a baby in her arms, which I think she didn't have before. In the turn-over of everything in those days," Dr. Bigelow continued, "both Kano Hogai and Hashimoto Gaho were without support. Kano could sell, but Hashimoto Gaho was not known. For a long time I kept him going; used to give him monthly pay and take whatever he chose to send me. Now his things are priceless."

Later Mrs. Winslow asked, "How far is it legitimate to try to become like a god in this life on earth?" To this Dr. Bigelow replied, "It is legitimate to try to become like any god, but the bigger the god is, the harder it is. Hence the reason for the use of all the lower and lesser divinities, Bodisattvas. They are the beings who have the power of expanding to infinity but have not done so but have kept enough in touch with the finite to be easily accessible to ordinary human beings." Then Dr. Bigelow spoke of the "direct transfer of consciousness from one mind to another. If the teacher knows some higher truth than the pupil, which is obviously the nature of the case, he can transfer that knowledge to the pupil without the pupil's realizing where it came from. Nothing is so common in this world as thought transference, and most of the good and most of the mischief in the world is due to that; not by talking but by transference. That is why it is desirable to keep in contact with decent people rather than with roughs. It is not what they say; it is getting their minds hitched up with yours more or less and dragging your mind down to the level of theirs so that you get to like what they like, admire what they admire and dislike what they dislike,—the wrong things right through."

Dr. Bigelow said, "The object of training is to disregard sensory experiences at will. Give your faith a clear swing. Be free to build up a universe by imagination . . . Protestant sects that have extemporaneous prayers do themselves great injustice by not using formal prayers. Lose value of constant association of words and ideas . . . Characteristic of Buddhists not to press or force people's interest; never to interfere with a man who doesn't come to them first and ask for help." On still another occasion he said, "Mind must be active—must be doing something of itself in order not to be swept off its bearings by an outside force. Mind should be able to hold a single idea voluntarily, to make that idea a matter of course . . . What you think of is unimportant. It is merely practice in thinking of some-

thing that does not exist, something that is the contradiction
of the evidence of your eyes and ears. Faith is saying you
believe something when you know it isn't so. Be able to con-
struct your own world, your own conditions without regard
to the conditions that are imposed on you through your
senses. In all Western science passivity is the test of truth.
You are passive to things that come through your senses,
whereas the great object of training is to get your mind
so accustomed to acting independently of your senses as to
be able to think what you want without regard to them."
Question: "In the East do they ever get to a point where they
believe in passivity?" *Answer:* "Never. On the contrary, passivity is thoroughly bad—a thing to be kept away from. It holds
you down. It is all in the direction of the material world,
which is just what you want to get away from."

VIII

Fenollosa's daughter Brenda, who was born in Tokyo, later
wrote a description of the family house there. "The entrance,"
she said, "was through a porch, enclosed by glass in winter,
some eighty feet long, and filled with tropical flowers and
shrubs. I still remember the beauty of the dwarf weeping plum-
trees, which bloomed there in the spring, amidst the multi-
coloured azaleas. At the end of this porch was my playroom,
where I kept my toys and where my dolls were ranged in their
full regalia. The house itself was on one floor, with a big tiled
Japanese roof. There was an entrance hall, library, two large
drawing-rooms with their respective fireplaces, the dining-room,
our five bedrooms, two bathrooms, and, not least important,
the small passageway with its low roof, to which we all rushed
at night whenever there was an earthquake—a thing which

happened quite often and which shook the house and made frightful rumbling noises. The servants' quarters were rambling and in Japanese style . . .

"In the summer we were wont to go to the mountains. At Nikko we lived in a real Japanese house that had sliding panels between the rooms and matting on the floors. The surrounding grounds were enchanting, with a broad stream, which dashed over rocks amid its trees and flowers. Bishop Brooks of Boston and Bishop McVickar from Pennsylvania came to visit us at Nikko, during their sojourn in Japan. So weighty were these pillars of the Church that all our wicker furniture creaked and groaned for many weeks after their departure; and, so tall were these two gentlemen, that their heads almost touched the ceiling whenever they walked through our house . . . At Nikko, near where we lived there was a very ancient and famous temple to which Ah-Ching (the Chinese nurse) would sometimes take me for a walk. The building was superb, covered with red lacquer and carved gold. Its marvellous roof, made of enormous tiles, sloped up with the angle which distinguishes Fugi Yama. One day, when we were there, I stood lost in admiration of the great bronze gong, some eighteen inches in diameter, and the bronze gong-master, which looked like a small torpedo and which hung from a chain, perfectly balanced and floating, as it were, in the air. Suddenly I decided to see if I could whang that great gong. Before Ah-Ching noticed me, I had climbed on to the flat wall surrounding the temple and, jumping up into the air, I reached for the gong-master, striking it with my hand. A resonant deep dong ensued. And then, with one hand over my mouth, Ah-Ching whisked me away . . .

"In our garden were the most beautiful of dragon-flies, multi-coloured and with iridescent wings. There were also many butterflies, and in our mountain stream stood white herons and storks. On occasion I would put a drop of honey on the end of each finger, and run off to the garden to entice the dragon-flies to come to me. Many a time I have had a dragon-fly perched on each of my ten fingers, sipping the honey ... Mother, who did a good deal of photographing in those days, had a dark room at the end of a passage in our house at Nikko. One day, as she was coming from the dark room, she beheld a priest, dressed in his gorgeous vestments of Japanese brocade, standing at the entrance of the corridor. She spoke to him, but he did not answer her. Suddenly, as she approached him, he vanished. She was amazed. The house in which we lived had belonged for many years before his death to a priest, and we were told in the village that this same priest always came back on moonlight nights that he might gaze over the valley to the mountain beyond and see the beautiful view that he had so well loved in life. Often, it was said, he had been so seen standing there on a balcony at the end of the passage.

"The summer over, we returned with all our luggage to Tokyo by many jinrickshas. This journey took two days, which required spending the night at a Japanese inn. Here we slept on the floor on mats, as is the custom in Japan. We were sprinkled with flea-powder in the hope of escaping the fleas. The road we took was narrow and rough, with mud up to the axles of the wheels, but the scenery was lovely with distant prospects of the mountains and nearer hills and rice-fields in the foreground. Tall cryptomeria trees lent shade to our journey, as these dark evergreens lined the road on either side ... Many were the changes that we found when we reached our home in Tokyo, for the parents had decided to give up the jinrickshas. A landau and a pair of beautiful high-stepping stallions had been purchased, for to Tokyo belonged the distinction of being the district set aside for stallions. So we found ourselves with a coachman, a footman and a stable-boy instead of the three jinricksha men. Then Father bought a horse to ride, also a stallion, and I used to watch him leave home in a cloud of dust . . . How beautiful was Mother dressed in her Court presentation costume! With pleasure I remember her, dressed in gold and white brocade with the long Court train of crimson satin embroidered with gold chrysanthemums. On her head were white ostrich feathers with a white tulle veil behind. Father had been knighted by the Emperor of Japan for his mission to Europe.

"After our return to Tokyo, our house, from time to time, became filled with objects of art: screens of gold leaf, over which were painted in brilliant colours scenes of Japanese life, of birds, and of landscapes; kakemonos in their rich brocade frames; wood-block prints of many famous artists; bronze hibachis—braziers in which the Japanese burn charcoal and over which they sit on padded mats, warming their hands; bronze vases and bronze candlesticks; bronze bells from the temples; brass and silver incense-burners; cloisonné trays and boxes; exquisite lacquer tanses and an infinite variety of porcelain. How wonderful they were, and how I gloried in looking at each new object after their arrival! And they mysteriously disappeared, only to be followed by others, until these latter also went the way of the first. This was the beginning of my father's Japanese art collection, now in the Boston Museum of Fine Arts . . . Not only the Emperor and nobles, but the temples, too, had vast collections stored in godowns or warehouses. Occasionally the ornaments in their houses were changed for others in the godowns. Father was given entree to these godowns, which enabled him to coördinate Japanese art and to purchase objects for his collection.

"One day at an informal lunch-party, largely of men, I was allowed to be at the table and sat between Mr. Percival Lowell and Mr. Lafcadio Hearn. Dr. Sturgis Bigelow was also there. I was charmed with Mr. Lowell and in later years often saw him in Boston. But Mr. Lafcadio Hearn was replusive to look at; he had a wonderful voice, to be sure, and he talked well; but he was totally blind, and his food landed in strange places, much to my delight. In the middle of lunch there was a loud crash. Suzuki, our tall butler, disappeared; Father followed, and, of course, so did I, not heeding Mother's protests. In the hall we saw a great hole in the ceiling, and below the floor was covered with plaster in which a six-foot snake was wriggling. Our butler killed the snake and took him out. Meanwhile our guests came out from the dining-room. As soon as Dr. Bigelow saw what had happened, he exclaimed, 'Three cheers! I have heard that snake moving around over the ceiling in my bedroom. Thank God, he did not fall on me!'

"The last incident I remember before we left Japan to return to America, soon after I was seven years old, occurred in our park, Kaga Yasiki, while I was out taking a walk with my governess. Suddenly we saw a red fox come out of his hole and dart away. Then, as we felt the tremors of an earthquake, we turned towards home. On the way the ground in front of us was heaving up and down, like the waves of the sea; but the tremors did not last long."

IX

In 1890, Lafcadio Hearn arrived in Japan. He had returned to New York from the French West Indies, and he came to Yokohama vaguely commissioned to write sketches of travel for American magazines. To him, the little people seemed all

gentleness and kindness, and he felt that he was surrounded
by a smiling world, a world of hushed voices and slow movements. He was won over at once by the folklore of the Japanese, threatened by infiltrations from the scientific West. Interested in the common people and their half-forgotten legends,
their old myths and stories of ghosts, he was impressed by what
seemed to him the joyousness of Shinto and Buddhism, and
his favourite divinity was also Kwannon. He was attracted to
Jizo, the god of the ghosts of children. Disliking the new militant Japan, he thought everything that was ugly in the empire
was a result of the influence of the West, and he was convinced that science was bound to wipe out all memory of Buddha's words from the mind of Japan. He spent most of his
first summer in Yokohama, tutoring and going on pilgrimages
to well-known and lesser-known temples. He never forgot, in
the grounds of a certain temple, a grove of cherry trees in
bloom against a pale blue sky.

Hearn found that teachers of English were still in demand
in government schools, and, presently married to a Japanese
wife, he cherished in his house a world of ancient courtesies,
thoughts and ways. He became instructor in English in a
government college at Kumamoto, on an island at the south
of Japan; but, ultimately becoming a professor at the University of Tokyo, he was known as the recluse of the campus.
His house was an hour from the university by ricksha; it stood
on a high hill, and beyond a field was an ancient Buddhist
temple in a dense wood on a higher slope. Usually in garden
or study, he walked in the evenings with an old priest, and he
wrote to Fenollosa that friends were more dangerous than
enemies,—"Alas! I can afford friends only on paper. Visiting
is out of the possible." Fenollosa had given him the story,
A Mountain of Skulls, about the vast heap of death's-heads,

the skulls of one man's previous incarnations; and he had
enjoyed, he said, more pleasant hours in the Fenollosa house
than in any other foreign house in Tokyo. Fenollosa too was
an advocate of Herbert Spencer; but Lafcadio Hearn wrote of
"the isolation indispensable to quiet regularity of work, and
the solitude which is absolutely essential to thinking upon
such subjects as I am now engaged on. My friends! Ah! My
friends! . . . But I have not been the loser by my visits to you
both—did I not get that wonderful story? And so I have given
you more time than any other person or persons in Tokyo.
But now—I must again disappear."

For Fenollosa the great years of romantic interest of living
in Japan had been from 1880 to 1890, and he was prepared
to return to Boston to spend five years as curator of the Oriental collections in the Museum. He arranged the treasures there,
wrote various catalogues and became interested in art education in the United States. He was opposed to the enforced
drawing from plaster casts,—"tracing the shadow of a shadow."
The keynote of his teaching was "spacing," and for a while
he worked with Arthur Wesley Dow at the Pratt Institute in
Brooklyn. In Boston he gave public lectures on Japanese and
Chinese history and art, and in 1893 he represented Japan
at the World's Fair in Chicago, where Japanese art was classified for the first time not among the industries but among
the fine arts. In the Puvis de Chavannes frescoes at the Boston Public Library he saw "the supreme triumph of the decorative idea," though he said they pushed too far towards the
pole of decoration as Abbey's pictures pushed too far towards
the pole of expression. He spoke of Sargent's first fresco as
"blazing up the firmament of art like a new comet." During
these years he showed the youthful Bernard Berenson his
collections of Oriental art, which Berenson defended in opposi-

tion to Norton; and Mrs. Jack Gardner saw much of Fenollosa. She remembered his "fresh enthusiastic greeting" when she was in Japan in 1883, and at her house he met Paul Bourget and his wife when they visited Boston in 1893. But she declined the honour of receiving at Fenway Court a distinguished Japanese who wore European dress. A believer in the maintenance of native customs, costumes and ceremonies, she found the ways of the Orient picturesque and interesting, and Japanese were welcome in her box at the opera only if they came in Japanese clothes.

Why did Fenollosa sever his connection with the Boston Museum? In part, no doubt, because of a scandal. He had left his wife and presently married Mary McNeil, who had grown up in Mobile, Alabama. Mary McNeil had been married before to a diplomat at Tokyo, and she had lived for several years in Japan, the setting of two or three novels she later wrote under the pen-name "Sidney McCall." After her husband died, she married Fenollosa in 1895, when he was still curator at the Boston Museum. The two returned together to Japan, where they lived in Tokyo from 1897 to 1900, and Fenollosa studied the Noh drama and Chinese and Japanese poetry and began to plan his history of Far Eastern art. Japanese artists, poets and priests gathered in his house there; Japan excited him more than ever, and, to Robert Underwood Johnson of *The Century Magazine* in New York, he wrote: "This is the first time I have ever lived. There seems no end to the material that is offering itself to us here. Meanwhile, we keep ourselves well-informed of the Western world through a liberal supply of papers and magazines . . . Here it was my intention, for the first time in my life, to enter upon a literary career; and the choice of residence and conditions was a matter involving much time. At last in the middle of June I was able to hire a suitable house in Tokyo, and soon had all my furniture, books and papers from America unpacked and arranged about me. It was then only that I could settle down to my writing . . . There can be no question that this is the place in which Oriental history should be written. Already I have vistas of years of fruitful collaboration with my Eastern friends. My closest friend and co-worker is Okakura."

"Let me hope," Fenollosa continued in a letter to Johnson in 1897, "that a word describing my new life may interest you. Besides working on the history of art, I have projected the early writing of treatises, which I have been preparing for years on the Theory of Art and on Art Education. In collaboration with my wife, I shall carry forward the translation of Chinese and Japanese poetry . . . A young lady is with us, a Miss Dyer of New Orleans, of a remarkable mind, a writer who will be heard from in the future. She, Mrs. Fenollosa and myself have three separate studies, where we work undisturbed for five hours every morning. In the afternoon we take exercise, view the city, or receive our friends. In the evening we meet for regular study together. Monday evenings our subject is Philosophy, and at present we are studying Hegel's Logic. On Tuesday it is Poetry, and we have begun with the Elizabethan dramatists. Wednesday, History, at present English, Thursday, the History of Art, Bosanquet's Aesthetics. Friday, Science, just now mechanics. Saturday, Japanese language. A number of years spent in this fashion will carry us over much ground." Fenollosa was preparing some articles on Japanese art for *The Century*, and he wrote to Johnson in 1898, "The time is more than ripe for the appearance of my articles, as yet the first accurate information on the subject, and that for which the world has been waiting for fifteen years. I cannot guarantee their primacy much longer, and my reputation demands that, in some way, my twenty years of effort should enter the field first . . . There have been efforts on the part of both foreigners and natives to publish on Japanese art . . . So far, we have the field pre-empted. Nobody has opened my historic mine, nobody has used such illustrations. But the drift here is rapidly toward a national interest in these things, which is stimulating many a scheme of art publication. The government's former prohibition of the public's photographing treasures in temples has been greatly relaxed. To have our illustrative material remain unique we must be quick in its use. As for the text, pardon my self-confidence if I say that I wish the early publication of my sketch to deter, by its evident reserve of strength, any rash and ill-equipped interlopers in this field."

Two years later, in 1900, the Fenollosas returned to America, but not before Fenollosa had published in the *Japan Weekly Mail* his ode on the marriage of the Crown Prince of Japan. Much Japanese history appeared in this *Epithalamial Ode*, which was written in the lofty style of Milton. Fenollosa lectured from San Francisco to New York, and, invited by President Theodore Roosevelt, he even lectured at the White House. He noted that he was regarded as a "Japanese man," and sometimes he heard students at a university say, "Oh, where is the Jap?" At least he believed that Japanese art had an immense amount to teach Americans. At this time he and his wife went to live for a while in Mobile, at Kobinata, named after Fenollosa's former house in Tokyo, where were installed not only many objets-d'art but also shrubbery brought back from Japan. There, when Fenollosa was absent on his lecture tours, "Sidney McCall" began to write her novels. She also wrote poems with Japanese themes, but, along with *The Dragon Painter*, the story of an actual artist with a violent

style, her most important book was *The Breath of the Gods,*
largely about an American senator who has idealized Japan before, as ambassador, with his family, he goes to live there. He
is convinced, like Fenollosa, that the Japanese can "fuse the
experience, character, insight, humanity of both our long-
suffering hemispheres." His own old mule, on the farm in
Illinois, called Kuranasuki, did better work than any span of
horses.

In a New York apartment, in the summer of 1906, Fenollosa completed a rough draught of his *Epochs of Chinese and
Japanese Art,* hastily writing in pencil and often omitting
Chinese names, the full names of artists and the names of
temples. He left blank the location of many T'ang paintings
in Japan, intending to insert these when he could get back
to Japan again, consult with old colleagues and have access
to archives. Making no claim to being a scholar, he wrote
for those who could try to form a clear conception of the
humanity of the Far Eastern peoples; but this was the first time
that anyone had attempted a treatise on its vast subject, "a
single splendid sweep." He discussed together Chinese and
Japanese art as if they were a single aesthetic movement, as
closely interrelated as Greek and Roman art, seeing each epoch
as having its own beauty of spacing, colour and line, permeat-
ing ceramics and textiles along with painting and sculpture.
He foresaw a time when the art-work of the whole world
would be looked upon as one, variations in a single kind of
mental effort.

In 1908, Fenollosa undertook a tour of Europe, leading a
class of young men to whom he lectured in art museums. For
The Craftsman he reviewed the spring Paris Salon of which
he said the live historical genius had fallen on a rocky soil
from Spain. Then, in September, on the eve of sailing for

home, he died suddenly in London, a victim of angina pectoris, and his ashes, placed at first in Highgate cemetery, were enclosed in a bronze casket and conveyed to Japan. They were buried on a hill overlooking Lake Biwa, under a group of large cryptomeria trees, in the grounds of the temple of Miidera, to which old lichen-covered steps led the way. There Fenollosa had spent many days meditating upon the sutras, and the ceremony was performed by Ajari Mobayeshi and his attendant priests chanting the sacred Kyomon. At the time of the funeral a memorial exhibition was held of two hundred paintings loaned by collectors in Tokyo, Kyoto and Osaka, for which two temples were turned into art galleries. Later a stone monument, twelve feet high, was erected in the grounds of the Tokyo Art School, with a chiselled portrait bust surmounting a long biographical inscription, shadowed in spring by cherry blossoms. Fenollosa, the poet Yone Noguchi said, was "the very discoverer of Japanese art for Japan."

Two years later, Mrs. Fenollosa left Kobinata and took the manuscript of his *Epochs* to Japan, where, working with Dr. Ariga Nagao and Kano Tomonobu, she completed the book as well as she could. Kano Tomonobu was the only blood descendant of his already forgotten school who was alive and practising his family art as he had learned it before the Revolution. The book, still full of errors, remained a great romance, and, as Langdon Warner said, "Though Western knowledge of Oriental art has progressed since [Fenollosa's] death, it has followed the path blazed by him." Meanwhile, the shadowy head of Christ behind Saint-Gaudens's "Phillips Brooks," at the side of Trinity Church in Boston, was modelled from Fenollosa's head. "He was in certain ways a great man," Dr. Bigelow wrote to the first Mrs. Fenollosa. Dr. Bigelow was to outlive him by several years. His heart too remained in Japan, and, while his family arranged for funeral services in Trinity Church, no one was permitted to see the body; for Dr. Bigelow had insisted on being dressed for burial in the Oriental robes of a Buddhist neophyte. He too was buried, near Fenollosa, on the shores of Lake Biwa. As for Edward S. Morse, the first of all these pilgrims to Japan, his five thousand specimens of Japanese pottery had long since been acquired by the Museum in Boston; but he continued to live in Salem, and Japanese visitors were astonished by his perfect rendering of long poetical passages from the Noh plays.

x

"The life of Ernest Fenollosa was the romance par excellence of modern scholarship," Ezra Pound wrote in 1916. After Fenollosa's death, his widow cast about for someone who could render into poetical English his unedited fragments of Chinese and Japanese poems and plays, and she became convinced that Ezra Pound was the "poet-interpreter" for whom she was searching. She forwarded her husband's notes to him, and Pound, enthusiastic, said that the writers before the Petrarchan age of Li Po were "a treasure to which the next centuries may look for as great a stimulus as the Renaissance had from the Greeks." Pound began with work on the Noh plays and presently went on to the Chinese poems, saying, "The first step of a renaissance, or awakening, is the importation of models for painting, sculpture and writing. The last century discovered the Middle Ages. It is possible that this century may find a new Greece in China." He drew a parallel between Chinese and Imagist poetry, explaining Imagism in terms of the idiogram of the Chinese written character, a "verbal medium consisting largely of semi-pictorial appeals to the eye."

For this written character was based not on sound but on form; the word was a picture of an object. He called Fenollosa's essay, *The Chinese Written Character*, "a study of the fundamentals of all aesthetics"; in its strong reliance on verbs it erected all speech into a kind of dramatic poetry. But George Kennedy, the sinologist of Yale, found this essay a mare's-nest, all self-contradiction and confusion, in which it was apparent that the Chinese language did not rely on verbs but rather on nouns.

In his summing up, however, Ezra Pound wrote truthfully of Fenollosa, "His mind was constantly filled with parallels and comparisons between Eastern and Western art . . . He looked to an American renaissance . . . In his search through unknown art, Fenollosa, coming upon unknown motives and principles unrecognized in the West, was already led into many modes of thought since fruitful in 'new' Western painting and poetry." Ezra Pound concluded with the remark, "He was a forerunner without knowing it and without being known as such."

FANNY WRIGHT

I

IN THE autumn of 1819, the Englishman John Garnett had
been living for twenty-two years in New Brunswick, New
Jersey, where this elderly philosopher of ample means had
bought the Whitehouse farm to bring up his four personable
daughters. A citizen of the world himself, he had travelled in
France and Italy; he had known, in Switzerland, Bonstetten
and Lavater; and, an ardent follower of the French Ency-
clopædists, he built an observatory beside his roomy dwelling.
For he was a student of astronomy and mathematics who gave
lessons in navigation and nautical science to Charles Wilkes,
the future discoverer of the Antarctic continent. John Garnett
had sent for an English governess to supervise the daughters,
one of whom wrote in later years a tale called *The Jersey
Laurel* about the shrub that grew by the Raritan river. Prosper
Mérimée, whom she was to know in Paris, compared her style
to Dr. Johnson's.

The Garnetts were cosmopolites, and among their neighbours in New Brunswick were the Hyde de Neuville family
who had escaped from France after trying to persuade Napoleon to recall the Bourbons. They were Bonapartist émigrés
as others in America had been exiled earlier still by the French

Revolution, and they lived for three years in New Brunswick
before the "shepherd of the Raritan" became the Minister of
Marine of the Bourbon king. The Hyde de Neuvilles were
royalists as the Garnetts were republicans, but they mingled
very happily in New Jersey, although John Garnett had more
in common with the Englishman Joseph Priestley who had
settled on the Susquehanna at about the same time. Garnett
had come to America in 1797, Priestley in 1794, hoping to
establish a settlement for the friends of liberty there. A few
years earlier Coleridge and Southey had planned to organize
their Pantosocracy on the banks of the Susquehanna; while
they gave up this plan, Priestley expressed the frame of mind of
many of the emigrants to the United States, "Whatever was
the beginning of this world, the end will be glorious and
paradisaical, beyond what our imagination can now conceive."
The age of Enlightenment was in full flood, and America was
the Eden of the new world.

Suddenly, in 1819, two attractive Scottish girls arrived in
New Brunswick to visit the Garnetts, Frances and Camilla
Wright, who had just come down from Montreal in the course
of a journey through the new republic. Frances Wright, or
Fanny Wright, as everybody called her, was tall and slender,
twenty-four years old, with blue eyes, high spirits, an air of
command and a manner that was often called enchanting. Her
pretty sister Camilla was a year younger. The two had stayed
in a boarding-house near the Battery in New York, then they
had moved to the house of the widow of Wolf Tone, the
leader of the Irish rising of 1798; but they had come to New
Brunswick with an introduction from John Wilkes, who was
very English himself in manner and appearance. This banker,
—the father of the explorer,—who lived in Greenwich Village,
wore a blue coat with a buff waistcoat, and his long hair was

slowly turning white. Fanny was anxious to be known as a
young author, and she had published the tragedy of *Altorf*,
a Byronesque play in five acts that was produced at the Park
Theatre in New York. It dealt with an imaginary incident in
the struggle of the Swiss against the encroachments of Austria
in the fourteenth century. Fanny had hoped that Kemble
would produce the play in Glasgow at a time when she was
living there, but it was brought out in New York with the
elder Walleck in the principal part and John Wilkes and
Cadwallader Colden sitting in boxes. Then, before it was
printed by Mathew Carey, it was produced again, with the
praise of William Dunlap, in Philadelphia. Thomas Jefferson,
who read the play, also praised it in a letter to the author.
It was supposed for a while to have been written by the young
Wolf Tone, whose mother was now married to a brother of
"Christopher North," the principal writer of *Blackwood's
Magazine*. Fanny, who had been engaged for a long time to
her cousin in England, fell in and out of love with this other
young man, as keen a radical as herself, who read the pro-
logue to *Altorf*, a play expressing views that were hateful to
the Tories. But Fanny, who spoke Italian and French, still had
conservative friends, like Wilkes and Colonel John Trumbull,
the painter.

Fanny and Camilla stayed with the Garnetts for many
weeks, and before they left to return to England they swore
eternal friendship with Julia and Harriet Garnett, two of the
young daughters. But Fanny, who had lost her own father
when she was not three years old, was even more taken with
John Garnett, the venerable sage whose name and character
she planned to introduce in a long poetical work, *Thoughts
of a Recluse*. In fact, she was always looking for a father, and
she was to find one in Jeremy Bentham, in Robert Owen, and,

above all, in Lafayette. In the end she married an elderly
Frenchman. She had had, with Camilla, meanwhile, an unhappy childhood. Born in Dundee, the daughter of a merchant who had been under surveillance for treason, they had
been left orphans when they were just able to walk, and they
had been brought up by their mother's conventional family
and friends. Their father, a great numismatist, who collected
coins and medals and presented his valuable collection to the
British Museum, had financed a cheap edition of Thomas
Paine's *The Rights of Man* and remained a trouble-maker in
a time of reaction. These were the retrograde years that followed Waterloo, and the great landlords of Scotland were
turning their estates into game preserves, leaving their tenants
to emigrate or die by the roadside. It was almost a crime to
sympathize with the ideas of the French Revolution, punish-
able by imprisonment or transportation, and Fanny, who had
fallen under Byron's influence, seemed to take pleasure in
defying public opinion. She had observed that her grandfather
Campbell knew only "lords and generals," and she and her
sister never learned to dress themselves without help from a
maid, while they themselves were subjected to "violence and
insult." Or so Fanny averred in a letter to her aunt. Carefully
brought up in the Church of England, and with ample means
of her own, she happened on a copy of Botta's *American
Revolution* and, as she said, awoke to a new existence. She
confessed to the Garnetts her aversion to England, its government and society, saying, "Do not think me madly prejudiced
against this island. But I cannot see beggary in our towns and
villages, and read of injustice in every paper . . . and meet
political and religious hypocrisy wherever I turn, without feeling pain, indignation or disgust." She wished only to see the
United States, and she had sailed with Camilla to remain for

two years and a half and travel through the country. Camilla, "young, lovely, attractive in manner," as one of their friends said, "could have no happiness distinct from her glorious sister." Camilla, in short, lived in Fanny's light.

Their only pleasant home in England had been the house, near Newcastle, of the sympathetic widow of one of their uncles, and to this Mrs. Robina Millar, who had lived in America herself, Fanny wrote the letters that she presently published. She called her book *Views of Society and Manners in America,* and she recounted her travels among the "calm, rational, civil and well-behaved" American people. Slavery was the only blot she could see in a country "where the dreams of sages, smiled at as Utopian, seem distinctly realized . . . a nation of all others the most orderly and the most united"; but, as she made only a little excursion into Virginia, she was not greatly disturbed as yet by slavery. From the "pleasant, opulent and airy" New York, she went to Albany and Vermont, Niagara Falls, Philadelphia, Baltimore and Washington, and there she met Henry Clay who quoted in one of his speeches a remark of the "distinguished foreign lady." She visited Joseph Bonaparte, the ex-king of Spain, at Bordentown, among Canova's busts of the Bonaparte family in his villa there, and she found on American farms plenty at the board, an open door, light spirits and easy toil. In short, her picture was much like Cobbett's in *A Year's Residence in the United States* when this transmogrified Tory, returning to the country, found universal civility, cheerfulness and industry where he had found everything hateful before. Nothing was said, in Fanny Wright's view of the great experiment, about any of the elements that America lacked,—a fine literature, cathedrals, imposing ruins; one saw only what was visible through rose-coloured glasses of a country that was happily called a republic.

II

Soon after Fanny returned to England, John Garnett died in New Brunswick, and his wife and three unmarried daughters sold their Whitehouse farm and went to live on the Left Bank in Paris. They settled in the Rue St. Maur, as it was called in the eighteen-twenties. The Hyde de Neuvilles welcomed their old neighbours from New Brunswick, with Paul de Neuville, who had also raised sheep on the Raritan, and Madame Dupont de Nemours, who had gone back to Paris. It was Paul de Neuville's daughter whose scandalous elopement caused her to appear as Mathilde de la Môle in Stendhal's novel, *Le Rouge et Le Noir,* and Prosper Mérimée acted as an intermediary between the Garnetts and the rejected lover. For Grasset was forbidden to marry the young lady.

The Garnetts, who were far from rich, had their own salon, nevertheless, at which Prosper Mérimée and Stendhal constantly appeared, and when Macready, the actor, came to Paris, they gave a little evening party for him. Mérimée, pale and thin, came once with his arm in a sling, the result of a duel, though he said it was due to a fall from a cabriolet. The duel was fought over a lady at whose house he was staying, and the husband challenged him and shot him in the arm. Sismondi, the Swiss historian, who had gone to Italy with Madame de Staël on the journey that resulted in *Corinne,* had married a Miss Allen, a cousin of the Garnetts, and at his house in Geneva later they met the great Chateaubriand, who appeared to be as liberal as they were. "I forgot I was talking to a *great man,*" Harriet wrote to Fanny Wright. "His head is beautiful and his conversation full of spirit and feeling." In Geneva she also met La Guiccioli, "as fair as a lily, but not melancholy enough for Byron's mistress." A few years later

Mrs. Shelley arrived in Paris and saw the Garnetts again and again, "such a complete coquette," wrote Harriet, "that I have no patience with her. Pretty she is but so affected," flirting with Prosper Mérimée. While most of their friends were conservative, the Garnetts remained liberals, and they felt at home in the circle of Lafayette and his gay young follower Benjamin Constant. "The general,"—always Lafayette,—who, in his old age liked young girls, was the great attraction of their salon; and Harriet Garnett later translated his memoirs into English when his family consulted her about a previous bad translation. The Garnetts were invited to the weddings of his granddaughters and all the family ceremonies at La Grange, the great gloomy castle forty miles from Paris. Ever since he had been released from the Austrian prison of Olmütz, he had been active in the French Chamber of Deputies, fighting for the freedom of the press, the abolition of titles and religious toleration. He believed that France had only to turn itself into another America to achieve happiness for all men.

Meanwhile, Fanny and Camilla Wright had gone back to the north of England. There they stayed near Newcastle with their aunt by marriage who wrote that, after two years and a half in the United States, they had returned "wholly American in their sentiments and feelings." Fanny sent Harriet Garnett two poems she had composed in the stage-coach on her way to Ayrshire, and, writing her *Views of Society and Manners in America,* she met Francis Jeffrey in Edinburgh. Not yet Lord Jeffrey, he was the editor of the *Edinburgh Review* and the son-in-law of her New York friend John Wilkes, and Fanny wrote to Harriet, "Jeffrey was very polite . . . But I did not like him so well as the last time I saw him. His conceit and nonsense are rather sickening, and his vulgar flirting with a married woman on a side sofa was *greatly* sickening. We saw at his house that evening his peculiar coterie, and I thought it altogether insufferable—conceit, affectation and vulgarity all united. For heaven's sake, whisper this not abroad." Then she related how a certain bluestocking had met Mrs. Jeffrey, who took her into the nursery, seated her by the fire and ran away to find a pair of dry shoes and stockings. (They had been walking along roads ankle-deep in mud.) Just then Jeffrey returned from his ride, and, coming to the nursery, he saw, sitting with her back to the door, a female figure which he took for his wife's. He called out loud, "You great ass, what are you sitting there for?" No answer. "You great stupid brute, why don't you answer?" Still silence. "You great ugly beast, you great deaf fool." Then the figure slowly rose and, lifting up her veil, confronted him, a stranger. Fanny added, "Don't you see his hair bristling like a porcupine's, his face lengthening into an ell and a quarter and his two eyes expanding into saucers?" She could scarcely have wondered that he ignored, in the *Edinburgh Review*, her *Views of Society and Manners in America*.

But the book won the attention of liberals and radicals all over Europe, and even the Bourbon King of France, Louis XVIII, was impressed by her picture of the young republic. She had a letter from Jeremy Bentham, an old friend of her father's, and the great utilitarian invited her to visit him the next time she came to London. Priestley's *Essay on Government* had given him the formula "the greatest happiness of the greatest number,"—at sight of which he had cried out, like Archimedes, "Eureka!"—and Fanny had seen the connection between this and her own Epicurean doctrine that the desire for pleasure and the avoidance of pain were the underlying motives of human action. "I had contracted," Bentham said, "oh! horrible! that unnatural and, at that time, almost un-exampled appetite,—the *love of innovation*," although he had been opposed to the cause of the American colonists, owing to the inadequacy of its presentment by their friends in England. But he had given Mirabeau materials for some of his greatest speeches and the title "Citizen of France" had been bestowed upon him. He had belonged to a dinner club of which the despot was Dr. Johnson, that "pompous vamper," as he said, "of commonplace morality," and he called Sir Walter Scott "that servile poet and novelist," for he himself had become more and more a radical. He devoted to projects of prison reform years of his life and much of his fortune, and he urged the suppression of fox-hunting and cock-fighting because they entailed a prolonged and painful death. His sole measure of good and evil was the quantity of pleasure or pain, physical or intellectual, that an action caused, and his contempt for the past was general and marked. He never tired now of comparing the honest government of the United States with the corruption that he found in England, and he was eager to converse with anyone who could give him information about the American republic. He refused to see Madame de Staël, whom he called a "trumpery magpie," but he talked with Fanny Wright till eleven in the evening.

An old bachelor, cheerful and benign, with long flowing white hair, a Quaker-like coat and light brown cashmere breeches, he seldom left his "Hermitage" in Queen's Square Place where flowers grew in all the window-boxes. A piano stood in every room for Jeremy Bentham to play on. He read and wrote all day and dined at six, beginning with dessert, for he said it lost its flavour if he ate it after the more sustaining viands. In the evenings he conversed with his friends, the philosophical radicals whom he inspired,—James Mill,

Francis Place, the "radical tailor," the poet Thomas Campbell and George Grote, the historian of Greece. Fanny, who was often there, sometimes found herself alone at the fireplace of her old philosopher, the Socrates who carried his years as bravely as ever, she wrote, except that he had grown considerably deafer. An hour's conversation with him left her more fatigued than a walk of six miles. But she felt at home in Jeremy Bentham's house, he called her "the strongest, sweetest mind that was ever cased in a human body"; and to him she dedicated *A Few Days in Athens,* a little book about Epicurus. "Think for yourself" is the motto of the Epicurean garden, as the young Corinthian, a disciple, quickly learns, and Fanny, the bold free-thinker, had thought herself out of religion, which she described as "the dark coinage of trembling ignorance." The book became a favourite with readers of Volney's *Ruins* and Thomas Paine's *The Age of Reason.*

One day in September, 1821, Fanny received a letter from Lafayette, who had read her *Views* of the United States and begged her to see him when she came to Paris to visit the Garnetts. He was enchanted with this book, which did justice, as he said, to "the best and happiest people in the world"; and, when Fanny went over to Paris, Lafayette invited her to visit him and his family at La Grange. In the old château with its crumbling walls and five massive towers, there were usually twenty or thirty guests at dinner, the "exiled constitutionals," Spaniards, Italians, Portuguese and Poles, not to mention the needy Americans who sponged upon him. Then there was the family of nineteen persons, Lafayette's sons and daughters, with their husbands, wives and children, who walked, fished, rowed on the lake and visited the islands. They all assembled in the fine old dining-room, a stone hall with a groined roof. The conspirators who appeared there used La

Grange as a meeting-place, though the Carbonari, who were held together by hatred of the Bourbons, had their supreme lodge in Paris. Lafayette, who was up to the neck in Carbonarist plots,—with Ary Scheffer, the painter, and the two Thierrys, the well-known historians of later years,—often appeared at meetings in this lodge, inviolable himself as a member of the Chamber. Open-handed, immensely rich, he had fed seven hundred peasants a day in a year of agricultural depression, and he cultivated not only his land but his flock of merino sheep, his Devonshire cattle and his pigs from Baltimore and China. He sent sheepdogs to Jefferson at Monticello.

For Washington's former aide-de-camp had retained through half a century his friendship with the fathers of the American republic, together with his loyalty to the American people as "one large innocent family having everything in common." He said that Fanny's book made him live over again the days that he had spent with "an army of brothers." He had his private quarters in one of the towers at La Grange, a library and a study where always hung the portrait that Ary Scheffer painted of Fanny, and Fanny's room was directly underneath, so that they could spend many hours together. Fanny, his confidante, aware of all his plans, sometimes acted as his secretary, and, spending six months there once, with her sister Camilla and Harriet Garnett, she worked on a life of Lafayette that was never completed. "My beloved, my adored Fanny," as Lafayette called her, with her amber hair, tall and slender, wore trousers at La Grange, a tunic and a sash and a broad-brimmed hat instead of a bonnet. "What goodness, what adorable goodness is yours to me, O my friend, my father, my brother! How fortunate I am after all to have such a friend in whom I can confide all my thoughts, and who finds me worthy of a like confidence . . . I who was thrown in infancy upon the world like a wreck upon the waters." So she wrote to Lafayette. They all spent their winters in Paris, Fanny with the Garnetts, in an old building that had once been a convent, and Lafayette drove over in his coach two or three times a week to pass a few hours in Fanny's study. It was a little room that had once been a nun's cell. Once he found her correcting the proofs of a French translation of her book.

For three or four years Fanny went back and forth between Paris and London, where she found a second home at Harrow, not far away, in the house of the mother of Anthony Trollope. Short, plump and voluble, Mrs. Trollope, a country clergyman's daughter, had been a lifelong friend of the Garnetts, and she said that her husband was "a good honourable man" but that his temper was really "dreadful." He had violent headaches for which he took calomel, and "every year increases his irritability, and also its lamentable effect upon the children." A melancholy failure at both law and farming, he was absorbed in writing an Encyclopædia Ecclesiastica, and their son Anthony, as a day-pupil at the Harrow school, was laughed at for wearing his father's cut-down suits. Mrs. Trollope, a Tory at heart, had been brought up on Rousseau. She was liberal, and even gullible, at this time of her life, anything but the orthodox matron she became later, and, writing letters to her sons in French and Italian, she was much taken with Fanny and her sister Camilla. She could not say too much about the "glorious sister": "Never was there, I am persuaded, such a being as Fanny Wright . . . Some of my friends declare that if worship may be offered it must be to her—that she is at once all that woman should be—and something more than woman ever was—and I know not what beside—and I for my part applaud and approve all they say. Miss Landon [Letitia Elizabeth Landon, the poetess], to whom I had mentioned her being here has written to ask leave to look at the most interesting woman in Europe. I honour the little Sappho for the wish—and have granted it."

Fanny Trollope had just travelled to England with Fanny Wright on the top of a diligence to Calais, for she had been in Paris in 1823 when she met Washington Irving and Fenimore Cooper. She dined at the Garnetts' house with Sismondi and Benjamin Constant, and Lafayette, who was also there, invited her for ten days at La Grange. General Guglielmo Pepe, too, may have been present, the hero of the unsuccessful rising at Naples, for Pepe, with his aide-de-camp, Count Pisa, was often at the Garnetts' and the Trollopes'. These two were professional soldiers of fortune, always on the liberal side, and Fanny Wright found herself entangled in General Pepe's affairs, concerned as he was at the moment with a revolt in Spain. Mrs. Trollope was to cross the ocean a few years later with Fanny Wright, but at the moment Fanny was to go to America with Lafayette, whom President Monroe invited in 1824. Lafayette had been defeated in the elections of 1823, and the failure of all the Carbonarist plans had discredited the cause of liberalism. Moreover, Lafayette himself was in financial straits, and his family had been embarrassed by his relations with Fanny. With what she called their "little minds and petty jealousies," they had turned against her; but their feeling changed when they were convinced that his well-being and even his health would be affected by any break with his "adopted daughters." In fact, they urged Fanny and Camilla to go to America with him, provided they sailed on a separate ship. "The Atlantic to be sure is a broad ferry, but easily to be crossed," Fanny wrote to Julia Garnett, adding, "Without some fixed and steady occupation, of labour, of business, of study . . . it is impossible to make our existence glide smoothly

. . . I remember an observation of your father's, that geometry had been his best friend and consoling companion. Rousseau said the same thing of botany, and Gibbon of his social research and composition." Fanny was very busy planning and writing.

So she and Camilla returned to America with "General Rainbow," as he came to be called; or, rather, sailing on a slower ship, the sisters reached New York in time for the great reception at Castle Garden. Then they travelled for several months about the country in his train, sharing balls, dinners and fêtes, from Charleston to Boston. They heard Daniel Webster's oration on the fiftieth anniversary of Bunker Hill, and they spent several days at Monticello with Jefferson, to whom Lafayette had sent *A Few Days in Athens*. Fanny and Camilla set out on horseback for Natural Bridge, then, striking across to Harper's Ferry, through scenes that Jefferson had described, they rode for ten days to Washington. There, meeting Sam Houston and Andrew Jackson, Fanny told John Quincy Adams that Jeremy Bentham often spoke of him.

But, at a certain Virginia seaport where they were disembarking, Fanny saw a vessel sailing for New Orleans, crowded with blacks who were chained two by two and destined for the slave-market of the deep South. From that moment the question of slavery filled her mind,—what could she herself do about it?—and she gave up all thought of returning to France with Lafayette and began to think out a plan for emancipation. Before long she had bought from agents of General Jackson six hundred and forty acres near Memphis, Tennessee, formerly a station for the fur trade of the Indians and at the moment consisting of a dozen log cabins. Her land was below the cotton line of the South; it was gently undulating and hilly, though still infested with wolves, bears and panthers; and there she started a "model plantation" where a small number of slaves were to work out their freedom. She called it Nashoba, the old Chickasaw name for Wolf, and in preparation she rode on horseback forty miles a day, spending the night in the forest, on the ground or in cabins. For her bed she used a bearskin, with her saddle for a pillow. She had, she wrote, a perfect horse, gentle as a lamb but full of fire, who ate salt from her hand and ran like a deer. As for Camilla, she was more excited by the Western woods than by the prospect of emancipation. Fanny had parted from Lafayette at St. Louis, but she was to see him again two years later.

III

Lafayette sailed back to France in 1825, carrying with him a large box filled with American earth so that he could eventually be buried in it. Meanwhile, he was all sympathy with the "dear girls and their present concerns," for he was interested in every plan to abolish slavery: he had even attempted, long before, an experiment in gradual emancipation on his estate in French Guiana. This experiment had been cut short by the French Revolution, but he had proposed to Washington that they should purchase some land together and employ the slaves as paid agricultural hands after giving them their freedom.

As for Fanny and her plan, both Monroe and Madison gave her their blessing, and Jefferson heartily approved of Nashoba when the sisters joined Lafayette at Monticello. Jefferson believed that every plan should be adopted, every experiment tried that might do something towards the ultimate object, and he wrote to Fanny, "That which you propose is well worthy of trial. It has succeeded with certain portions of our white brethren, under the care of a Rapp and an Owen; and why may it not succeed with the men of colour?" Fanny revered the "greatest of America's surviving veterans . . . on the top of this little mountain . . . His face exhibits still, in its decaying outline and fallen and withered surface, the forms of symmetry and deep impress of character. His tall well-moulded figure remains erect and springy . . . but the lamp is evidently on the wane, nor is it possible to consider the fading of a light so brilliant and pure without a sentiment of deep melancholy." But, while Jefferson thought her plan was promising, he wrote, "At the age of eighty-two, with one foot in the grave and the other lifted to follow it, I do not permit myself to take part in any new enterprise,"—or any but his university at Charlottesville.

This was the age of communities, one hundred and seventy-eight at least, in the course of fifty years, in the United States, and there even existed at this time a Society for Promoting Communities in New York. George Flower, an Englishman of means, also a friend of Lafayette, who had his own community in Illinois, had journeyed with Fanny on horseback across the state of Tennessee searching for the right land for Nashoba. Finding it near Memphis on both sides of the Wolf River, Fanny bought eight slaves at Nashville, five men and three women, and a family of seven who had come from South Carolina. They were a mother and six daughters, the gift of a planter, and a carpenter and a blacksmith were expected from day to day. George Flower, who had gone home to Illinois, presently arrived again with his family and Camilla. They had had a tedious voyage on a flatboat, snagged in the Mississippi and getting off with difficulty. Travelling on the Mississippi was extremely hazardous, but "snags and foundered steamboats," wrote Fanny, "lost cargoes and drowned passengers, seldom inspire the precaution of lying in on a dark night, or of carefully firing the boilers, so as to prevent the addition of blowing up to the other perils of the navigation."

Soon a Scotsman, Richardson, arrived at Nashoba, with a young man, Richeson Whitby, who had been brought up in an easy-going Shaker Village; and they all piled brush and rolled logs, Fanny with the rest, fencing an apple orchard of five acres. They cleared two acres for cotton and five for corn. They built at first two log cabins, one for the Negroes, one for the whites, and at first they were cheerful and contented. "The axes are ringing and all is stirring," Fanny wrote to Julia Garnett. A fiddle, produced by one of the men who knew how to turn some merry tunes, struck up regularly every evening, and Fanny soon procured a flute for another. They had dances twice a week in a larger cabin which they presently built, dancing after a hard day's work of hewing and chopping, Fanny wrote, so heartily, "that I could wish myself one of them."

Fanny's old desire to be known as an author seemed to her very silly now. She was not interested in making her way to fortune and renown when there was a chance of gradually freeing the slaves without financial loss to the planters. She had spent, meanwhile, about $10,000, "more than a third of my property," she wrote, refusing the aid of Lafayette who watched over every move she made and who kept her friends the Garnetts well-posted about her. But she accepted a gift of goods from a Quaker in New York to help her in outfitting the community store. Moreover, George Flower transported down the river, in a flatboat, corn, hay, pork and beef, for she estimated that it would take three years of steady industry to bring the vegetable garden and the farm to bear. She had two cows to supply the dairy until they could send for the cattle and sheep, still in Illinois, in the autumn and spring. She planned to form a school where whites and blacks were to study together, proving their equality in brains, and a small cotton factory also, and she proposed to build on the pretty Wolf River a washing-house and another house for bathing. Then they were to open in time some wooded pastures and retired walks extending over meadows by the stream. Fanny rode three hundred miles into the Indian country, and she found in Memphis an interpreter for the body of Choctaws and Chickasaws who were trading there.

Fanny had no doubt that the Garnetts were going to join her, and she wrote to Julia Garnett, "When you come, bring a piece of stout cambric muslin—percale. Bring a few common beads, if cheap . . . Garnet red a favourite colour. Article of trade with Indians. A few cheap neck handkerchiefs, open net or silk, mixed with cotton or worsted. Showy cotton or marine handkerchiefs would sell well. Pincushions, bags, baskets, etc., also three plain looking glasses"; and she enclosed a draught to purchase these objects. Camilla added a request for two boxes of eau de Cologne, six yards of Swiss muslin for neck handkerchiefs, and two dozen cambric handkerchiefs for common use. Fanny wrote to Julia, "This state is one of the most favoured in the Union, abundantly watered by navigable streams flowing in all directions, and affording all varieties of soil and many of climate. Most of the productions of the North can be raised in perfection, and the Southern staple of cotton finds in this Western district a sun sufficiently genial and a soil particularly apt." Again she wrote, "The lovely face of nature—such woods, such lawns, such gently swelling hills, such glorious trees, such exquisite flowers, and the giant river wafting the rich produce of this unrivalled land to the ocean. I could have wept as I thought that such a garden was wrought by the hands of slaves." Fanny had spent seven of the nine months she had passed in America almost entirely within the slave states. On her earlier tour she had scarcely seen them at all, and she was now convinced that the cure for slavery lay in the amalgamation of the races.

Fanny owed the idea of Nashoba to the Owenite experiment which she had seen in its early stages; and she had even visited Economy, near Pittsburgh, where the Rappites were now living. George Rapp, a German vinedresser, had sold to Robert Owen the village of New Harmony in Indiana, although, moving to this new site, he continued the community that carried on its orchards and its vineyards. Owen, a rich Englishman, who had come to America with his four sons, hoped to prove in his village on the Wabash that men were what their environment made them, and his experiment in coöperative living largely inspired Fanny's single-handed attempt to liberate the slaves. Owen, a great manufacturer who had begun as a poor boy, had seen men, women and children demoralized and maimed by the wage-slavery of ordinary factory-life. Treated as mere instruments for the accumulation of wealth, they had worked in impossible conditions, and Owen was convinced that if the conditions were reversed the human results would be reversed as well. In short, he believed that men were perfectible if the environment was right. A friend of Bentham and William Godwin, he had conducted, at New Lanark, a laboratory for experiments in education, and, not believing in punishment, he had started schools for the factory-folk, teaching by means of maps and coloured blocks. The pupils danced and sang, following the methods of Pestalozzi, and studied in the open air, on country walks. When the control at New Lanark was taken out of Owen's hands, he had come to the United States hoping to establish his new world of the spirit in new-world conditions. He had addressed, in Washington, the House of Representatives, and the whole country was soon aware of this English socialist and his so-called "village of coöperation."

Fanny and Camilla were heartily with him. Camilla wrote to the Garnetts, "The principles advocated by Owen are to change the face of this world as surely as the sun shines in the heavens," and Fanny said, "Mr. Owen is working miracles and promises to revolutionize the North as I pray we may do the South." She dreamed that Nashoba might not only win for the Negroes political liberty but that it might lead to the moral regeneration of the race, and she set out to prove the equality of black and white by giving to mixed classes the same education. At the same time she agreed with Owen that "Christian fanaticism and subjection" were "the means employed for stultifying the intelligence," for she too was opposed to revealed religion. She was "not of any religion yet taught in the world"; moreover, she felt with Owen that marriage ought to be a free contract between willing partners. A little later Owen challenged the whole religious public to discuss the truth or falsehood of all religions, and Alexander Campbell challenged him, in 1829, in a famous debate in Cincinnati. Meanwhile, he had been to Mexico where he tried to convert Santa Anna, and he obtained a large tract of land in Texas, at that time Mexican, in order to start another community there. He had all but beggared himself in these enterprises. Lafayette wrote to the Garnetts, "You see, dear friends, that there is but one opinion, in Scotland and elsewhere, of Mr. Owen's exaggerations, while his virtues are as generally acknowledged."

Owen, returning to America after eight months in Europe, brought with him down the river his "Boatload of Knowledge,"

artists, teachers and men of science, among them Phiquipal
D'Arusmont, an eccentric little French physician. D'Arusmont
started his School of Industry in the old Rappite church building, with between sixty and ninety boys who produced enough
by labour to supply their daily needs. At the moment, both
Fanny and Camilla looked to New Harmony as a refuge in
case Nashoba was a failure, and Fanny was to go there when
it failed.

IV

In the spring of 1827, Fanny Wright returned to France in
the company of Robert Dale Owen, Robert Owen's son. Desperately ill with brain fever, she was carried aboard the ship,
the victim of malaria, the result of riding and sleeping in the
woods under the midday sun, in the dews at night. Richardson had recommended a sea voyage for her and a residence
in Europe during the summer, and there was also a question
of finding recruits in England and France and spreading the
good news of Nashoba. Camilla was left at the colony, the
only white woman there, with Richardson and Whitby, in
charge of their forest home. In New Orleans,—the "Babylon
of the Revelations," where slavery abounded, and the clank
of chains rose from the piles and gutters,—Fanny engaged a
Scotch woman to travel with her. She provided herself with a
box of lemons to make lemonade during the crossing. There
were two goats on the little ship, two pigs, two sheep and two
alligators; and among the passengers were six Osage Indians
who lay on the roof of the companionway. As they set out,
the Indians began singing hymns to the Great Spirit for the
success of the voyage.

For six days the ship was grounded on a sandbar, while
swarms of mosquitoes tormented the passengers, and, as Fanny

wrote, "If Moses had thought of Mississippi mosquitoes, one plague would have done the work of seven." But she acquired on the voyage new limbs, and a new head and eyes, and, when after fifty days at sea the ship reached Le Havre, she went to the Garnetts and then to La Grange to be with Lafayette. She found the château much improved, "as simple as ever but neat and fresh, the old faces—Nichola's primum flourishing through the room, broom in hand and brush on foot." From La Grange she wrote, "I see our forest home with its smiling faces of every hue almost as if I stood in our busy square . . . The children both of slave and free are now gathered together under the charge of Charlotte and Camilla, separated from the contamination of their parents whom they see only in presence of their directors."

Then, about Lafayette, she wrote to Sismondi, the cousin by marriage of the Garnetts, "It is soothing to the heart to see the autumn, for seventy years have not brought him to the winter of life, thus fresh and vigorous and so sweetened by well-merited honours and grateful retrospection." Sismondi himself wrote to Julia and Harriet Garnett, saying it was impossible to take their mother to Nashoba, "It is not at her age that one is able to go to look for death in the savannahs of the Mississippi in the midst of flood, and mosquitoes, in a miserable hut made of tree trunks, deprived of all the sweetnesses of life, of all society of her own age, of all medical care, even of furniture and common utensils, of food and drink which long habit has made neccessities." The year before, Sismondi had written, "Poor girls! Almost alone, without food for their mind, with the coarsest food for their body, weakened in their health, very likely disheartened in their schemes . . . You exaggerate strangely the influence I have over them. I love them almost entirely through you. They have seen me only once." He added, writing to Julia, "I wish much to see F. Wr. but chiefly to see her to persuade her to study here, in Italy, the systems of exploitation which have made the peasants happy, which have given them habits of order and intelligence, which have in short been the successive and necessary steps to advance from slavery to liberty and goodness. I am persuaded she will continue to combine her American experience with the old experience of Europe. I believe that before returning to Tenese [*sic*] she should see the peasants of Switzerland and also those of Tuscany . . . I regret especially that she has employed her heroic enthusiasm under the direction of a man [Robert Owen] whose mind is so little logical and who has delivered himself up to dangerous reveries on the ways to better mankind instead of studying what is, and what has been . . . In writing to Miss Wright, speak to her again of my admiration and attachment"; but a year later, referring to Fanny's "great presumption," he said, "I cannot admit that a young woman should be so bent on remaking the whole of human society."

Fanny, however, had no doubts, and she was convinced that she would find many recruits for her enterprise. In Paris she tried to make converts in liberal circles, and before going over to London she stayed long enough to witness the marriage of Julia Garnett to a young German historian. This was Georg Heinrich Pertz, whom Julia had met at one of Lafayette's *soirées* and when she was staying in Harrow at Mrs. Trollope's. They had played chess together and Pertz's conversation pleased her. Pertz had been in England collecting materials for his German history, and he eventually published texts of the more important writers on German affairs down to the year 1500, a work that made possible the existence of the modern school of scientific historians of mediæval Germany. Fanny had been for nine years, Julia wrote to Sismondi, "the

sole object of my thoughts,—almost the sole object of my love";
but Julia went to Hanover now, to remain for the rest of her
life, and henceforth Harriet Garnett was Fanny's correspondent.
Fanny still hoped that Harriet and Mrs. Garnett would join
her at Nashoba, and she wrote back from Harrow, where she
was staying at Mrs. Trollope's, asking Harriet to send two
pairs of sabots, "and do not forget to bring a pair for yourself. They will be very useful in the spring out of doors . . .
I say only delay until I see a comfortable residence for your
mother . . . If you come, dear Harriet, take pills regularly
while at sea and drink plentifully a thin gruel the first three
or four days . . . Pills of rhubarb and aloes mixed are as good
as any." If she could make the voyage on the first of October,
after the equinox had passed, she would have the best chance
for a good voyage. She would thus land in New York in
time to cross the Alleghanies "before the spring rains set in,"
and she would reach Nashoba in November or December.

In London, Fanny found much interest in her undertaking,
for she had returned, Sismondi said, with an "immense reputation"; and she was "engrossed," she wrote, "by a crowd of
visitors from morning till night." Robert Dale Owen thought
that Leigh Hunt and Mary Shelley would join them, and,
remembering that Mrs. Shelley was the daughter of Mary
Wollstonecraft, Fanny had written to her with high hopes.
For Mary Wollstonecraft had been the pride and delight of her
own life. She described herself as "a delicate nursling of
European luxury and aristocracy. I thought and felt for myself, and for martyrized humankind, and have preferred all
hazards, all privations in the forests of the New World to the
dear-bought comforts of miscalled civilization. I have made the
hard earth my bed, the saddle of my horse my pillow, and
have staked my life and fortune on an experiment having in

view moral liberty and improvement." She wrote again, "Yes, dear Mary, I do find the quiet of these forests and our ill-fenced cabins of rough logs more soothing to the spirit, and now no less suited to the body, than the warm luxurious houses of European society . . . I do want one of my sex to commune with and sometimes to lean on in all confidence of equality and friendship." But the gentle and womanly Mrs. Shelley, who found Fanny "like Minerva . . . a woman young, rich and independent," had had too much adventure in her pre-carious life, and she was more interested in Fanny herself than in her settlement in the Western woods. She introduced Fanny to her father, William Godwin, but she is supposed to have remarked, "Since I lost Shelley, I have had no wish to ally myself to the radicals—they are full of repulsion to me"; and she said, when she sent her son to Harrow, "For heaven's sake, let him learn to think like everyone else!" When Fanny finally sailed away, Mrs. Shelley came to the Town Steps in London to see her vessel off. She had made upon Fanny an ambiguous impression, but she had no intention of going with her.

About Mary Shelley, Fanny wrote to Harriet Garnett, "Deficient sensibility is a negative quality, but hypocrisy is a positive one of the worst character . . . 'Tis a bad and hollow world, my Harriet, as it is now, whatever it may be hereafter, and all I hear of or from it makes me rejoice in the breadth of the wilderness that separates Nashoba from it." There was another possible recruit with whom she perhaps fell in love, a young Frenchman, Antoine Dutrone, a member of the radical Carbonari, to whom she wrote a letter that she sent to the Garnetts, asking them to read it. You would have "to turn your back," she wrote to Dutrone, "on old institutions, on established customs, on the interests, the luxuries and the comforts of the Old World . . . There are many men of your age who are able to leap forward with enthusiasm, but few, very few, who are able to persevere in the face of obstacles and to press towards the goal without averting their eyes. I am not trying to discourage you. Far from it. I am too sensible of the need for companions in the work that occupies me, a work that needs for its success the efforts of all right-minded men. Only I wish to guard against illusions on your part, and disappointments on mine. May those who form our little battalion be at least brave and strong." Perhaps the young man felt that the prospect was too grim. At any rate, he went instead to Greece.

Were some of the recruits scared away by rumours that had begun to spread and that had reached Fanny already at La Grange? The moment she turned her back on Nashoba, things had begun to go wrong there, for Camilla, landlady of the tavern, was too easy-going to control the community, and Richardson and Richeson Whitby were no stronger. The very day that Fanny had left, Dilly and Redrick were reprimanded for interchanging abusive language, and Willis was made to retract the threat which he had uttered of avenging with his own hands the wrongs of Dilly. Henry declined to follow the plough on the plea of pain in his knee-joint, and some of the slaves broke the swing by using it in a riotous manner and had to be forbidden to partake of any such amusement. Black Peggy stole a pair of shoes, black Jenny quarrelled with black Joe, and Maria tried to hang herself for jealousy of Henry, in which the community could not support her. Kitty was reprimanded for washing the clothes of Mr. Roe, instead of carrying them to the washerwoman, Sukey. Maria began to cohabit with Henry, and Isabel laid a complaint against Redrick for coming to her bedroom during the night and endeavouring, uninvited, to take liberties with her person.

Moreover, Richardson informed the community that he and Mam'selle Josephine had begun to live together, and he wrote and published an article defending his conduct. He said that the proper basis of sexual intercourse was the unconstrained and unrestrained choice of both parties, and Camilla backed him up, affirming in print that the absent Fanny shared their views. Then Richardson thought he could not live in a co-öperative system and left Nashoba to play his part in the competitive world, while the mulatto Josephine sailed with her children to Haiti where they would no longer be described as "niggers." Camilla was left alone with Whitby as her only white companion, and they were presently married by a justice of the peace.

Now Camilla was opposed to marriage as "a subtle invention of priestcraft for poisoning the purest source of human felicity." Nevertheless, she had married in a quite official way, as her sister Fanny was to do in time; but when the rumour got about that Nashoba was a free-love community,—and one that ignored the colour-line,—their conventional friends were horrified, among them John Wilkes, who had heartily approved of their project for emancipation. There could be no more intercourse with the ladies of his family, John Wilkes said, although he continued to manage their financial affairs, and their Scottish uncle, James Mylne, was outraged by their insulting attacks on "the fixed opinions and the decent feelings of mankind." He felt obliged to conceal his relationship to the sisters. Julia Garnett wrote to Sismondi, "Mr. Owen has much to answer for—in sacrificing such beings as F. and C. Wright, he has done an irreparable wrong to mankind. Alas! What a mind he has ruined . . . I believe that Owen worked upon her mind at a moment when she was incapacitated by fever from judging sanely." The Garnetts had not objected to the free amours of their friends Benjamin Constant, Mérimée and Stendhal, but Anglo-Saxons were supposed to be different from the French, and in any case Harriet was loyal to Fanny. It was true that, two or three years later, Mrs. Garnett would not allow her to invite Fanny to come to see them. "The gates of the most rigid convent," Harriet wrote to Julia, "are not so insurmountable a barrier between the world and the nuns they enclose as public scorn makes against a woman who has joined such a community as Nashoba."

It is possible that Mrs. Trollope had not heard these rumours. However that may be, she wrote to Julia Garnett. "I feel greatly inclined to say, 'Where her country is, there shall be my country'. The more I see of her, the more I listen to her, the more I feel convinced that *all* her notions are right. She is pointing out to man a short road to that goal which for ages he has been in vain endeavouring to reach. Under her system I believe it possible that man may be happy." Mrs. Trollope was the only recruit who followed Fanny without any doubts, —the only one except Auguste Hervieu, the painter, who sailed eventually to America with them. Hervieu, a familiar visitor at Harrow, was a political refugee artist to whom Fanny offered the position of drawing-master at Nashoba. Mrs. Trollope, whom Fanny had met six years before at La Grange, saw Nashoba as the end of all her troubles, a comfortable rustic retreat where she could recoup the family fortunes and find a good school for her invalid son. Henry Trollope could be educated at Owen's socialist colony in Indiana. So, although her friend Macready tried to persuade her not to go, she had been too ready to be converted, and she was prepared to like everything there and everybody. She took with her all the furniture except enough to furnish two rooms for Mr. Trollope, whom she was leaving behind at the Harrow farmhouse.

v

On the ship to New Orleans, Fanny Wright haunted the steerage. She sat on a coil of rope reading to a sailor, who sat on another coil patching his breeches, and she expounded the wildest doctrines of equality and concubinage, or so Mrs. Trollope said later. Something, she felt, must have befallen Fanny when she went back to America that totally unsettled all her views, for obviously someone was to blame for Fanny's irregularities, either Lafayette or Robert Owen. In spite of Fanny's enchanting manner, Mrs. Trollope's feeling about her had in a measure changed on closer acquaintance. As for the young Hervieu, Mrs. Trollope discovered on the voyage that he was unfitted for anything but his art, and before their arrival she had told him so. But here again she was obliged to change her opinion. "Poor Hervieu! He seemed to live only in the hope of helping us," she was to write a few months later. Hervieu was virtually to support the Trollopes for two years in Cincinnati.

At Nashoba, Hervieu found that the school was not yet formed, and he went off in a rage to Memphis, where he painted a few portraits before he finally settled in Cincinnati. Mrs. Trollope was disillusioned in a very few minutes. There was no pump, no cistern, no drains, no milk, no butter, no meat but pork, no dustman's cart, no vegetables but rice and potatoes. Fanny made her own meals on a bit of Indian corn bread and a cup of very indifferent cold rain water, although with her persistent and indomitable enthusiasm she seemed perfectly at home in Nashoba. The savage aspect of the scene appalled Mrs. Trollope; desolation was her only feeling there.

The rain came through the roof of her bedroom, and the logs, flimsily plastered with mud, caught fire a dozen times a day. Camilla and Whitby,—the "surly brute,"—looked like spectres from fever and ague, and in fact the complexion of everyone on the river was a bluish white, suggesting the idea of dropsy. What a miserable and melancholy mode of living!—it was all vividly dreadful. Mrs. Trollope, who had made up her mind to be a "forest pioneer," stayed ten days at Nashoba. Then, alarmed for her children, she too went to Cincinnati. Fanny, the ever magnanimous, wrote, "F. Trollope has proceeded up the river with her friends to Cincinnati, more suited to her at present than our retirement. She is a sweet hearted being, though too much under her feelings and, as you know, not always judicious"; and Harriet Garnett wrote to Julia, "The more I think of it—and of her enthusiasm for the cause —of all the sacrifices she made to accompany Fanny—of the difficulties she conquered—of the public opinion she braved— the more astonishing does it seem to me that she should so soon have been discouraged by the difficulties she encountered there."

In the "triste little town" of Cincinnati, as she described it later, Mrs. Trollope, resolved to invest the last remnant of her capital, built "Trollope's Folly," as it came to be called. This was the castellated bazaar in which she struggled to make a living, the Egyptian mosque with Moorish pilasters, Gothic battlements, a colonnade and a dome surmounted by a Turkish cresent. It contained a great ballroom and a rotunda for exhibiting pictures; and later it was used as an inn, a theatre, a military hospital, a dancing school and a Presbyterian church. Mrs. Trollope intended to sell the latest luxuries, watch-guards, pincushions and toilet-table ornaments, but her husband sent her a consignment of just the wrong objects which she could not sell by any means. She was obliged to auction them off to pay for the building; then, after a long interval, she went to live near Washington with a married sister of the Garnett girls. She proceeded to write the book, *Domestic Manners of the Americans,* to show that the Americans had no domestic manners at all. For Mrs. Trollope had seen in the West only dishonest transactions, craft, coarse familiarity and a dreary coldness. She saw none of Burke's "unbought grace of life," and, while Washington Irving described the book as an abominable fabrication, Sismondi was shocked by Mrs. Trollope's prejudices. "In America, the heart speaks more nobly than with us," he said, reflecting the great mood of the Revolution. Lafayette, urging Fanny Wright to defend America against the book, said, "Her abuse of the American character and American manners has not a little contributed to make her fashionable in the fine circles of England." It was true, she had entered America by the "back door" at New Orleans and had seen little but the pioneering regions. Regarding these, Mark Twain later said that she described a state of things which "lasted well along in my youth, and I remember it."

Mrs. Trollope, who had been called "the old woman" in Cincinnati, where at that time they did not like the English, remarked that once she would have "thought only, what will be said of it? Now, alas, my only anxiety is, what will be paid for it? This same poverty has a mighty lowering affect on one's sublimities." Later, with tongue in cheek, no doubt, she wrote another book about the country of the Stars and Stripes, "the most glorious country . . . beyond all reach of contradiction, the finest country in the whole world." Her heroine, Mrs. Barnaby, who has lost her money in England and who writes *Justice Done at Last,* is rather inclined to agree with Anne Beauchamp, the American girl, about her "poor paltry miserable atom of an island." But this was long after Mrs. Trollope had settled for a while in Bruges to escape punishment for debt, leaving behind in America the name of "Old Madame Vinegar", along with Auguste Hervieu and Hiram Powers. Hervieu, hoping to find an opening in the line of historical pictures, painted "Lafayette Landing in Cincinnati," and he opened in 1828 a gallery of historical paintings that included a number of his own. Among these were "General Bolivar Hunting Bisons," "Napoleon and His Army Crossing the Alps" and the "City of Lyons, Capital of Southern France," painted on four hundred square feet of canvas. Hervieu decorated the Western Museum in Cincinnati, where Mrs. Trollope's invalid son, who spoke seven languages, made a great success as the "Invisible Girl." Hiram Powers mended some wax figures broken in transit, which he arranged as a group of banditti. Hiram Powers, who had come from Vermont, had worked in a provision store selling flour, whiskey and salt pork; then he invented a machine for cutting wooden clock wheels and made in bees'-wax his first bust. A pet of Mrs. Trollope's, who conceived the idea of presenting scenes from Dante's *Inferno*, he created mechanical figures for the Infernal Regions that remained for decades an amusement in Cincinnati. When, many years later, Mrs. Trollope settled in Florence, she was not surprised to find Hiram Powers "fully emerged from the boyish chrysalis state into a full-fledged and acknowledged man of genius."

Meanwhile, Fanny Wright abandoned Nashoba in 1828. Her whole heart and soul had been occupied by the hope of raising the African to the level of the European intellect; but in her absence the colony had run down completely, and she knew she must give it up altogether or devote herself entirely to it. Remembering the painful impression the forest home

had produced upon her, Mrs. Trollope wrote to Mary Mitford, "Miss Wright has abandoned for the present (and I
think forever) her scheme of forming an Eden in the wilderness and cultivating African Negroes till they produced accomplished ladies and gentlemen." Thus ended the first serious
attempt that had ever been made to emancipate the slaves. A
year or two later, chartering a brig, Fanny carried her slaves
to Haiti: there were twenty or thirty of them now, and the
President promised to look after them. Richeson Whitby accompanied them to New Orleans, and Phiquepal D'Arusmont,
who had lived in the West Indies in early life, went with
Fanny on the voyage. She was convinced now that the example
of Haiti would cause the gradual emancipation of the slaves
of the South.

Then Fanny went to live in Robert Owen's New Harmony,
resolved to instruct the young in the rational principles of the
Enlightenment, and she joined Robert Dale Owen in editing
the *New Harmony Gazette,* in which she continued *A Few
Days in Athens.* In this she made an open plea for atheism,
and at the same time she began to lecture as "the advocate
of opinions that make millions shudder and some half-score
admire." It was Mrs. Trollope who said this, and she went on,
to Miss Mitford, "Her subject is *just knowledge,* and in strains
of the highest eloquence she assures the assembled multitudes
that throng to hear her that man was made for happiness and
enjoyed it till religion snatched it from him, leaving him fantastic hopes and substantial fears instead." Fanny was disturbed by the great revival in Cincinnati and the talk of
original sin and the torments of hell, and, taking up the cause
of "insulted reason and outraged humanity," she attacked
"the ghostly expounders of damnation." She opposed the Christian party that was believed to have set out to unite Church

and State and dominate the nation, and her lectures on free enquiry and the advancement of factual knowledge were full of the ideas of Bentham and Owen. Her dress of plain white muslin looked like the drapery of a Greek statue, and Mrs. Trollope could not say enough of "the splendour, the brilliance, the overwhelming eloquence" that went with "the wonderful power of her rich and thrilling voice."

Fanny lectured on "existing evils," capital punishment, imprisonment for debt, and she demanded women's rights and advocated birth control, saying "turn your churches into halls of science." She spoke in the principal cities of the West, and men and women crowded to hear the "priestess of infidelity," as the religious called her. In Cincinnati, five hundred persons were turned away from the lecture-hall, and Camilla, who was present, wrote, "The whole town was in a state of excitement." But Sismondi, who was anxious for Fanny and who was troubled by "the vague and disordered spirit of Owen," regretted that she had ruined the cause of the Negroes by declaring war on public opinion. He sent her a long letter, expressing his "eager affection" for her, but directly opposing her whole system; and to Julia Garnett he wrote, "After all, your friend, for all her aversion to religion, is a religious madwoman . . . She is a new St. Theresa in whom the love of principle and usefulness moves, but not that of the soul or the love of God." James Madison, writing to Lafayette, deplored her views on religion and marriage, "the effect of which your knowledge of this country can readily estimate . . . With all her rare talents, she has I fear created insuperable obstacles to the good fruits of which they might be productive by her disregard, or rather open defiance, of the most established opinion and vivid feelings."

What, meanwhile, had become of Camilla? She left Nashoba

to join her sister in New York, when Fanny moved there in 1829. She had remained until her child was born, then, breaking with Nashoba where Richeson Whitby continued to live alone, she never saw her husband again. "Fortunately," wrote Harriet Garnett, "he seems satisfied to remain in the woods. He was not a man she could bring to New York." Mrs. Trollope had written, "Fanny Wright has made herself too unpleasantly conspicuous for any person so insignificant as myself to venture to brave public opinion by holding intercourse with her, but I do not believe it possible that any circumstances can occur which should prevent my seeking the society of Camilla Whitby, wherever and whenever I could obtain it." Later, after the separation had taken place, she continued, "Our dear Camilla is wonderfully recovered in health and in looks since I parted with her at that miserable Nashoba. She is again the sweet, the elegant Camilla I knew in Europe."

Fanny had taken to New York the *New Harmony Gazette,* which she renamed the *Free Enquirer,* and she printed this in the basement of the house in Yorkville where she set up a printing-press. She had leased this roomy old dwelling, with ten acres of land, a cow-house and a poultry yard and garden, on the bank of the East River, not far from the house where Margaret Fuller was to live twenty years later. There, besides Fanny, were Camilla and her baby, Phiquipal D'Arusmont, three French boys who had been committed to her care, and Robert Dale Owen, who had come with the magazine which he helped Fanny to edit. The office was in the basement of the Hall of Science, remodelled from the old Ebenezer Church in Broome Street, near the Bowery, which Fanny had bought and which was largely supported by receipts from her lectures. There were evening classes for young mechanics in chemistry, physics, geology, history and political economy. Fanny had really come to New York with the purpose of taking command of the workingmen's parties in the city; and there she continued until 1830, when she broke up the home of the Free Enquirers and returned for five years to France.

VI

In Paris, Fanny soon married Phiquepal D'Arusmont, an ugly fidgety little man, many years older than herself, but an ingenious, experienced, capable teacher. She had been staggered by the death of Camilla in a lonely lodging there,—the baby had died of cholera some time before; and it was supposed that, after her marriage, Fanny would give up public life and devote herself wholly to her husband. Meanwhile, her feelings seemed to have changed as much towards her friends as their feelings had often changed towards her, although Lafayette and Harriet Garnett remained loyal to the last. She ceased to write to them, or even to see them, and Lafayette was especially hurt, for no one had cared more deeply for the "angelic girls" than he. Fanny Wright had ceased to appear at Lafayette's *soirées*. But to Harriet he wrote in 1832, "I had a visit from dear Fanny before I left town. She no doubt has informed you of the death of her child. [For Fanny's first child had died, like Camilla's.] Poor Fanny! Her portrait in my room incessantly retraces to me the days of hers, Camilla's, Julia's and your happy presence at La Grange."

Fanny had not even announced to Harriet the birth of her child, and Mrs. Garnett wrote, "How completely she is changed. I suppose Harriet has told you [Julia] she wishes, I should say, to be forgotten, and of course will be." Fanny and her husband lived near the Luxembourg, "And I cannot therefore often see her," said Harriet, especially because

Mrs. Garnett forbade any intercourse with her and the younger sister took her mother's part. "She has lost the recollection," Harriet wrote, "of her former affection for us," and Harriet ceased to write to Fanny, who lived only five minutes' walk away. "Why should I write? She will only think it is a trouble to answer my letters. She does not think of any of her friends—of those who have been so much attached to her." Later she wrote to Julia in Hanover, "I have received a letter from F. W. but a letter that gave me no pleasure . . . it is so cold, so changed from her former letters that I have not had courage to reply to it." Fanny herself told Harriet it was not for want of affection that she did not write but because doing so awoke too many painful ideas of the past. In 1831 Harriet wrote again to Julia, "I have seen F. W., now Madame D'Arusmont . . . Fanny received me kindly but coldly; old friendships I think she had forgotten; old scenes have vanished from her mind . . . She looked well and not older except for the deep furrows of her forehead; that sweet playfulness of her manner is gone; it was her and yet not her. This I felt as I saw her caressing her naked girl [the second child, Sylva]—for a naked child is an ugly object. A bedroom, a dirty girl, a naked child, Fanny in robe de chambre, a stove and a child's victuals cooking—how different from the elegant boudoir in which we used to find our loved Fanny writing. I thought of the past, of you and poor Cam—and I felt, I own, very unhappy. I have not had courage to return and shall probably seldom see her I have loved so well—too well, alas."

In America, Mrs. Trollope had observed this change long before. "I saw Fanny at Cincinnati," she told Harriet, "about three months ago. Every time I see her I am struck by the increase of that dry, cold, masculine, dictatorial manner that has been growing upon her since she commenced her public lectures. Oh, how unlike the Fanny of former days!" and she continued, to Julia, "How easily do the wonders of a day pass away! Last year I hardly ever looked at a paper without seeing long and repeated mention of Miss Wright. Her eloquence and her mischief, her wisdom and her folly, her strange principles and her no-principles, were discussed without ceasing. Now her name appears utterly forgotten . . . If you mention her, the answer begins with, 'Oh—the woman that made such a fuss at New York. I don't know what's become of her. I expect she's dead!' Or—'That joke is over. We must have something nearer to talk of. But she was only mad, Madam. I guess she was not half so bad as what was said,' and so the subject is dismissed. But there are some of us who have felt her influence too deeply to forget it so easily, though my sanguine spirit leads me to hope that no heavy evil will be the ultimate result."

Fanny was plainly the victim of that sclerosis of the temperament which often goes with humanitarian activities. A case in point was Robert Owen who "became a humanitarian and lost his humanity," as one of his admirers said. "He became an embodied principle and forgot his wife." Still more, she resembled Hollingsworth, in *The Blithedale Romance,* whose heart was "on fire with his own purpose, but icy for all human affection." For, "by and by," as Hawthorne said, "you missed the tenderness of yesterday, and grew drearily conscious that Hollingsworth had a closer friend than ever you could be; and this friend was the cold, spectral monster which he had himself conjured up, on which he was wasting all the warmth of his heart and of which, at least . . . he had grown to be the bondslave. It was his philanthropic theory . . . This was a result exceedingly sad to contemplate, considering that it had been mainly brought about by the very ardour and exuberance of his philanthropy . . . He had taught his benevolence to pour its warm tide exclusively through one channel, so that there was nothing to spare for other great manifestations of love to man, nor scarcely for the nutriment of individual attachments, unless they could minister, in some way, to the terrible egotism which he mistook for an angel of God." Moreover, Fanny was not in love with her husband, for she made seven more trips between Europe and America, and her husband made nine, but they never travelled together. Phiquepal D'Arusmont wrote to her many years later. "Your life was essentially an external life. You loved virtue deeply, but you loved also, and perhaps even more, grandeur and glory; and in your estimation, unknown, I am sure, to your innermost soul, your husband and child ranked only as mere appendages to your personal existence." Husband and wife were divorced before they died. But now, in Paris, where Lafayette said that all happiness was over for Fanny, she obtained for D'Arusmont, the disciple of Pestalozzi, a post as head of an agricultural school. Of their new circle one member was Auguste Comte, whose religious belief in humanity went even beyond Robert Owen's and took the place of the Christian idea of God. He too recommended the reorganization of society in the interest of the working classes.

This was Fanny's doctrine when, in 1835, she returned to America and lectured in New York. There, and in Cincinnati, she and D'Arusmont remained for another four years before they returned to Paris. Thenceforward, they were constantly crossing the ocean until at last Fanny, left alone, died in 1852 in Cincinnati. In the ferment of Jacksonism, she lectured on the history of civilization, opposing abolitionism because of its alliance with religion and growing more and more apocalyptic. D'Arusmont wrote a book on a new system of education. Fanny said, "It has long been clear to me that in every country the best feelings and the best sense are found with the labouring and useful classes, and the worst feelings and worst sense with the idle and useless"; and many years before Marx she envisaged the struggle of the classes. "The intelligent enthusiasm and pure feeling which sparkled in the eyes or burnt on the cheek," she said, "of many young and old hearers in the crowd who stood as if still listening when I had ceased will, I think, never leave my memory." On the platform, at least, she was human enough, and even enthusiastic, she whom a dream had possessed and who charmed others.

One of those who listened to her at Tammany Hall, on Sundays, was the young son of a carpenter, the future author of *Leaves of Grass*, who spoke of her, in his old age, as "glorious Frances." The Whitman family, who lived in Brooklyn, read the *Free Enquirer*,—there were always copies lying about the house,—and, for Walt Whitman, Fanny Wright and Robert Owen wrote in the free-thinking spirit of Jefferson and Paine. Their faith was based on the love of man for man, and Whitman, who had been blessed as a boy on a street in Brooklyn by Lafayette, found "daily food" in *A Few Days in Athens*. There were some people, he said, who were shocked by the bare mention of Fanny's name, but "she was a brilliant woman of beauty and estate who was never satisfied unless she was busy doing good . . . always to me one of the sweetest of sweet memories . . . Fanny Wright (we always called her Fanny for affection's sake)—Fanny Wright had a nimbus, a halo, almost sacerdotal . . . She was beautiful in bodily shape and gifts of soul . . . We all loved her, fell down before her,

her very appearance seemed to enthrall." When a disciple said, "I have never known you to speak of any woman as glowingly as you do of Fanny Wright," Walt Whitman answered, "I never felt so glowingly towards any other woman."

JOHN LLOYD STEPHENS

I

Towards the end of the eighteenth century, in 1795, the French savant Constantin Volney appeared in the United States. He had escaped the guillotine and hoped to find in the new world the refuge he had lost in the old one, and he travelled through Kentucky as far west as Detroit before he returned to France, which was then under Napoleon. Volney had previously spent four years in Egypt and Syria, and, seated among the ruins of ancient cities, he had meditated on the causes of the downfall of empires. His book *The Ruins* ended with a prophecy of the assembly of peoples and the universal republic of humankind, an idea developed earlier by Joel Barlow, who translated the book at Thomas Jefferson's suggestion. *The Ruins* was read, like *The Age of Reason,* through the woods and clearings of the West and discussed, with Thomas Paine, in village stores, and Volney's sombre meditations on the fate of empires in the antique world captivated the American imagination. Along the Hudson river, artificial ruins rose at Hyde Park and further up-stream, and among these dilapidated arches were placed large Mayan sculptures brought back from the jungles of Central America by John Lloyd Stephens. For ruins existed there like the ruins of Egypt, relics of an

unknown race and a forgotten people. The fashionable feeling
for the picturesque delighted in this contrast with the hurry
and bustle of the new-world civilization.

II

The "American Traveller," as he was called, John Lloyd
Stephens, had also visited, like Volney, Syria and Egypt, and,
even more adventurous, he had made his way through the
valley of Edom, the only man who had been known to do so.
For this was the land of Idumen, the desolate region that
Isaiah had cursed, saying, "None shall pass through it for ever
and ever"; and, though several had crossed its borders and
three Europeans had attempted the journey, they had left no
written record of it. Stephens had visited the Holy Land, as
well as Greece, Russia and Poland, before he explored the
green forests of Chiapas and Yucatan. A small, wiry, nervous
man, the son of a prosperous merchant in New York, he had
been born in New Jersey in 1805; but, taken to the city when
he was a year old, he had grown up in Greenwich Street.
Fulton's "Clermont" was anchored in front of the house on
the river. The Bowling Green had been his playground, he
had climbed its fence hundreds of times, and he had been one
of a band of boys who held on to it long after the Corporation
invaded their rights. Brought up in a school kept by an Irish-
man, "wondrously good at drill and flogging," he had entered
Columbia College at thirteen, and then he had studied law
under Tapping Reeve at the first American school of law at
Litchfield.

After that, with his father's approval, he had taken a long
trip in the West into the heart of the Shawnee country. He
and a cousin travelled in a Conestoga wagon, and, presently,

starting from Pittsburgh, he had floated to New Orleans in a flat-bottomed boat down the Mississippi. They had stopped along the bank at night as, later, Stephens stopped on the Nile, in one case under the ruins of an ancient temple, in the other under the wild trees of the forest; but whereas in Egypt the men sipped coffee around a fire, smoked and lay down quietly to sleep, the roaring boys of the West fought and frolicked, with fighting cocks or at cards or pitching pennies. Stephens, who had come home smoking long black cheroots, with an ample growth of reddish whiskers, a violent partisan of Andrew Jackson in 1828, became well-known in New York as a political speaker. In fact, he was the favourite speaker at Tammany Hall.

At twenty-nine, a promising lawyer, suffering from an affection of the throat, the result of too much public speaking, he was sent abroad for treatment in Paris, and from there he went to Rome and, presently, to Greece, carrying a copy of Volney's *Ruins* with him. His cutter was driven by the wind into the harbour of Missolonghi, where Byron had died ten years before, a long stretch of shanties that had been run up since the destruction of the old town in the Greek revolution. There was not even a hotel where he could get breakfast: it reminded him of "Communipaw in bad weather." But he was invited to call upon the widow of Marco Bozzaris about whom his friend Fitzgreene Halleck had written a poem. Still under forty years old, tall and stately, she was living with her children in a large square house. The tomb of Marco Bozzaris consisted of a pile of round stones, and Stephens remembered how this chieftain had resisted the whole Egyptian army, defending the town with a few hundred men. All Europe had condemned as foolhardy the Greek revolution, but Stephens, as a Columbia student, had solicited funds for Greece, and he knew every campaign by heart. Later, when he returned to New York, he told Halleck about his visit there, and Halleck sent a copy of his poems to the widow of Marco Bozzaris.

Travelling with a carpet-bag and a Greek servant, Stephens filled his journal with impressions of war-devastated Greece. He set out on horseback for Athens by way of Corinth and the village that had been the birthplace of Euclid. The road ran along the sea to Piræus, a ruined village with a starving population, standing on the site of the ancient Eleusis where were held the mysterious rites of Ceres. At Athens, he visited, first of all, the American missionary school where young Americans were teaching the elements of their own tongue to the descendants of Socrates and Plato. For the only door of instruction in the city where Cicero had gone to study had been opened in 1832 by American Episcopalians, and there were now five hundred pupils of whom not more than six of the first ninety-six had been able to read. There Stephens shook hands with a little Leonidas and a little Miltiades, together with a son of the Maid of Athens, who had married a Scotsman, the chief of police.

Stephens surveyed the ruins of Athens, where the modern Greeks had built their miserable dwellings with the plunder of the temples, and he detested the insolence with which the Germans, under their king, lorded it over the emancipated natives. One of these Germans, on the Acropolis, showed him plans of "city improvements," with new streets laid out and a projected railroad, a great hobby of his own New York, and he caught himself laying out streets in his mind, a Plato and a Homer street, on a spot where solitude and silence bred thoughts that were very remote from lots in Athens. He drove over the plain of Argos in a bright yellow carriage, with a big Albanian for coachman, and, poring over the Iliad, he saw Agamemnon's

tomb, well preserved but empty and forsaken. In one corner
a goat was dozing and a shepherd drove his flock within for
shelter. The rocks and caves of Delphi, the seat of the muses,
were the abode of robbers. On the field of Marathon, he saw
the large mound of earth erected over the Athenians who fell
there, and, sitting on the top, he threw the reins over his
horse's neck and read in Herodotus the account of the battle.
He passed the region of the Nemean grove, the haunt of the
mythical lion and the scene of the first of the labours of Her-
cules, and several times he jumped over the Ilissus and trotted
his horse over the garden of Plato. Then he sailed to Smyrna
on a rickety brig with hardly ballast enough to keep the keel
under water, Smyrna, ten times destroyed and ten times risen
from her ruins, exalted by the ancients as the pride of Asia.

It was at Smyrna that Stephens began to write, or rather
to compose out of his journal; for he sent a long letter about
his travels to Charles Fenno Hoffman, the friend who was
editor of the *American Monthly Magazine.* Hoffman published the letter, under the title *Scenes of the Levant,* in successive issues of the magazine, recording Stephens's admiration of the ladies in the city of raisins and figs, with large
dark rolling eyes under their enchanting turbans. From Constantinople, he crossed the Black Sea to Odessa, a city laid
out on a gigantic scale that had risen in thirty years over a
village of a few fishermen's huts. He carried with him the
poems of Byron, prohibited in Russia, his companion in Italy
and Greece, but, omitting to mention it, he put the book under his arm, threw his cloak over it and walked out unmolested. A brigadier-general in the Russian army, an American
from Philadelphia, was the inspector of the port of Odessa,
and Stephens rode out to the country-house of this grand
counsellor of the empire who was living with the true spirit

of an American farmer. They compared his wheat with the wheat that was raised on the Genesee flats with which the general was perfectly familiar. Then Stephens set out on a journey of two thousand miles through Kiev to the city of churches, Moscow.

He had bought a carriage, a large calash, with a postillion in a sheepskin coat and four shaggy wild-looking little horses, engaging for a servant a bewhiskered Frenchman who had been exiled by the Restoration. The steppes over which they drove were desolate and bleak, and great herds of cattle passed them with long trains of wagons, fifty or sixty together, drawn by oxen. At Kiev, the old capital, the holy city of the North, with gilded domes and spires glittering in the sun, Stephens found it cheaper to give his carriage away and take the newly established diligence to Moscow. They passed processions of pilgrims on their way to Kiev, bands of a hundred or so, men, women and children, led by a white-bearded monk, barefoot, with a staff; and Stephens was struck by the elegance of the opera-house in Moscow before he went on to St. Petersburg over a new road. He procured a *carte de sejour* that enabled him to remain two weeks on the understanding that he would not preach democratic doctrines; then he set out for Warsaw, another thousand miles, travelling in a round-bottomed box that was called a kibitka. It had straw to lie on but no springs. Warsaw, on the Vistula, was a gay city of nobles and peasants, with no middle class between them, and Stephens, who all but remembered the American revolution, visited, at Cracow, the tomb of Kosciusko. There, on an eminence, stood an immense mound of earth that was visible for miles in every direction.

In Paris, when he was intending to return to New York, Stephens picked up a folio on the quays along the Seine. It contained enchanting lithographs of Petra, a city of Arabia cut out of the rock; and this *Voyage de l'Arabie Petrée* by Léon de La Borde sent him instead to Egypt on the way there. For all ruins had for Stephens an irresistible attraction. The Pasha at Cairo, who favoured Americans after the war with Tripoli, gave him a permit for an expedition up the Nile, and he set out in a falookha, in January, 1836, carrying Volney's *Ruins* and a dictionary with him. Besides the captain and the crew, ten men in all, he took, as a dragoman, Paolo Nuozzo, a Maltese whom he had met at Constantinople, thirty-five years old, honest and faithful and, like himself, a great lover of ruins. An Arab tailor made for him a star-spangled banner to float over the falookha during the voyage, for it was necessary to place himself under the flag of his country to prevent the men from being taken for the army. The boat was forty feet long, with two lateen sails. A swinging shelf over the bed contained his books, together with his pistols and a shotgun.

At every village on the Nile, Stephens was struck by the misery of the peasants in their mud-huts, whether this was the result of their character, or the climate or the government of the great pasha at Cairo; and he could understand why in Egypt the centre of interest was the dead, why death had been the paramount preoccupation. Only in the world of the dead could people imagine security and peace, and, where the Greeks had resisted and turned toward life, the Egyptians had turned towards death, the releaser and rewarder. In Greece the theatre flourished, in Egypt the tomb, and many of the peasants lived in tombs, great buildings with domes and minarets, crawling in with their dogs, sheep, goats, women and children. Every sarcophagus was broken, the bones had been scattered, and in many cases the hollow shell was used

as a sleeping-place, or the mummy-cases were used for fire-
wood and the traveller might cook his breakfast with the
coffin of a king. There were supposed to be eight to ten
millions of mummied bodies in the vast necropolis of Thebes,
and the Arabs had been in the habit of selling the mummies
to travellers until an order from the pasha put an end to this.
The open doors of tombs appeared in long ranges on the western bank of the river, and on the plain large pits had been
opened in which were found a thousand mummies at a time.
From one tomb Stephens saw an enormous wolf run out, followed by another, furiously fighting; and, entering one of the
tombs, he found the ceiling covered with paintings, some of
them as fresh as if they had just been executed. Passing into
the inner chambers, he heard a loud rushing noise; he fired
his gun; the report went rumbling and roaring into the dark
passages; then the light was dashed from Paolo's hand, a soft
skinny substance struck his own face and thousands of bats,
wild with fright, came whizzing forth from the recesses. At one
point a long funeral procession followed a corpse on the way
to a burying-ground at the foot of a mountain. Having the
permission of the sheik, Stephens walked over to the tomb,
built of Nile mud, with a round top and whitewashed.

With no plan yet of writing a book, he sailed to the first
cataract whose roar in ancient days frightened the boatmen:
the fall was only about two feet, although poetry and history
had invested these rapids with extraordinary terrors. The river
was filled with rocks and islands, among them the island of
Philae, carpeted with green to the water's edge and lovelier,
Stephens thought, than the Lago Maggiore with the beautiful
Isola Bella and the Isola Madre. The temple, on the southwest corner of the island, about a thousand feet long, had been
approached by a grand colonnade. An Arab village was built

among the ruins of Thebes: the plough had been driven over the ruins of the temples and grass was growing where palaces had stood. The sun was beating down with meridian splendour when the falookha made fast at the ancient port where boatmen had tied their boats thirty centuries before. Thebes had once been more than thirty-three miles in circumference, and the whole of this great area was more or less strewn with ruins, broken columns, avenues of sphinxes, colossal figures, obelisks, pyramidal gateways, porticoes, blocks of polished granite, while over them, in the unwatered sands, stood the skeletons of gigantic temples solitary and silent. The road to Karnac was lined with rows of sphinxes, each of a solid block of granite. Two miles away was the temple of Luxor on the summit of which, a year before, John Lowell of Boston had drawn a long codicil to his will providing for the well-known Lowell lectures. Stephens's boatmen, having little to do, lay all day about the deck, gathering towards evening round a large pilaff of rice, turning their faces, as the sun was setting, towards the tomb of the Prophet, while they knelt down on the deck and prayed. Stephens was still dreaming of a visit to Arabia Petræa, suggested to him again by a party of four Englishmen who were hoping themselves to make the attempt.

Returning to Cairo, he fell in with La Borde's companion who told him about their earlier expedition. With a retinue of camels and horses, they had made a great display to overawe the wild Bedouins of the desert. Stephens provided himself with the costume of a Cairo merchant, a long red silk gown with a black abbas of camel's hair, a sword and a pair of large Turkish pistols. He wore a red tarbooch with a green and yellow handkerchief rolled round it as a turban, white trousers, a blue sash and red shoes over yellow slippers; and he took

with him, besides Paolo, eight men, with pistols and muskets, six camels and the dromedary that he rode. The caravan
struck into the desert towards a range of sandstone mountains,
following the wandering steps of the children of Israel when
they flew from their land of bondage before the anger of
Pharaoh. Virtually the only object on the route to Suez was
a large palm, standing alone, green and living, which they
saw for two or three hours before they reached it: watching
this, while they travelled at the slow pace of the camels, filled
their minds for a great part of the day. Then they caught
sight of the Red Sea, rolling between dark mountains; and
they watered the camels for the first time since they had left
Cairo at a well on the hither side of Suez. Crossing the Red
Sea in small boats, they camped on the sacred spot where the
Israelites, rising from the dry bed of the sea, watched the
divided waters rushing together, overwhelming Pharaoh and
his chariots and the host of Egypt.

After Suez, their road lay between wild and rugged mountains, and the valley itself was stony, broken and gullied by
the washing of the winter torrents. A few straggling thorn-
bushes were all that grew in that region of desolation, and on
the sides of the mountains, deformed with gaps and fissures,
not a blade of grass or a shrub was to be seen. Stephens could
think of nothing but water. Rivers floated through his imagination, and, moving slowly on his dromedary, with the hot
sun beating upon his head, he wiped the sweat from his face
and thought of the frosty Caucasus; and when, through an
opening in the mountains, the others saw a palm-tree shading
a fountain, the caravan broke into a run and, dashing through
the sand, threw themselves to a man on the living water.
Reading this, when Stephens's book was published, Herman
Melville, as a boy, remembered seeing the author in church

in New York, and his aunt whispered, "See what big eyes he has. They got so big because when he was almost dead with famishing in the desert, he all at once caught sight of a date-tree, with ripe fruit hanging on it." When church was out, the boy wanted his aunt to follow the traveller home. "But she said the constables would take us up if we did; and so I never saw this wonderful Arabian traveller again. But he long haunted me; and several times I dreamt of him and thought his great eyes were grown still larger and rounder; and once I had a vision of the date-tree."

At the foot of Mount Sinai stood the convent of St. Catherine, surrounded by high stone walls, with turrets at the corners: the convent looked like a fortress. It was sometimes attacked by the Bedouins, so the walls were mounted with cannon, and only after the caravan had set off two volleys of firearms did a monk with a long white beard appear at a slit in the wall. He let down a rope thirty feet for the letter of introduction which the Greek patriarch at Cairo had given to Stephens; and, when the rope was let down again, Stephens tied it about his arms and swung to and fro against the wall. Then he found himself clasped in the arms of a burly long-bearded monk who kissed him on both cheeks and set him on his feet. All the monks pressed forward, took him in their arms and gave him a cordial greeting. The superior told him that God would reward him for coming from so distant a land to do homage to the sacred mountain; and, leading him through a long range of winding passages, he and Stephens came to a small room spread with mats. Presently arrived a platter of beans and a large smoking pilaff of rice. In his wanderings, Stephens had invariably found the warmest feelings toward his country from boatmen, muleteers and ploughmen in the fields, and this was also glowing in the wilderness of Sinai. The monks, with their superior, were all Greeks.

From the door of his little cell, Stephens saw the holy mountain and longed to stand on its lofty summit; and the superior led him through galleries built of stone, with iron doors, to the outer garden. There bloomed almonds, oranges, lemons, apricots and dates, shaded by arbours of grapevines; and they began to ascend in the company of a Bedouin dwarf and an old monk with long white hair. Paolo and Stephens followed: the rest of their caravan remained outside the walls and continued to sleep there. At every point was a legend or a chapel. At length they stood on the peak of Sinai where Moses had talked with the Almighty amid thunder and a fearful quaking of the mountain. On the way down, they came to a long flat stone, with a few holes indented on its surface, the stone upon which Moses broke the tablets of the law when he found the Israelites worshipping the golden calf. Then they saw the rock of Horeb, which Moses struck with his rod, causing the water to gush out. At parting the superior gave Stephens a small box of manna, the same, as he believed, that fed the Israelites during their sojourn in the wilderness; and he begged Stephens to come back and live there if, returning to his own country, he found his kindred gone.

Stephens had found, on the rocks of the wilderness, certain strange characters that Edgar Allan Poe reproduced in his account of the South Sea island of Tsalal, in the *Narrative of Arthur Gordon Pym*. Reviewing with admiration the *Incidents of Travel in Arabia Petræa*, Poe doubted the assertion of Stephens that he had passed through the valley of Edom, there being some question about its proper boundaries; but Stephens had certainly been one of the first to visit the city of Petra since it had been rediscovered in 1812. He had been the first American to do so; and his view of the "rose-red city, half as old as time" * remained forever fixed in his imagination. The capital once of a Roman province, it had been forgotten; for many hundred years only the Bedouins knew it, and Stephens found written on the façade of the temple the names of an Englishman who had entered the city, two Frenchmen, an Italian and the discoverer, Burckhardt. Two miles long, it lay between high and precipitous ranges of rocks with ivy, oleanders and wild fig-trees growing out of the sides of the cliffs, while, among the open doors of tombs, stood the beautiful temple, hewn out of the rock, with rows of Corinthian columns in the sunlight, fresh and clear. There was a large circular theatre, with thirty-three rows of seats, capable of containing more than three thousand persons. The sides of the mountains were cut smooth and filled with long ranges of dwelling-houses, excavated out of the rock, with columns and porticoes and pediments, palaces and triumphal arches, a waste of ruins prostrate, in confusion. Stephens clambered up broken staircases and among the remains of streets until he had made the whole circuit of the desolate city. The valley continued as before, presenting sandy hillocks, thorn-bushes, gullies and the dry beds of streams, and presently, on the summit of Mount Hor, Stephens caught sight of the tomb of Aaron, the first high-priest of Israel, covered with a white dome. Climbing the mountain, rocky and naked, he held on to the rough and broken corners of the porous sandstone rocks, and he found the tomb was about thirty feet square, entirely bare save for a few ostrich eggs suspended from the ceiling.

* This line from the Newdigate Prize Poem at Oxford in 1845, written by John William Burgon, seems to have been suggested by Stephens's book.

Then he beheld the Dead Sea that rolled its dark waters over the guilty cities of Sodom and Gomorrah.

He had noticed a change for the worse in the appearance of the Bedouins, and he had heard that those with whom he now set out belonged to one of the most lawless tribes of a lawless race. They were by far the wildest and fiercest looking he had yet seen, with complexions bronzed and burnt to blackness, dark eyes glowing with fire, and sinewy figures, thin and shrunken. But the appearance and habits of the Arabs were precisely the same as those of the patriarchs of four thousand years ago: with their flocks and herds they might have been Abraham, Isaac or Jacob, and the women winnowed and ground the grain, or pounded and rubbed it between two stones, in the same primitive manner that was practised of old. The beauty of the weather atoned to Stephens for the desolation of the scene, and, mounted on the back of his Arabian horse, he felt, with his elastic spirit, a lightness of frame, and he was happy to accept an invitation to supper from an old Bedouin whom he met. This patriarch, wearing a large loose frock, a striped handkerchief on his head, bare legs, sandals and a long white beard, took up his shepherd's crook, after they were seated, and selected a lamb from the flock for the evening meal.

Stephens had followed the wandering path of the children of Israel from Egypt to the borders of the Promised Land, and he came to another field of ruins where the relics of an Arab village were mingled with those of a Roman city. Then he arrived in Hebron, the old capital of David, where Sarah had washed the clothes of Abraham and Isaac at a large fountain just beyond the mosque. The chief rabbi of Hebron gave him a warm welcome, and there Stephens threw off most of his Turkish dress and continued his journey in a blue roundabout jacket. He wore grey pantaloons, boots splashed with mud, a red sash and a tarbooch with a black silk tassel; and he moved through the Holy Land with three mules, one for himself, one for Paolo and the third for his luggage. After visiting Bethlehem and Jerusalem, Nazareth, Mount Tabor and Jericho, he became ill at Beirut; and his travels in the East came to an end there. He got on board a vessel that was bound for Alexandria and presently found himself in London.

III

Now Stephens had been guided in his tour of the Holy Land by a map executed by "F. Catherwood." He had seen the name Frederick Catherwood signed in convent registers and on monuments in Egypt, where, in point of fact, Catherwood himself, an Englishman, was teaching architecture at the University of Cairo. Stephens knew nothing of architecture; he had never measured a building, and his whole knowledge of Egyptian antiquities was little more than enough, he said, to enable him to distinguish between a mummy and a pyramid. He could not have gone far in archæology without some knowledge of architecture or, at least, without a companion who was familiar with it; and here in London he fell in with Catherwood himself, the architectural draughtsman who was to illustrate his later books. The two men were to explore together Central America and Yucatan. Catherwood was lecturing in Leicester Square on the Panorama of Jerusalem, painted from the drawings that he had made in the holy city at the time when he had drawn the Mosque of Omar there, half expecting at any moment to be torn to pieces. For Christians were not admitted and the crowd was only pacified when the Governor appeared and announced that Catherwood had come to repair the dilapidated mosque. In

London, as a panoramist, he had given the producer Burford his drawings also of Thebes, Karnac and the ruins of Baalbec. The rotunda, which was presently reproduced in New York, exhibited pictures of battles, coronations and far-away cities. It was sensationally popular at the moment.

Six years older than John Lloyd Stephens, Catherwood, born in a suburb of London, had made a topographical journey through England, then he had studied at the Royal Academy, under Sir John Soane, where he had heard much of Piranesi. Soane was mad about Piranesi, who had engraved the ruins of Rome, and Catherwood, who had seen Keats off on his brig to Italy, had followed his own friend Joseph Severn there. He went to Sicily to paint the ruins of Taormina, and then to Greece where he was shut up in Athens during the Greek revolution, besieged by the Turks, but, escaping to Syria, dressed as an Arab, he had made his way to the Nile, drawing the ruins of the ancient cities on the river. A good linguist who read Hebrew and spoke Arabic and Greek, he arrived in Egypt during the year in which Champollion found the Rosetta stone and used it as a key to the hieroglyphics. He had hired with two friends a vessel to ascend the Nile, and there he drew three pyramids to scale, with a coloured plan of Thebes and the ruins of Memphis and Abydos, Karnac and Luxor. The Pasha employed him as an engineer to repair the mosques of Cairo; then he climbed Mount Sinai, sketched it and visited the ruins of Baalbec, pitching his tent among the fallen columns. It was Catherwood's drawings, made into a panorama, that first made Baalbec widely known; and he showed Stephens in London a crude book he had picked up about an ancient city in Guatemala. The city was called Palenque, and it had palaces and pyramids buried in the jungle of which no one had ever heard before. Stephens and Catherwood discussed, if

nothing more, in London, a plan to visit Central America and
search out these ruins.

Meanwhile, after two years in the East, John Lloyd Stephens returned to New York, where Catherwood presently
followed with his panorama of Jerusalem. Catherwood built a
rotunda at the corner of Broadway and Prince Street, exhibiting
other panoramas of Niagara and Thebes, establishing himself
as an architect who was much in demand after the fire of 1835
had destroyed so many buildings. He made a drawing of the
tower at Newport that was supposed to have been built by the
Norsemen, and his rotunda was as popular, at the time, as Catlin's Indian Gallery and Niblo's Garden. Stephens, opening
a law office, resumed his public speaking on behalf of Martin
Van Buren, the successor of Jackson, but he set to work at
once writing *Incidents of Travel,* the first about Egypt, Arabia
Petræa and the Holy Land, the second on Greece, Turkey,
Russia and Poland. Both books were popular, the first especially so; they went through five or six editions in one year,
and the British continued to reprint for thirty years the account of travels in Arabia Petræa. The review of this book
by Poe made Stephens famous. Stephens and Catherwood were
often seen together at the Astor House Book Store, the rendezvous of the literati, and the bookseller John Russell Bartlett
showed Stephens two books that had appeared on the mysterious ruins of tropical America. These books were exaggerated,
shadowy and vague; and the original cities were ascribed to
the Egyptians, the Phœnicians, the Scythians, the Scandinavians or the Chinese. Even Humboldt had never heard of
the ruins south of Mexico, forgotten, buried in the jungle. It
had come to be generally supposed that the lost tribes of Israel
had built up this unknown civilization, for no one dreamed
that it could have been the work of American Indians, the

savages whom the Americans knew so well. The names of Uxmal, Palenque, Copán, reverberated in Stephens's mind. He was overwhelmed by what he read.

IV

Catherwood, too, was excited by this new prospect of exploration, and, turning his back on everything else, he set out with Stephens, in October, 1839, for Belize. The capital of British Honduras was a range of white houses extending a mile along the shore, thronged with Negroes, a fine-looking race, tall, straight and athletic. It happened that the minister to Central America had died, and Stephens, who applied to Van Buren for the post, received his appointment before the friends sailed together; a Broadway tailor shaped for him a blue diplomatic coat with gold braid and gold buttons. The British brig "Mary Ann" carried them to Central America, and they engaged at Belize a servant, a French Spaniard, born in Santo Domingo, Augustin by name. Then they sailed down the coast of Honduras one hundred and fifty miles to Punta Gorda, a settlement of Carib Indians that produced cotton and rice, bananas, cocoanuts, pineapples, oranges and lemons. There the natives gathered under the trees to be baptized and married by the padre who had sailed down also from Belize. From Punta Gorda,—or, rather, from Izabal, to which they had taken another steamboat,—Stephens and Catherwood set out with five mules, each armed with a brace of pistols and a large hunting-knife carried in his belt. Four Indian carriers, besides Augustin, went with them, entering a land of volcanoes and earthquakes, torn and distracted by civil war, on the so-called high road to Guatemala City, a place of importance in the Spanish-American world. They dragged their way through mud-holes and gullies, knocking against trees, stumbling over roots, meeting a large party of muleteers, encamped for the night, with bales of indigo and mules peacefully grazing. They passed an occasional palm-leaf hut and mountains thousands of feet high, while flocks of parrots, with gorgeous plumage, flew over their heads, catching up their words and filling the air with their mockings.

It was a wilderness of flowers and bushes clothed in purple and red, and they soon came to the great plain of Zacapa, bounded by a belt of mountains with the town at the foot. Their host had heard of the United States: he had read about it in *The Spy*, called in the Spanish translation a history of the American Revolution, in which Washington appeared under the name of Harper. They passed in a day, in this region of desolation, no less than seven Hispano-Moriscan churches, some of them roofless and falling to ruin as a result of earthquakes or scourged by the current civil war. The states of Guatemala, Salvador, Honduras, Nicaragua and Costa Rica, liberated from Spain in 1823, and originally forming a single nation, had broken apart into five separate republics: General Morazán, the head of the Federal party, was now in Salvador, defeated at the moment, while Carrera, whom Stephens was soon to meet, was the absolute master of Guatemala. A band of Carrera's soldiers arrested Stephens and Catherwood at another village along the way. Indians and mestizos, ragged and ferocious, armed with swords, clubs, muskets and machetes, carrying blazing pine-sticks, burst in upon them, and their young officer said that Stephens's passport was not valid. Though they were released a few hours later, Stephens was presently told that a plan had been formed to rob and murder him. A man passed who said he had met two of the robbers on the road and they were intending to catch him in the morning. They had got it into their heads that he was an aide-de-camp of Carrera, returning from Belize with money for the troops, but Stephens evaded the robbers by crossing the mountains in the evening instead of, as usually, in the afternoon. He knew that two English travellers had recently been arrested. Their muleteers and servants had been murdered, and he himself was beginning to feel heartily sick of the country and its incessant petty alarms.

In a spot that was wildly beautiful, in a hacienda, Stephens and Catherwood spent one night, driving out the dogs and pigs and lighting their cigars in a room that was full of women, most of them servants. Later Catherwood alone returned to Quiriquá, with its ruined terraces and mounds, and statues some of them twenty-six feet tall, and meanwhile they approached Copán and the modern village of half a dozen wretched huts that were thatched with corn. The appearance of the travellers created a sensation, and all the men and women in the village gathered round to look at them; for the people were less accustomed to the sight of strangers than the Arabs about Mount Sinai, and they were more suspicious. The skin of an ox was spread in the piazza, ears of corn were thrown upon it and all the men sat down to shell the corn. The cobs were carried to the kitchen to burn, the corn was taken up in baskets and hogs were driven in to pick up the scattered grains. But no one in the village had ever heard of the ruins that stood a few miles away, and the visitors were sent to the hacienda of Don Gregorio, where the fire was kindled in the cosina. The sound of the patting of hands gave notice that tortillas were being made, and in half an hour dinner was ready.

Stephens, with Catherwood, spent thirteen days at Copán, and he knew that the Hondurian natives, who had no traditions of the past, were the actual decendants of the builders.

In short, they were Mayans, a word of which Stephens was unaware, but he could see that the work of their forbears was different from that of any other people, and by no means derived from the old world. It had grown up in this jungle like the indigenous plants and fruits, and the builders were as aesthetically advanced as the people of Egypt. They had been neolithic, cutting stone with stone, and between the first and the ninth Christian centuries the old empire of the Mayas had invented a solar calendar, hieroglyphic writing and a well-developed agricultural system. As subsequent explorers found, the city of Copán had stood from 436 to 810 A.D. Stephens first caught sight of a great wall, about a hundred feet high, that followed the bank of the river, and his business was to follow the Indians who cleared a path among trees and shrubs in order to excavate monuments for Catherwood to draw. They began with a regular survey of the ruins. They had good surveying compasses, and Catherwood worked the theodolite while Stephens used the tape-reel that Catherwood had employed in a survey of Thebes on the Nile. Stephens directed the Indians in cutting straight lines through the woods, sticking their hats on poles to mark the stations. On the second day they were thoroughly in the spirit of it, and in three days of hard and interesting labour they finished the survey.

They found several pyramids with flattened tops on which temples had once stood,—two of them one hundred and twenty feet high,—a stairway rising almost a hundred feet and a chamber ten feet long in a mound of ruins. In a sepulchral vault they found red earthenware dishes and pots, more than fifty of these full of human bones. They came to a large fragment of stone elaborately sculptured, and, working their way through the woods, they happened on a square stone column that was carved in bold relief from the base to the top. The front was the figure of a man curiously and richly dressed with a face fitted to excite terror. There was a gigantic head, six feet high, and near by two other colossal heads turned over and partially buried, with various fragments of curious sculpture protruding from decayed vegetable matter. No doubt there were many others completely buried that could be brought to light by digging. A dozen monoliths still stood erect, some with elegant designs and some in workmanship equal to the best of Egyptian carving. One was displaced by enormous roots, while another had been hurled to the ground and was bound down by huge vines and creepers. Before this could be drawn, it was necessary to disentangle the vines and tear the fibres out of the crevices. There was a remarkable altar, of a single block of stone, with thirty-six tablets of hiero-glyphics, and with channels in the stone to carry off the blood of the victims whose hearts had been cut out and exposed to the sun. Halfway up the side of one of the pyramids there were sculptured rows of death's heads. The only sound that disturbed the quiet of the buried city was the noise of monkeys moving among the tops of the trees and the crackling of dry branches broken by their weight. Processions of forty or fifty walked on the ends of boughs, springing from tree to tree with a sound like a current of wind as they passed on into the depths of the forest.

Stephens remembered the ring of the woodman's axe in the forests at home, and he longed for a few Green Moun-tain boys to do the cutting for him. In this jungle of lizards and snakes, the Indians thought he was engaged in some black art to discover hidden treasure. One Indian found the legs and feet of a statue, another found a part of the body to match, and they set it up without the head. Stephens discovered more than fifty objects for Catherwood to draw in his manner that recalled Piranesi, as he stood with his feet in the marshy ground, while he drew with his gloves on to protect his hands from the mosquitoes. He was already ill with fever and ague and rheumatism and from standing all day in the mud of the jungle. But the beauty of the sculpture, the sombre stillness of the woods and the mystery that hung over the desolate city created in Stephens an interest higher, if it was possible, than he had felt among the ruins of the old world. These ruins had put to rest for him all uncertainty in regard to the character of American antiquities: the people who had lived there had not been savages, for savages had never reared these structures or carved these stones. All the arts that embellish life had flourished in this forest, although no associations were connected with the place. The jungle had shrouded the ruins, and when one asked the Indians who had made them, their only answer was, "Who can tell?"

Finally, Stephens bought the ruins. He paid $50 for them. The owner thought he was only a fool: if Stephens had offered more, he would have thought something worse. Stephens was dreaming of a museum in New York that would house these relics of the continent, but he found it was out of the question to transport more than a few fragments. Catherwood, meanwhile, had acquired a reputation for his medical skill, although, as he was ill himself, he was obliged to give it out that he had discontinued practice. However, his fame had extended far, and he had many applications for remedios, —for one, the wife of the owner of the ruins was ill with malaria at Copán. People came from more than thirty miles to be cured by this medico who never killed anybody, and it was hard to send them away without doing what he could for them.

It was on the Copán river that Stephens and Catherwood separated, Catherwood to remain behind and go on with his drawing, Stephens to proceed to Guatemala City and try to find the government. So Stephens rode forward alone through grand and even magnificent scenes, along the beds of streams and down ravines that were deep, narrow and wild. He passed through the village of San Jacinto in a primæval wilderness, a collection of huts, some of them plastered with mud, and, entering Esquipulas, he rode up to the convent, where he was welcomed by the cura. There was the great church of the pilgrimage, the holy place of Central America where pilgrims came every year from Peru and Mexico, eighty thousand people, trading on the way. The town contained about fifteen hundred Indians, living on a road a mile long, with mud houses on each side. Under the shed of a deserted house he had seen an old Indian teaching their catechism to ten or twelve Indian girls, dressed in red plaid cotton drawn round the waist and with white handkerchiefs over their shoulders.

Arriving in Guatemala City, Stephens looked around to find the Minister of Foreign Affairs, but he was told that no government existed: Morazán had retreated and Carrera was expected. Stephens took possession of the American Legation, and then the master of Guatemala appeared. Stephens found him sitting at a table counting silver coins, and the conqueror rose, pushed the money to one side, gave the American minister a chair and received him with courtesy. About twenty-three years old, boyish in manner but unsmiling and grave, Carrera had begun with thirteen followers armed with old muskets, and, wounded himself in eight places, with five musket balls in his body, he was evidently ignorant and evidently sanguinary. In the meantime, Stephens, struck with the beauty of Guatemala, climbed to the top of the Volcano de Fuego.

It was fourteen thousand feet above the level of the sea, and from the top he saw the old city of Guatemala, thirty-two villages and the Pacific Ocean. He descended into the crater, swept by a whirlwind of vapour and cloud, until his clothes were saturated with the rain and the mud. The ancient capital had been destroyed by an earthquake, and the ruins of convents and churches stood in masses about the plaza with their fronts still erect and trees growing inside the walls. Stephens visited the hacienda of a cochineal planter whose plants were set out in rows like Indian corn: a piece of sugarcane was pinned with a thorn to every leaf and thirty or forty insects gathered in the hollow. He overtook on the road a man and a woman on horseback, he with a gamecock, she with a guitar. The cock was wrapped in matting under the man's arm.

Stephens had made up his mind to go down to Salvador, the seat of the Federal government, if such a thing existed, inasmuch as Morazán was there; so, discharging Augustin and procuring a man who knew the route, he set out for the port of Istapa. It was a place, now desolate, but once the focus of romantic adventure where Alvarado had embarked to dispute with Pizarro the wealth of Peru. Istapa consisted now of a few miserable cabins with half-naked Indians sitting on the shore. Stephens sailed on a French ship within sight of six volcanoes, one emitting smoke, another flames, and he himself was again ill with malaria, light-headed, with chills and fever: in fact, wild with pain. However, the French crew doctored him, and, reaching Salvador, he found Morazán at Ahuachapam, a handsome man with dark eyes, somehow suggesting Bolivar, and with an expression that was intelligent and mild. He stood, by the light of a candle, in the corridor of the cabilda, full of sorrow for his unhappy country but with not a word about his own misfortunes. The best man in all Central America, Stephens strongly felt, his troops were sleeping in the plaza under arms. In the morning, calling upon Stephens, Morazán spoke of Carrera without malice or bitterness, and Stephens bade Morazán farewell with an interest greater than he had felt for anyone else in the country. There was a range of gigantic volcanoes along the coast, one of them spouting into the air an immense column of stones and smoke; and, while the earth shook under his feet, he ascended a mountain behind the volcano, commanding a view of the crater. He had been sleeping in a bed that was full of cockroaches and spiders and the ashes now fell about him with a noise like the sprinkling of rain.

When later he returned to Guatemala, Stephens wrote to Washington, to the Secretary of State, resigning his position. "After diligent search, no government found," he said; for there was indeed no government in Central America, and the five republics were all involved in the civil war. But now, in order to study the much talked of canal route, Stephens took another ship to the Gulf of Nicoya in Costa Rica. Again he came down with chills and fever; nevertheless, he mounted a horse for the return journey to Guatemala, five hundred miles more or less. It was a country with no provisions for travellers, with rumours of horrible atrocities, murders in the forest; but Stephens plunged into the wilderness alone, riding through clouds of locusts, beating them off with his hat. He heard the surge of monkeys moving along the tops of the trees, and he rode north through Nicaragua and Salvador, the richest of the Central American states, extending a hundred and eighty miles along the shore of the Pacific. The wild woods were constantly swept by tornadoes. At one hacienda a noise over the supper-table brought the good-natured host out of his chair; it was another sudden earthquake; everyone rushed out of doors and the earth rolled like a pitching ship. In the darkness Stephens's feet barely touched the ground, and he threw out his arms involuntarily to save himself from falling. Riding all day in the forest, where the ground teemed with noxious insects, he stopped at a stream and tore them out of his flesh; and, sleeping among the trees at night, wrapped in his poncho, he heard the howling of wolves and the screams of the mountain cat. He had been told in Nicaragua that the troops had marched into Honduras, and that the troops of Honduras were invading Nicaragua. Then he met an American named Hardy of whom he had first heard at the Cape of Good Hope, hunting giraffes. Later he had fallen in with Hardy in New York. With an elephant and two drome-daries this man had travelled through Central America where no one had ever seen an elephant before. Meanwhile, Stephens was able to send the Department of State at home a good report of the possibilities of the Nicaragua Passage.

At Christmas he returned to Guatemala City, encountering a religious procession with priests and monks bearing lighted candles, preceded by men throwing rockets. A letter came from Catherwood, saying he had been robbed by his servant, adding that he was ill and had left the ruins and was on his way to Guatemala City. Then he arrived, armed to the teeth but also pale and thin, half eaten by mosquitoes, ticks, wasps and ants, happy at reaching the capital, but not half so happy as Stephens was to see him. They resolved not to separate again. Catherwood had explored several ruins, especially Quiri-guá, which no one in Guatemala had ever visited. He had found a pyramidal structure like the pyramids of Copán, to-gether with a colossal head, two yards in diameter, covered with moss; near by stood a large altar and a collection of monuments much like those at Copán but twice or three times as high. In the centre of a walled circle there was a large round stone, with sides sculptured in hieroglyphics. The ruins were by no means appreciated in Guatemala, and the owner said that, if his family had not been impoverished, he would have been proud to present them to the United States. Stephens and Catherwood went to a bullfight in Guatemala City, where Carrera entered the captain-general's box, dressed in a blue military frock-coat, embroidered with gold. All eyes turned towards this man who, a year before, had been hunted among the mountains and treated like an outcast. Stephens shook hands with him and presently called upon him, telling Carrera that he had met Morazán. He had shaken hands with men who were thirsting for each other's blood, and he met Carrera's wife, a pretty delicate-looking mestiza who was not more than twenty years old. Carrera had an idea that Stephens was a great man in his own country, although he was vague about where the country was. Stephens had obtained from the Archbishop of Guatemala letters to all the padres along their route through Chiapas; for they were soon to enter this state of Mexico in search of the ruins of Palenque.

At Tecpan, still in Guatemala, near the magnificent church, the second that was built after the conquest, the ground was covered with mounds of ruins where they spent two hours, while they rolled back and forth in another earthquake. They were travelling with a cargo mule apiece, each with an oxhide trunk, secured with a chain clumsily padlocked, and each containing a small cot, doubled with a hinge, and with pillows and bedclothes wrapped in another oxhide. They had added to their equipment undressed goatskins embroidered with red leather to protect their legs from rain in the wintry ascent through high and rugged mountains. The scenery was grand

and beautiful, with gigantic volcanoes and lakes, and on the narrow road they met caravans of mules loaded with wheat and cloth for Guatemala City. In the afternoon, looking back, they counted six volcanoes, two of them nearly fifteen thousand feet high. At Quiché a mestizo advised them to carry their weapons, for the people were not to be trusted; two travellers had recently been speared by the Indians and the wife of another had been murdered on the road: her fingers had been cut off and the rings torn from them. They had stopped at Quiché to measure and examine the ruins of Utatlán, where they found confused and shapeless masses of stone. Even the palace had been largely destroyed to afford building material for the present village. However, the floor remained unbroken, with fragments of partition walls, and the inner walls were covered with plaster that had remains of colour on them. In one place, on a layer of stucco, they had made out part of the body of a leopard that was well coloured and drawn. Stephens found a large plaza or courtyard with the relics of a fountain in the centre. On a quadrangular stone structure had once stood an altar where human beings were carried up naked, stretched out with four priests holding the legs and arms while another priest tore out the heart and offered it to the sun. The Indians, impressed as they were by the pomp of religious ceremonies, and by the splendour of the churches, were still full of idolatry and superstition, and in the mountains and ravines they kept their idols and practised their ancestral rites in secrecy and silence.

So Stephens and Catherwood were told by the padre of Quiché, of whom they first caught sight near the ruins of Utatlán, toiling along under a red silk umbrella. A Spaniard and a Dominican, he had witnessed the battle of Trafalgar, looking down from heights on the shore, and he had seen

enough, he said, of wars and revolutions and had come to
Guatemala with twenty other Dominican friars. With a broad-
brimmed black glazed hat, an old cassock reaching to his heels,
a waistcoat and pantaloons to match, he laughed at everything
in a good-natured way and told them stories of the country.
He said there was a city in the cordilleras where the Indians
still lived as they had lived before the conquest, and he had
himself climbed the topmost range of the sierra and seen this
city at a great distance with white turrets glittering in the
sun. The people there were said to keep their roosters under-
ground so that their crowing might not attract the white men.
The padre pointed out on a map the position of the mysterious city in a region that did not acknowledge the government
of Guatemala; and Stephens, excited by the tale, would gladly
have climbed the cordilleras in order to have a glimpse of the
white city. But to attempt this alone, speaking none of the
twenty-four dialects that, as he knew, were spoken in Guatemala, would have been out of the question; and he decided
not to let anything deter him from reaching the ruins of
Palenque. But Barnum, the showman in New York, reading
later Stephens's book, got up his hoax of the two "Aztec children," found in the Indian city that Stephens half believed
in and had longed to see in Guatemala. Barnum said the city
had high walls and parapets, with hanging gardens and vestal
virgins, and, taking to London the Aztec children, he induced
the Prince Consort to come and see them in his exhibition.
He even published a descriptive guide that was said to have
been written by Stephens and that Catherwood denounced
as the fraud that it was.

When Stephens and Catherwood crossed the border into
Mexico, the rainy season was approaching, and they were told
that the roads would be impossible. But nothing could stop

them, and Mexico struck Stephens as an old, long-settled, civilized, quiet, well-governed country. However, while most of Mexico was quiet, Tabasco and Yucatan, two points in their journey, were in a state of revolution, and the government of Santa Anna had issued a peremptory order to prevent all strangers from visiting the ruins of Palenque. What the revolution was about Stephens had not any idea, although it was true that the central government used its distant provinces as quartering places for rapacious officers. However, Stephens made up his mind to go on to Palenque, nevertheless, as one of the principal objects of the expedition. He had just met Henry Pawling, an American from Rhinebeck on the Hudson, who had been connected with Hardy's travelling circus. Pawling had arranged in Central America its places of exhibition, and then he had managed the cochineal plantation that Stephens had seen near Guatemala City. For seven years he had not spoken a word of his own language, and, tired of the chaotic state of the country, he had raced along the road to catch up with these explorers who spoke English. Later, Stephens arranged for Pawling to make plaster casts of the sculptures at Palenque that were presently seized and destroyed by a "patriots' committee."

On a poor little trail through the forest, winding about through mountains and ravines, with vultures overhead and scorpions below, and with aguanas, rattlesnakes and lizards, they made their way by Ocosingo, the city that had a pyramidal fortress and two stone figures lying on the ground. They crossed an ancient suspension bridge, made of osiers twisted into cords, passing roofless churches standing in places that were unknown: their altars were thrown down and trees grew within the walls. The cold was still severe; there were many rugged peaks with gigantic cypress trees growing on

their sides; and they crossed a river where alligators were in
undisturbed possession, basking on mudbanks like logs of
driftwood. The river was dotted with their heads. One monster,
twenty-five or thirty feet long, lay on the arm of a tree that
hung over the water; and, when Stephens shot him, he fell
with a tremendous convulsion, reddening the water with a
circle of blood. There were corn patches in deep ravines and
on mountain heights, and the Indians were notoriously hostile; but Stephens and Catherwood reached Palenque safely,
a village that was eight miles from the ruins. They found
coffee in three small village shops, with rude pottery cooking
utensils and hard vegetable shells for cups. One Indian carried a cowhide trunk with a chicken on each side, another had
a live turkey on top of his trunk, and a third carried beside
his load several strings of eggs, each egg wrapped in a husk of
corn.

At the ruins of Palenque, best known of the ancient
American cities, they came first upon masses of stones, then,
climbing to a terrace covered with trees, they saw the front
of a large building which the Indians described as the
Palace. It was richly ornamented with stuccoed fragments
on the pilasters; and, tying their mules to the trees, they ascended a flight of steps and entered a corridor and a courtyard.
There were many rooms in the Palace, with a three-
storied tower in the centre, and there were apartments under-
ground containing tables that were about eight feet long. An
aqueduct was supplied by a stream that ran at the base of
a terrace, and a broken but level esplanade led to a pyramidal
structure. From the tower they discovered another building
more than a hundred feet high, the Temple, with great bushes
dislodging stones from the roof; the carved wooden lintels
were covered with a complex stucco design, all overgrown

with trees. A monument lay on its face, half buried under earth and stones, which the Indians turned over, having cut down saplings for levers. It was like the Egyptian statues, ten feet, six inches tall, and beautifully carved on the under-surface. The figure wore a lofty spreading headdress. There were large tablets of hieroglyphics, half obliterated by the action of the rain and the decomposition of the stone, covered with a coating of green moss which they had to wash and scrape away. Stephens cleaned the lines with a stick and scrubbed the hieroglyphics with blacking brushes, preparing the monument for Catherwood to draw. The hieroglyphics were exactly like those at Copán, three hundred air-miles away, separated by rivers, mountains and jungles, showing that the whole country had been occupied by the same race and that the Indians had once spoken the same language.

Stephens fired off his gun, knowing the Indians would report it and that it would prevent them from making a visit during the night. Then he and Catherwood hung their hammocks in the corridor, uneasily conscious of snakes, scorpions and lizards and finding the mosquitoes beyond all endurance. They were also disturbed by the screams of the bats that hung from the ceiling and whizzed through the corridor all night long. The next morning they escorted through the ruins three padres who had come especially to see them and who were attended by more than a hundred Indians, carrying chairs, hammocks and luggage. They were all great card-players, but the padre of Tumbalá, who weighed two hundred and forty pounds, played his violin while the others played monte, and Stephens, who had been impressed by the kindness of the padres he had seen, was convinced that they were all diligent in their vocations. In short, they were good and intelligent men, without reproach among the people. The ruins were wet, and the continuous rains worked through cracks and crevices and pushed the stones asunder. Catherwood was wan and gaunt, wracked with malaria, his face swollen with insect bites and his left arm crippled with rheumatism. Then the nigua insects attacked Stephens's feet, which were soon inflamed and swollen to twice their natural size. For a day or two he could not leave his hammock. But at Palenque he had taken elaborate notes and Catherwood had made about fifty sepia drawings.

When finally they abandoned the ruins, Stephens and Catherwood left their beds, together with their pots and calabashes, hoping that later visitors could use them, and, riding in their wet clothes, with another long journey before them, they presently took a Spanish brig for Sisal. This was the port of Mérida to which they drove in a calash, without springs, painted red, green and yellow, looking in the capital for Don Simon Péon, the owner of the hacienda and ruins of Uxmal. Stephens had met him in New York at a Spanish hotel in Fulton Street, where he had been himself in the habit of dining, and, finding that Don Simon Péon had gone to Uxmal, he and Catherwood decided to go on at once. They set out on horseback to ride the fifty miles, escorted by a servant of Señor Péon and preceded by Indians carrying a load provided for his guests in which a box of claret was conspicuous. At the hacienda there were two major-domos, one of whom Stephens had also known in New York, a waiter at Delmonico's, a young Spaniard from Catalonia who had taken part in some unsuccessful insurrection. Through a noble stretch of woods, Stephens and Catherwood walked to the ruins, emerging suddenly upon a large open field that was strewn with vast buildings and terraces and pyramidal structures. Although it was never mentioned in history, Uxmal had obviously been, at one time, a large and populous city, and the ruins were in a fine state of preservation. They re-called the descriptions of the old chroniclers of the conquest, who spoke of the splendours that met their eyes in their progress through the country. Cortes must have passed within a few miles of Uxmal, ever since exposed to the deluge of tropical rains and with trees growing through the doorways. The Indians regarded the ruins with superstitious reverence, believing that immense treasure was buried in them. Stephens was struck at the first glance with the wonder and admira-tion with which he had caught sight of the ruins of Thebes. Volney would have found here another occasion to meditate and moralize on the ruins of empires.

At Uxmal, Catherwood began to draw a panorama; then, with a violent attack of fever, he suddenly collapsed and had to be carried back to Mérida. He felt as if Stephens, on horse-back, was following his bier. Stephens, who had returned for one more view of the ruins, decided that they must come back later to pursue their explorations. Meanwhile, in July, 1840, they sailed for New York. The sharks played around them as they were transferred from a Spanish brig to the jolly-boat of the "Helen Maria." They reached New York exactly ten months after they had originally sailed for Belize.

v

When Stephens and Catherwood arrived in New York, the campaign was at its height for William Henry Harrison as President of the country. Stephens, after visiting Washing-ton to call upon Daniel Webster, set to work at once on his new book. *Incidents of Travel in Central America, Chiapas and Yucatan* created, at the moment, a great sensation: it went through twelve printings in three months, and Edgar Allan Poe called it in a review "perhaps the most interesting book of travel ever published." William Cullen Bryant, the editor of the *Evening Post,* especially admired the wash and sepia drawings for which Catherwood had engaged five different engravers; and Albert Gallatin and H. H. Schoolcraft, authorities on the American Indians, called upon Stephens in New York. Schoolcraft presently contributed an appendix to Stephens's later book. The historian Prescott, who had begun to dictate *The Conquest of Mexico,* was enthusiastic about this explorer's work; he was deeply indebted to the author for his discoveries in Central America and for his pictures and comments on the Mexican scene.

Scarcely more than a year later, in October, 1841, the two friends sailed back to Sisal, the port of Mérida, in Yucatan. It was a voyage of twenty-seven days, and the barque "Tennessee" carried, as cargo, gunpowder, six hundred kegs, with turpentine, muskets and cotton. Along with a daguerreotype apparatus, the explorers took with them a modest young Harvard man from Boston, Dr. Samuel Cabot, later well-known as a surgeon, who had studied medicine in Paris. Dr. Cabot was also a naturalist, deeply interested in ornithology, and he looked forward to finding in Yucatan a great number of rare tropical birds. He was not to be disappointed, for the state had never before been explored ornithologically, and he found egrets and pelicans, the white-winged king vulture and the ocellated turkey, which Audubon described. He was to see, near Tulum, a tree covered with white ibises, its green foliage appearing like a frame for their snowy plumage, and he was to shoot a trogan, one of the most unusual birds, adorning with its brilliant plumage the branches of an overhanging tree. Then there were scarlet ibises and roseate spoonbills and many new varieties of bitterns and hawks. In addition, Dr. Cabot knew how to cure strabismus, and there was much squinting in Mérida, there were many cross-eyed people: in the Maya world it had been attractive to be cross-eyed and one of the gods had been so represented. Without any anæsthesia, one cut a small muscle to let the eye fall back into its normal position, and Dr. Cabot operated on a fourteen-year-old boy, an old Mexican general and a pretty young girl. The general, an exile in Mérida, had served as an aide-de-camp to General Jackson at the battle of New Orleans. Dr. Cabot's room was crowded with curious people; and in the street passers-by pointed to him and said, "There goes the man who cures the biscos."

There was a great cathedral in Mérida, with a Franciscan convent. The bishop lived in style in the palace, and Stephens, Catherwood and Dr. Cabot were conducted through three stately rooms, all with high ceilings and lighted lamps. The bishop, handsomely dressed, seated in a further room, was like some priestly warrior or grand master of the Temple, as he spoke of generals, seiges, blockades and battles, and he said his house and table were at the service of the Americans and asked them to name a day for dining with him. Since 1840, Yucatan had been an independent state, and the general aspect of Mérida was Moorish, for it had been built at a time when the Moorish style prevailed in Spanish architecture. The houses were mostly of one story, with balconies and court-yards. The three friends took a small stone house, where they set up the daguerreotype apparatus, and they began to photograph the young ladies of Mérida: there were three who came first, with their fathers and mothers, dressed in their prettiest costumes, with earrings and chains. One was a deli-cate and dangerous blonde, from the point of view of Ste-

phens, whose name, he said, was poetry itself and who presently sent them a large cake, three feet in circumference, and
six inches deep, which Stephens smothered into his saddle-
bags. There it spoiled some of his small stock of wearing ap-
parel. His business in Mérida was to enquire about more
ruins and arrange for the journey into the interior, and all
three set out, on horseback, with their luggage on the backs
of mules, for Uxmal and, presently, Mayapán. This ancient
city, once the capital of the fallen empire of Maya, had never
been visited by strangers.

At Uxmal again, they went first to see Don Simon Péon, the
proprietor of the ruins, on his hacienda, with a large cattle-
yard, great trees and tanks of water; then they went on to the
ruins and swung their hammocks, alone in the palace of unknown kings. The buildings there still had doors that could
be opened and shut, and, according to the tradition, the
Indians had been going there one hundred and forty years
after Mérida was founded, observing their religious rites far
from the eyes of the Spaniards. Stephens had ladders made,
and Catherwood climbed up to make his accurate drawings
of the Governor's house, the largest building in Uxmal and
the most interesting of all the Maya buildings anywhere: the
façade of carved stone was largely unbroken. They cut roads
from ruin to ruin, to make a line of communication, and
first they took a stroll along the whole front of the house, with
no great wish to go to bed. But their mosquito-nets were a great
success, and they made one of the Indians the ruler over their
fireplace, with all the privileges and emoluments of sipping
and tasting.

Stephens and Cabot cleared the buildings so that Catherwood might draw them, measuring the walls and making
floor-plans. From the House of the Magician they could see

most of the ruins, scattered over an area of two miles, stone buildings with elaborate façades and terraces, now indistinct, and truncated pyramids with stairways on the sides. There was the House of the Doves, resembling a dovecote, and the House of the Turtles, so called because of the row of turtles carved on the cornice: it had been tottering when they had been there the year before and the centre, within this year, had fallen in. After a few more returns of the rainy season, the whole building would be a mass of ruins. The hieroglyphics were like those they had seen at Copán and Palenque; and there was a sculptured beam, a rare piece of carved wood, that Stephens hoped to have in his museum: covered with hempen bagging, it was carried away by the Indians and presently reached New York in good condition. But with no one to cook well for them they had been all but helpless until Chaipa Chi appeared, an Indian woman, with the look of a Maya portrait, a slanting forehead and hooked nose, who came up the steps, carrying her clothes on her head. The only interest her soul loved was the making of tortillas. In the six weeks he spent at Uxmal, Catherwood did his finest work. He had his happiest period drawing there. But the ruins were unhealthy, and at the end of that time all three were carried away on the backs of Indians, delirious with malaria. They left the famous Uxmal, silent as they had found it, to crumble and fall like other cities in the forest.

Before he himself collapsed, Stephens had ridden off one day to visit the fair at Jalacho, on the main road to Campeachy, thronged with Indians moving to the fiesta, all in freshly washed garments, from the villages roundabout. On the plaza, tables were set out with necklaces and rings, and in rustic arbours opposite were vendors of toys and trinkets and looking-glasses in frames of red paper. There was a procession of toreadors headed by an Indian, squint-eyed and bandy-legged, carrying a drum under his arm, dancing grotesquely to his own music; then followed the band and the picadors, a cut-throat looking set, who presently took part in a sanguinary bullfight. Stephens discovered on the way the ruins of Maxcanu, with a great cave where he explored the recesses, tying to his left wrist the end of a ball of twine and entering the labyrinth with a candle and a pistol. Riding through thick canebrake he visited ruins at another hacienda in the neighbourhood. The Indians who had not gone to the fair sat in their yards in the village streets, plaiting palm-leaves for hats and weaving hammocks, while the women sewed in their doorways and the children played naked in the road.

When all three men were well again, they set out for Mayapán where they found a circular building on a mound from which projected double rows of columns. The road was a mere bridle-path through the woods, and, stopping at one hacienda, Dr. Cabot operated on the owner's wife, this time not for strabismus but to remove a wen. Dr. Cabot's presence in every village was known at once and patients crowded round him to cure their biscos. For there were no doctors in Yucatan except in Campeachy and Mérida, and in villages the whole duty of attending to the sick devolved upon the usually devoted cura: he had, as a rule, a "sister-in-law" who did not impair his usefulness but was supposed to give him settled habits. The ruins of Mayapán covered a great plain with sculptured stone strewn about the ground, human figures and animals with hideous expressions. There were many ruins near Uxmal, ruin after ruin in the jungle, Kabah, for instance, with pyramids, terraces and arches, six tigers with stone masks and a figure carved in wood, with a headdress of quetzal plumes, standing on a snake. Then there was Nohcacab, where the padre hurried to meet them, exclaiming, *"Buenas noticias! Otras ruinas!*—Good news! More ruins!" At Nohpat they found the figure of a great lord lying on its back, and at Labna there was a row of death's heads in stucco, painted figures and a beautiful arched gateway. On many of the ruins they found the stamp of a red hand, a symbol of mastery or power, as bright as if it had been newly made, that brought one close to the Indian builders; but the rankness of the tropical vegetation was hurrying to destruction all the walls and all the cities. The gnarled and twisted roots of the trees encircled the stones with a ruthless grip and the fibres gradually overturned the walls. When the jungle had overtaken the farther flung cities, the Maya people had returned to their original home, and from the tenth century till the coming of the Spaniards they had gathered in the northern tip of Yucatan.

Presently, from Kabah, the friends proceeded on horseback, on the flat plain, toward Campeachy, with hammocks, a tin table service, a few changes of clothing, a candlestick, bread, chocolate, coffee and sugar. Catherwood could sketch, without dismounting, from his horse and Dr. Cabot could shoot from the back of his. Entering a region that was occupied wholly by Indians, they came to the ruins of Sayil, a name that had never been uttered by civilized man; and at the rancho of Sannacté the Indians were wild in appearance. The women disappeared at once and the men crouched on the ground, their long black hair hanging over their eyes. Stephens, Catherwood and Dr. Cabot explored the woods for ruins, Mani, Sabactche, Kevic, Xampon, where the walls had furnished materials for the church and all the stone houses of the village. Stephens rode off alone to Ticul for a bullfight and a dance and there he saw sculptured heads fixed as ornaments on the

fronts of houses. The plaza was overgrown with grass, while
a few mules pastured upon it, the perfect picture of stillness
and repose. But then again he was overtaken by malaria. An
icy chill succeeded a fire in his body, and the padre in an old
Franciscan habit took him to the convent and cured him with
orange and lemon juice flavoured with cinnamon.

The friends met again at Bolonchen, where the water was
taken from a deep well and Catherwood made some of his
finest drawings. There was a ladder wide enough for twenty
men to descend abreast, with water-jugs strapped to their
heads, and Catherwood climbed down one hundred and
twenty feet and made several sepia drawings in the dripping
half-darkness. The most dramatic of all was his picture of the
ladder. The three proceeded to the hacienda of Santa Rosa
Xtampak, where, peering through the trees, they saw the
white front of a lofty building, the grandest they had seen
in Yucatan. They found interior staircases for the first time,
and, mounting to the top, where the wind swept over the
ruined building, they caught sight of an eagle hovering aloft.
Dr. Cabot recognized it as one of a rare species but, before
he had time to shoot it, the proud bird soared away. The moon
beamed over the clearing, lighting up the woods and illuminating the great building from the base to the summit, and then
a short walk brought them into an open country and among
the towering remains of another city. There were lofty mounds
and ranges through which white masses of stone were glim-
mering and rising in quick succession.

Stephens had discovered the stone roads of Yucatan, which
had once traversed the whole country, binding together all the
Maya cities. These roads were eight feet wide, well kept in
Maya times, and one of them wound its way to Chichen Itza.
Ever since he had left home he had had his eyes upon this

place, the greatest city of the later Maya empire, and a centre of religious pilgrimages, where he, with his companions, was to spend eighteen days, and Catherwood was to make more than fifty drawings. All the great buildings were in full view, casting prodigious shadows over the plain, and the morning after they arrived, guided by an Indian, they prepared for a preliminary survey. While the field of ruins was partially wooded, most of it was open, crossed by cattle-paths here and there. A great truncated pyramid had staircases on all four sides, and the balustrades were decorated with gigantic serpents, intertwined, portions of which were still in place. The decoration on another building was a procession of tigers or lynxes, and there were paintings in vivid colours of human figures, battles, houses, trees, scenes of domestic life and a large canoe. The heads were adorned with plumes and the hands bore shields and spears. One of the buildings was more than two hundred feet long with a staircase fifty-six feet wide rising to the top, and in the gymnasium or tennis-court, so called, the Mayas had played a game with hardened rubber balls. In the interior of Yucatan, Chichen Itza had been the spot where the conquering Spaniards had first settled. For two centuries the whole Maya empire had been ruled by the lords of Chichen Itza.

To visit the northern and eastern coast, Cozumel and Tulum, the ruined city that could be seen from the ocean, they followed the route to Valladolid, nine leagues away, where great buildings towered on both sides of the road. The first stranger to visit Chichen Itza had been an American who was now living in Valladolid, a living city that still bore the mark of ancient grandeur going to decay: there were houses blazoned on the front with the coats of arms of Castilians whose race had been forgotten. Stephens and his friends arranged then for their further journey through seventy miles of the densest forest; and, although they were warned that it was impossible, they had no thought of turning back. Moreover, they were charmed by the welcome of the cura of Valladolid and the comfortable appearance of the convent, where the parlour was furnished with engravings from the novels of Sir Walter Scott that had been made for the Spanish market. Presently they set out for the port of Yalahau, over a road that was lonely and rugged, past bushes covered with garrapatas that swarmed in thousands over them until the body itself seemed to be crawling. This port, recently a haunt of pirates, was now the abode of smugglers, a business they combined with the embarking of sugar and other products of neighbouring ranchos. The coast had been infested with bands of desperadoes, doomed to be hanged on sight, whenever they were caught; and the principal men of the town were notorious quondam pirates who were living there, now greatly respected. A canoe was pointed out, lying in front of their door, that had once been used in pirate operations. Dr. Cabot found a new field opened to him in flocks of seafowl strutting along the shore and screaming down from over their heads.

At Yalahau they laid in a stock of provisions, two turtles, beef and pork in strings and implements for making tortillas, and they set out in a canoe following the track of the Spaniards along the east coast of Yucatan. They had undertaken to find vestiges of the great buildings of lime and stone that had astonished the Spanish conquerors, and they reached first the island of Mugeres, the resort of Lafitte, the notorious pirate who had been buried in a church near by. Then, after a few days, they came to the island of Cozumel, finding there a well of pure and abundant water upon which they fell at the moment of landing. Cozumel had been called by the chroniclers a place of many temples, a sanctuary for the aborigines; but the island was overgrown with trees and only after a long search did they find a tower standing on a terrace. Then they discovered another building, with the remains of a Spanish church in which a tree grew out of the main altar. Returning to the mainland, they travelled down to Tulum, where they found an ancient sea-wall, fifteen hundred feet in length, and the remains of several buildings with the Castillo on a high cliff, one hundred feet long, in full sight. There, again, were prints of the red hand, and they discovered on another building the figure of a man with head down and legs and arms spread out. From there they returned to Silam, the port of Izamal, with the towering remains of another ruined city. The whole of Izamal was built from the stones that lay in the mounds, and Catherwood made a splendid drawing of a gigantic head that was seven feet high and wide and covered with stucco. On the way back to Mérida, fifteen leagues from Izamal, they stopped to visit the ruins of Aké, where they found a great platform with thirty-six columns but with no trace of a building or a roof.

Once more in Mérida, Stephens could say that he had introduced the first circus company that had ever been in Yucatan. For a man named Clayton had brought there a portable theatre with spotted horses, riders, clowns and monkeys, and he said that Stephens, whom he had met in New York, had induced him to come to Mérida. Stephens had encouraged this in the belief that it might be a first step towards breaking up the popular taste for bullfights, the bullfights that even Jacques Casanova considered "a most barbarous sport and likely to operate unfavourably on the national morals." The circus threw into the shade the daguerreotype and the curing of biscos. Then Stephens and his companions, bidding fare-

well to the house of Péon, set off with their luggage to the
port of Sisal. They carried with them Stephens's notebooks,
Catherwood's huge portfolios and Dr. Cabot's collection of
Mexican bird-skins. Stephens, in his irregular route, had discovered the crumbling remains of forty-four ancient Mayan
cities, some of them certainly never seen by the eyes of a
white man and most of them never visited by any stranger.
Many had been occupied when the Spaniards had invaded
the country, but time and the tropical rains were hastening
them all to destruction; and in a few centuries great buildings,
already cracked and yawning, were destined to become mere
shapeless mounds.

VI

From that time forth, in Latin America, John Lloyd Stephens was to be known as the "father of Mayaism." But what
was to be his own future, and what became of Catherwood?
To the Rotunda in New York, with Catherwood's panorama,
Stephens had sent many relics, Mayan sculptures, vases, figures,
the lintel covered with hieroglyphics and carved beams from
Uxmal, Kabah and Labna. There were hundreds of Catherwood's drawings and water-colours, and all were destroyed
when a fire consumed the panoramas that Catherwood had
made of Jerusalem and Thebes. The few sculptures that were
saved Stephens gave to John Church Cruger, his friend who
owned the island in the Hudson, and the "Stephens stones"
were built into the wall that had been erected there to suggest one of the fragments of Volney's ruins. They were bought
generations later by the Museum of Natural History from a
descendant of John Church Cruger. After the fire Catherwood
set up again as an architect; then he was sent to British Guiana
to build a small railroad that would enable the planters to

bring their cotton and sugarcane to market. He bought land in California, invested his savings in a railroad there, and, going to England, he was lost, coming back, in 1854, in a collision at sea.

Stephens had died two years before him. The two had met once again on the river Chagres in Panama, where Stephens had begged Catherwood to take charge of the administration of the railroad that he was building there. Stephens himself had gone to Bogota to arrange with the government for the lease of the land for the railroad. As agent for a steamship company, he had sailed to Germany where he had a long conversation, at Potsdam, with Humboldt, "the greatest man since Aristotle," in his opinion, and "a part of history, belonging to the past." Stephens had published in 1843 his *Incidents of Travel in Yucatan,* republished every two years until 1861. The discovery of gold in California hastened the building of the railroad, and among the gold-seekers on the isthmus Stephens met Hermann Schliemann, the future discoverer of the city of Troy, who was bound for Sacramento. But the so-called "Chagres fever" soon got the better of him, and, picked up unconscious under a gigantic ceiba tree, he was carried to New York and presently died there. He was hastily buried in the tomb of a well-known family, with which he was not known to be connected, and only a century later, when the coffin was discovered, was the name of the father of Mayaism famous again.

GEORGE CATLIN

I

THE eighteen-thirties were a heyday of the Indians, and when George Catlin ascended the Missouri in 1832 he saw them in all their splendour of gait and costume. He sailed up the river on the first voyage of the "Yellowstone," the "Big Thunder Canoe," as the Mandans called it, a journey of three months from St. Louis, two thousand miles north, to Fort Union at the mouth of the Yellowstone river. The boat, on its way up, puffing and blowing, bumped against floating trees and hidden sandbars, and the Indians and buffaloes on the banks were terrified and fled when the twelve-pound cannon was discharged at a tepee village. The Indians ran to the tops of the bluffs or lay with their faces to the ground or shot their horses and dogs to appease the Great Spirit, who had been offended, they thought, by the belching of the gun. But to Catlin the country seemed like fairyland, both sublime and picturesque, as his eyes roamed over the hills, the bluffs and the dales. It was like the ruins of an ancient city with ramparts, domes, towers and spires of clay; and he was astonished by the herds of buffaloes, elk and mountain goats that bounded over the green fields of the unending prairies.

Catlin had come out to the Far West to make portraits of

the Indians, who were still uncorrupted beyond the frontier, and at St. Louis, where he had already spent two years, he had met and painted General William Clark. The survivor of Meriwether Lewis, of the Lewis and Clark expedition, had crossed the Rockies twenty-eight years before, following the Columbia river to the Pacific ocean, and the old general was superintendent of Indian affairs in the Western country and knew more about the Indians than anyone else. He was drawn to Catlin, impressed by his sincerity; and Catlin painted portraits also of the chiefs of the delegations who visited the superintendent at St. Louis. The two men went up to Prairie du Chien, where General Clark made treaties with the Ioways, the Sioux, the Omahas and the Sacs and Foxes, and Catlin, painting all the time, rode through the country of the Konsas, who ornamented their heads with crests of deer's hair. Then he travelled through passes in the mountains to Great Salt Lake when the Mormons were still living in Illinois. He was at home in the saddle and a master of woodcraft who had lived as a boy on a farm on the Susquehanna.

Before going up the Missouri, Catlin had returned to Albany. There he had married, in 1828, the daughter of a magnate who had bought up a good part of the town, a rival in this respect of the first William James who had also made his fortune in real estate at Albany. But Clara Catlin was to have much to put up with, for her husband was destined to live a nomad's life, one who took, as he said, "an incredible pleasure in roaming through nature's trackless wild." Born at Wilkes-Barre in 1796, he had heard trappers and Indian fighters talking at his father's forest farm; then, studying law at Litchfield, like his father before him, he had set up as a lawyer for two or three years. But, exchanging his law books for paint-pots and brushes, he had gone to Philadelphia to study with

Thomas Sully and the Peales, delighting in the Peale museum where were exhibited, among minerals and birds, relics
of the Lewis and Clark expedition. Becoming a well-known
portrait-painter, travelling from city to city, he had painted
Dolly Madison and De Witt Clinton. Especially he painted
reservation Indians, Senecas, Oneidas and Tuscaroras, among
them the old chief Red Jacket, standing on the brink of Niagara Falls where he thought his spirit would linger after he
was dead. Catlin had already made up his mind to visit the
unknown Far West and become the "historian," as he put it,
of the Indians there.

II

General Clark in St. Louis approved of Catlin's plan to
travel in the "Yellowstone" up the Missouri. It would be early
summer when the Indians were gathered round the agencies
to fit themselves out for their autumn hunts. Then he said,
"I need your help in a losing battle," for he believed in the
Indians and felt they were doomed. He had his own private
museum of Indian costumes and weapons, with heads of elk
and buffalo and portraits of chiefs, which were poor indeed
beside Catlin's, smooth and academic. The "Yellowstone" was
stocked with blankets and red flannel shirts, tomahawks, bush-
els of beads and kegs of tobacco, together with the vermilion
the Indians daubed on their bodies and faces and that caused
them to be described as red men. For their natural colour was
a sort of cinnamon brown. Catlin, who had come aboard with
his easel, canvas and bladders of paint, soon saw what the
general meant by a "losing battle," for the traders and the fur
men talked about the Indians and how many beaver-skins
could be traded for a bottle of whiskey. Catlin, determined to

champion their cause, also believed in them "before they were put in frock coats with velvet collars," and he was convinced that, before they were spoiled by the craft and cunning of the whites, they were proud, honourable and honest. He was to find everywhere, in his eight years with the Indians, universal hospitality and kindness, but there was an example on the boat of the effect that white civilization had upon these children of the prairies. A young man named Wi-jun-jon, or the Pigeon's Egg-Head, the son of a chief of the Assiniboines, had spent a winter in Washington, where he met the Great White Father, and was returning home in full-dress regimentals. Whistling "Yankee Doodle," he strutted on the deck, while he had slept in his uniform, his white kid gloves were almost black and two bottles of whiskey stuck out of his pockets. The village had assembled to welcome the son of the chief, who walked ashore with a blue umbrella in his hand, and Catlin later heard the rest of the story. His wife, thinking his coat was useless, cut it off at the waist in order to make leggings for herself; she made of his hat-band a pair of garters; and the Pigeon's Egg-Head himself, bragging about the white man's ways, was finally killed as a liar and a good-for-nothing.

The steamboat, with its Yankee trappers and French-Canadian *coureurs de bois,* was grounded several times on sand-bars in the river, and Catlin, who went ashore and painted portraits among the Sioux, fell in with an old chief who had been exposed. Too infirm to follow his tribe, which was driven afar by hunger for buffalo meat, he had asked to be left alone to starve,—a custom of all the prairie tribes,—and Catlin could only shake the hand of the poor old forsaken patriarch and leave him to the mercy of the bears and the wolves. On another occasion, with seventeen fellow passengers, he walked across the country two hundred miles to Fort Tecumseh, where the Teton river flowed into the winding Missouri. With his sketch-book slung on his back, rifle in hand, he learned how much easier it was to walk with his toes turned in, through the long grass, in the Indian fashion. There were six or seven hundred skin lodges grouped about this fort,—the site of the future capital of South Dakota,—for it was a centre of trade with the Sioux whence buffalo robes in great quantities were transported to be sold in the Eastern markets. There were games and horse-races and the Indians gave the white men a feast of dog-meat, killing their most faithful companions to bear witness to their friendship. Each guest had a wooden bowl with dog's flesh floating in the soup and a large spoon made of a buffalo's horn, and everyone knew the solemnity and good feeling behind the feast and the necessity of devouring a little of the brew. Catlin saw one chief take from his bowl the victim's head and descant on it with affection and with tears in his eyes.

At Fort Tecumseh, Catlin painted One Horn,—Ha-wan-je-tah,—the great chief of the Sioux, whose white elkskin tunic was fringed with scalp-locks and quills; and he made a portrait of Mah-to-tchee-ga, the Little Bear, in profile, merely for the sake of variety, from his point of view. But he did not foresee the consequences. A surly member of another band, Shon-ka, watching as he painted, remarked, "The Little Bear gets only half a face because he is only half a man." When the Little Bear asked, "Who says that?" Shon-ka, the Dog, replied, "Shon-ka says it," whereupon the Little Bear answered, "When the Dog says it, let him prove it." Then the Dog said again, "He knows that half of your face is good for nothing, so he has left it out of the picture." Presently two shots rang out, the Little Bear was killed and the Dog fled, to be killed later; and Catlin was blamed for this by the medicine-men who said that all the men he painted were bound to die, for they could not live in two places at once. A portrait, to them, was obviously alive: the eyes in the picture were always open, the subjects could not even sleep at night, and the picture would go on living when the subject was dead. Presently the Indians left the fort: their wigwams lay flat on the ground, horses and dogs were loaded and the cavalcade crept off. Catlin painted this scene, too, and noted it in the letters he was sending to a newspaper in New York.

By the time when the "Yellowstone" reached Fort Union, the end of its run of two thousand miles, Catlin knew much about the northwestern Indians. The fort, the principal depot of the American Fur Company, was built with palisades and two stone bastions, and there were eight or ten log-cabins, store-houses, sheds and living quarters within the enclosure. It was a rendezvous of several tribes who came to trade there, Crows, Blackfeet and Assiniboines among them. Sometimes, in fact, a whole tribe camped there; and Kenneth McKenzie, a Scotsman, the master, locked up all their weapons, so that hostile tribes were obliged to keep the peace. The agent of the company as far west as the Rocky Mountains, he kept a vast stock of goods for trading, and the hunters came in from the further West, laden with packs of furs, with Indian chiefs, sachems, warriors, women and children. Catlin was given a painting-room in one of the bastions of the fort, and there he worked, with his easel before him, sitting on the breech of a twelve-pounder. The room soon became a lounge for the worthies of the tribe, where Crows and Blackfeet, deadly enemies outside, gathered and quietly smoked together. At McKenzie's table, Catlin dined on buffalo meat and buffaloes' tongues and on beavers' tails with marrow-fat for butter, and with port and Madeira for lunch and dinner.

There Catlin painted for several weeks, while he took part in buffalo-hunts, ball-plays, foot-races, horse-races and wrestling, or chased the little wild horses that ranged from Lake Winnepeg to the Mexican border, the shyest animals of the prairie. Milk white, or jet black, sorrel, bay, iron grey or pied, with long tails that swept the ground, strays from Mexico, where the Spaniards had introduced them, they scoured the plains in herds of thousands. Just so the buffaloes also ranged as far north as Hudson's Bay, and the Indians, who killed them with arrows or with lances, lived altogether on buffalo meat. Their flesh was delicious, Catlin thought, like that of fat beef, but the Indians used every part of the buffalo, not only the flesh for food but the skin for clothing. They used the skin also for covering their lodges and for constructing saddles, bridles and thongs, as they used the horns for ladles and spoons, the hoofs for making glue and the bones for saddle-trees and war-clubs. They braided the buffalo hair into halters and made strings of the sinews and the women used the sinews in their sewing. The Indians hunted the buffaloes even in winter on snow-shoes, but this was mainly for buffalo robes to sell; for they usually killed and dried the meat in the autumn when it was especially fat and juicy. Carts were sent out, following the hunters, to collect the buffalo-meat, which was then thrown into the ice-house. Catlin enjoyed these buffalo-hunts, with the great animals eddying and wheeling, plunging and butting at each other and attacking the horses; and, with his sketch-book and rifle, and his canvas rolled up in a case on his back, he sometimes took notes and drew when he was in the saddle. At the end of the day, the hunters returned to relate their adventures to the women-folk. But the buffaloes were doomed like the Indians who fed upon them. Catlin related that a band of Sioux brought in fourteen hundred buffaloes' tongues for which they received a few gallons of whiskey. The skins and the flesh were left on the prairie for the wolves.

The Blackfeet and the Crows, the aristocrats of the Indian world, were the finest in appearance at Fort Union, the Blackfeet, the largest and most warlike of the tribes, and the Crows, known for their tall figures, who made the most beautiful lodges. Their wigwams were hung with skins that were dressed to look almost as white as linen and were most picturesquely ornamental. Catlin painted the Four Wolves, a fine looking fellow of six feet, whose hair as he walked trailed on the grass, and he also painted Pe-toh-pee-kiss, the Eagle Ribs, a Blackfoot brave, holding two medicine-bags made of the skins of otters. Medicine was their word for mystery, and Catlin himself was called the White Medicine painter, for no Indian had seen a life-like portrait before; and painting was held to be the most unaccountable of mysteries, while guns and pistols were great medicine also. So were the lucifer matches that Catlin carried with him. Young Indians, "making their medicine," wandered off alone, neither eating nor drinking until some experience or dream told them what their medicine was to be, and whatever bird, animal or reptile they first dreamed about became their special medicine and their protection. Then they hunted for the creature, otter, badger, loon or wolf, or perhaps even a mouse, to be saved for its skin which was to become the basis of the medicine-bag they were to wear on all occasions. They carried these medicine-bags into battle, disgraced if they lost them or if their enemies captured them and displayed them later as trophies of war. Once Catlin witnessed the procedure of a Blackfoot doctor or medicine-man over a brave who was dying. Dressed in the skin of a yellow bear, he growled and groaned and gesticulated, hopping over the patient while he pawed about with his hands and feet, exactly in the manner of a bear. Attached to the skin he wore were the skins of other animals, snakes, frogs and bats, with the beaks and tails of birds and with antelopes' hoofs. Catlin obtained this costume for his Indian collection, with other headdresses, pipes, war-clubs, lances and arrows. He collected rattles, whistles, drums and flutes, and the staves of medicine-men, hung with bats' wings, ermine skins and bears' claws, perfumed with the scent of the skunk. He had bows of ash-wood, lined for their elasticity with the sinews of the buffalo and the deer.

Most of Catlin's portraits were painted in half-length, the head of the White Buffalo, for example, with his mystery drum over his left arm; but he painted the Iron Horn at full length in a very splendid costume. Then there was Mah-to-toh-pa, the Four Bears, for whom Catlin was obliged to wait till noon with his palette and colours all prepared, for this important man had spent at his toilet the whole morning until he was finally satisfied with his looks and equipment. He entered like a tragedian treading the stage, in a headdress of war-eagle's quills extending to his feet and a necklace of fifty claws of the grizzly bear. His shield was the hide of a buffalo's neck, hardened with glue from its hoofs, and he was a picture of manly dignity and grace with his leggings, knife, medicine-bag, tomahawk and war-club. He was accompanied by a crowd of women and children who gazed at him with admiration, and, taking a position in the middle of the room, he sang his medicine-song and looked the painter straight in the face. For if a warrior was painted not looking straight forward, if in the portrait he looked away, it was necessary for him to challenge the painter to fight. Catlin acquired for his collection the great man's painted robe, adorned with twelve battle scenes on the back, and he also acquired the scalping-knife with the blood of the victims dried on the blade and certificates of its identity and history. No warrior, in fact, would stand for his portrait until he had spent all the time from sunrise until eleven or twelve o'clock arranging himself in his war-dress and war-paint, oiling with bear's grease his long locks and bedaubing and streaking himself with red, green and black. Catlin painted the head chief of the Blackfeet, who sat for his picture superbly dressed and surrounded by his warriors and his braves, the warriors being those who had taken one or more scalps while the braves had not taken scalps but had only fought. The Stone with Horns,—Toh-ki-ee-to,—was tattooed by pricking in vermilion and gunpowder in elaborate profusion. When a portrait was finished, the sitter usually lay down in front of it, admiring his own beautiful form from noon till night.

Distinguished personages of each tribe lounged about the room, narrating stories of the battles they had fought and boasting of the scalp-locks that were attached to their tunics and their leggings. Their likenesses were recognized by stamping and yelling, while the women covered their mouths, a sign of surprise; and the painter was considered the greatest of all medicine-men, for the eyes of the picture moved and smiled. Guards were stationed at the door in order to keep the crowds away, and, when he was summoned, Catlin stepped out and the women gazed and gaped at him: the braves offered him their hands and the little boys struggled to touch him with their fingers. The portraits were held up over the door together, so that the whole tribe could see their chiefs, and the painter was presented with a doctor's wand and a dog was sacrificed to him and hung by the legs over his wigwam. The chiefs decided who was worthy of the honour of being painted, but Catlin occasionally made mistakes. There was a kind of dandy who strolled about in a beautiful dress but without scalp-locks or claws of the grizzly bear. In each tribe there were a few of these young men, pluming themselves with swan's-down, sweet-scented grass and the quills of ducks, and they were held in low esteem by the chiefs and braves because they had an aversion to arms and fighting. Faint hearts, gay and tinselled bucks, decked out in all their finery, they were always taking up attitudes at Catlin's door, and Catlin began to paint one of them when two or three chiefs were in the room, whereupon the chiefs rose and went outside. Presently an interpreter came in saying, "My God, you have given great offence to the chiefs. If you paint that man's picture, you must destroy theirs." Generally, when Catlin was painting, he induced the other young men to perform their dances so that he could study their expression and their character. Their songs were made up of yelps and barks, harsh and jarring gutteral sounds, but they were handsome and picturesque beyond description, and he greatly admired their grace and perfection of form. Among many, he painted the White Buffalo, the Bear's Child and the Eagle's Rib, together with the wife of the chief, the Crystal Stone.

Meanwhile, he took wild rambles about this country of green meadows, enamelled with myriads of flowers,—there were lilies, wild roses and sunflowers everywhere,—a country where everything was topsy-turvy, where men were red and wolves were white, rivers were yellow and frogs had horns and where magpie and paroquet replaced the bluebird and the robin. There were no laws here but those of honour and only the sun and the rats were the same as at home. The steamboat, the "Yellowstone," was returning to St. Louis, transporting a heavy load of buffalo skins, but Catlin was planning to paddle down the river in a canoe with two companions, Bogard and Ba'tiste. Bogard was a Mississippian, Ba'tiste was a weather-beaten *voyageur,* and both had been employees of the Fur Company, engaged in trapping beavers on the northern Missouri or at the base of the Rocky Mountains. They all bade farewell to their friends at the fort and set out in their frail little bark canoe, Bogard in the bow, while Ba'tiste paddled from the middle and Catlin steered, sitting in the stern. He had, besides his canvas, easel and paint-pots, and the pictures that were dry and rolled together, several packs that contained his Indian collection, and the canoe was stocked with beavers' tails and dried buffaloes' tongues, fresh buffalo meat and a good supply of pemmican. They counted on Bogard with his rifle to replenish their larder. They had also brought three tin cups, a coffee-pot and a plate, together with a frying pan and a tin kettle. They travelled at the rate of four or five miles an hour, camping at night on buffalo robes on the shore, and they were in high spirits, under the rugged and varicoloured bluffs, because the coffee was good and the weather was fine.

At the fort, Kenneth McKenzie had given them a war-eagle, the bird which the Indians esteemed for its valour and the quills that were used for the heads of warriors and chiefs. It was full-grown and domesticated. Catlin had a perch erected for it, six or eight feet high, over the bow, and there, without being fastened, the great bird rested quietly, silently survey-ing all that passed. Fed with fresh buffalo meat or fish, it usually held to its perch all day, and could not be made to leave the canoe. When the companions woke up in the morn-ing, there the bird was on its stand, but, tired of its position, during the day, it sometimes raised its long broad wings and, spreading them, hovered a few feet over their heads. Occasion-ally it soared for miles together, looking down over them, shading and fanning them with fresh air. Once, waking up, when they slept on a beach, Catlin heard Bogard exclaim, "Look at old Cale, will you?" Caleb, or Cale, was the word for a grizzly bear, and there the monster stood, a few feet away, with his mate and two cubs standing beside him. The bears had been in the canoe, and had pawed out every article, untying two packs of Indian dresses, shirts, leggings and robes which were daubed with mud and spread out as if to dry; and they had devoured most of the eatables that Bogard had to replace by shooting an occasional antelope that was gazing at them. For that matter, they were well supplied with clams, frogs, snails and rattlesnakes, delicious when they were properly dressed and broiled. The canoe passed a prairie-dog village, and a herd of buffaloes crossed the river, swimming about and blackening the stream. Catlin painted the scene and described it in his journal. Once he left Bogard and Ba'tiste, stretched out on the grass, where they enjoyed a mountaineer's nap, while, taking his rifle and sketchbook, he roamed from hilltop to hilltop, picking wild flowers and looking at the valley beneath him. He carried his easel and canvas to the top of a bluff and painted views up and down the river, the gracefully sloping hills and domes of green that vanished into blue in the distance. He followed the traces of a grizzly bear and pursued a wild war-eagle in sight of a herd of buffaloes on the rugged cliffs. There were thousands of white swans and pelicans where the river expanded itself into what appeared to be a beautiful lake.

III

Catlin had made up his mind to visit every Indian tribe and record with brush and pencil its habits and amusements, its mysteries and religious ceremonies,—the grass-builders, the earth-builders, the bark-builders and the timber-builders,—in all their native simplicity and beauty. Documenting their everyday life, he had set out to defend them and explain why they resented the invading white men who stole their land away from them, dug up their graves and scattered the bones, debauched them and destroyed them with whiskey and small-pox. The Mandans, whom he stopped to see, with whom he spent several weeks indeed, were to be exterminated by small-pox two or three years later: only about thirty were left out of two or three thousand, and twenty-five thousand Blackfeet were exterminated also. Two or three traders had introduced among them a disease from which they had no immunity. The Mandans were a small unwarlike tribe who lived in a fortified village,—two villages, in fact, two miles apart,—protected by the river and a high stockade, with dome-shaped lodges all close together, circular, with walls of timber and earth on top. They sat on the roofs of these lodges, which looked like inverted potash-kettles, with their dogs, sleds, pottery and buffalo skulls, and they cultivated corn, pumpkins and small turnips, while most of their time was spent in gossip and games. For the Indians were not taciturn, reserved or morose, they were actually more talkative than civilized people, garrulous, fond of story-telling, laughing easily at a slight joke, full of fun as they sat cross-legged, in winter, by the fire.

Two hundred miles south of Fort Union, the "polite and friendly" Mandans, as even the traders called these leisurely people, the "people of the pheasants," as they called themselves, lived on the future site of Bismarck, the capital of North Dakota. All hilarity and mirth, they spent much of their time in gambols and games, ball-plays, horse-racing and archery, the "game of the arrow," or in dancing the scalp-dance, the boasting dance, the begging dance, or in their hot vapour baths or swimming in the river. The buffalo dance, with much beating of drums, stamping, bellowing and grunting, sometimes lasted four days until the buffaloes finally came. They had rain-makers, when the earth was dry, and rain-stoppers, when the earth was wet, and, instead of burying their dead, they wrapped up the corpses carefully and placed them on high scaffolds out of the reach of wolves and dogs. Catlin, with so many picturesque subjects before him, was busy all the time with his easel and brushes. The art of portrait-painting was unknown to the Mandans, and this was a new era of medicine for them. There were glistening eyes at every crevice of the painter's lodge, with braves at the door and a hush when he was painting. Catlin straddled a naked horse, all unclothed himself, for the Mandans rode naked on unsaddled horses.

Lewis and Clark had spent in their villages the winter of 1804-1805, and Prince Maximilian of Neuwied also spent the winter there a year after Catlin visited the Mandans; and when Schoolcraft, the Indian scholar, said Catlin was untruthful, Prince Maximilian came to his defence. He had told the exact truth in describing the ceremony of O-Kee-pa, the annual commemoration of the Deluge. For all the Indian tribes had this tradition of the great flood that left only one man alive and of the Big Canoe that landed on a mountain. The ceremony of the Mandans had a three-fold object, to celebrate the settling of the waters, to dance in order to bring buffaloes and as an ordeal for the young men; and it began on the day when the willow-leaves were full-grown, for the medicine-bird had brought a twig with full-grown leaves upon it. A stranger from the West entered the village and, playing the part of the only man who had been saved, he related the story of the Deluge. Then he proceeded to open the medicine-lodge. Catlin was present at the sacred transactions that took place within the lodge, probably the first white man to have seen them, when the youthful candidates were put through frightful tortures to prepare them for manhood in the tribe. Catlin, convinced that a better, more honest or kinder people were not to be found, painted, among many others, a Mandan chief. He bought the costume of the chief but finally sold it for two horses, keeping only the headdress for his collection.

Then, taking to the canoe again with Bogard and Ba'tiste, he recommenced the journey to St. Louis, eighteen hundred miles down the river, stopping at the village of the Minatarees, where he painted the Black Moccasin, the patriarch who was more than a hundred years old. Catlin was an inmate of the chief's hospitable lodge, where he slept on a buffalo-robe with curtains of elk-hide, and he painted the courteous old man who sat on the ground smoking his pipe with a fine Crow robe wrapped about him. He also painted Red Thunder in his war-dress. The Black Moccasin remembered Lewis and Clark, who had visited the tribe, and, hearing that "Long Knife" Clark was still living at St. Louis, he sent warm regards to his old friend. Catlin brought Clark the message and showed him the portrait, which he recognized at once, saying the old man had treated him with great kindness.

Once more on the river, the three men camped on the bank as usual. Catlin would steer the canoe silently into a little cove and drop his line under the willows to catch fish for their supper. They shot deer, ducks, wild geese and prairie chickens, and once two or three big grey wolves approached them in the night and chewed off the corner of Catlin's buf-falo-robe. They stole, around midnight, with muffled paddles, past the Riccarees, who had once been friendly to the white men. Lewis and Clark had found them hospitable, but their

experiences with traders had made them hostile. At last
they reached St. Louis, the gateway of the West, the headquarters of the fur companies and of Catlin himself, who
sent there from all points, to be kept till he arrived, his
packages of pictures, note-books and Indian treasures. He lifted
his pretty canoe to the deck of the steamer, lying at the
wharf, to remain for a few hours while he found a place to
store his portraits; but when he came back it had been stolen,
though he finally recovered about fifteen of the twenty packages that he had brought to St. Louis. For weeks, at Indian
villages, the canoe had lain unmolested, although there had
been no laws to guard it, and Catlin was reminded all over
again of the honesty of the Indians, not one of whom had
stolen from him a penny's worth of property. No Indian
had ever struck him, nor had he ever had to raise his hand
against an Indian. They were high-minded and honourable,
the honestest people he had lived among. No Indian ever
questioned the ridiculous fashions of the civilized world or
asked why the white man did not paint his body, why he
wore a hat on his head and buttons on the back of his coat
or why he wore whiskers and a shirt collar up to the eyes.
Catlin agreed with Columbus, who wrote to Ferdinand and
Isabella, "There is not a better people in the world, more
affectionate, affable and mild. They love their neighbours as
themselves and they always speak smilingly." Far from being
sullen, they were proud before they had teachers or laws and
best, as Rousseau said, in their primitive state. They were
cruel, but their hearts were good, and they had the most un-
principled part of civilized society to deal with. Considering
the boundless system of plunder that was practised on these
rightful owners of the soil, how natural that they should

appropriate a few horses or kill a few trappers who took their beavers.

There was Black Hawk, for instance, who had called for war against the whites and who was now a prisoner at Jefferson Barracks, with a ball and chain fastened to his ankle, the old chief against whom Abraham Lincoln had fought, along with Lieutenant Jefferson Davis. Catlin painted Black Hawk who held up his cannon ball and said, "Make me so and show me to the Great White Father," for he had done nothing of which an Indian should be ashamed. Jefferson Davis had sat by Catlin and watched him painting portraits and he knew how accurate this painter was, and later, in the Senate, he said in a speech that it would be a shame if Catlin's Indian collection were sold in a foreign land. Yet when the bill came up to buy the collection for the Smithsonian, and Senator Daniel Webster defended the bill, Jefferson Davis voted no "on principle"; for Jackson had removed the Southern tribes west of the Mississippi so that the land might be covered with slave labourers, and Jefferson Davis wished to protect this arrangement. Meanwhile, from St. Louis Catlin went East in order to rejoin his wife at Pittsburgh, where he himself was desperately ill for a month. Yet he exhibited his paintings there and at Cincinnati presently, where Harriet Beecher Stowe and her father heard him give a lecture. Then he and his wife went on to Louisville and presently to Florida, where they spent at Pensacola the winter of 1833-1834. It was a land that Audubon knew, the artist who was compared with Catlin,—the painter of Indians as he painted birds,—a land of cypress and myrtle, live oak and magnolia, of pines, swamps, alligators, sandhill cranes and wolves.

In the spring, when the swans and wild geese were flying north, the Catlins sailed up the Mississippi to Natchez, whence

Catlin set out for Fort Gibson on the Arkansas river, the future site of Tulsa, Oklahoma. His wife went on to Alton, where he planned to meet her later, after he had "reverted again to the wild and romantic life that," he said, "I occasionally love to lead." Fort Gibson was the last southwestern outpost of the frontier, and again he wrote, "You will agree with me that I am going farther to get sitters than any of my fellow-artists ever did." The whites and the Indians were rapidly destroying the furs and game of the Western country, but there were still thousands of Indians to paint; and Catlin, with pen and brush, depicted the Osages, who shaved their heads, wore crests and slit their ears. He painted the chief Clermont at full length, in a beautiful dress, with his favourite war-club and leggings fringed with scalp-locks, and Tchongtas, the Black Dog, who was seven feet tall and whose body was wrapped in a huge Mackinaw blanket. For several months Catlin travelled and hunted with three young Osages, whose portraits he painted together on one canvas, visiting with notebook and easel the villages of Cherokees and Creeks, who had been driven West from Florida and Georgia. It was a country of oak ridges, wild currants, prickly pears and occasional huge yellow rattlesnakes. He painted a game of lacrosse between two of the tribes. Then he set out for Texas with a regiment of eight hundred dragoons, among them Lieutenant Jefferson Davis, under the command of General Leavenworth, who invited Catlin to share his tent while he explored these savage and beautiful regions.

The expedition soon found itself in the land of the bold Comanches, who hung on the sides of their horses when they were fighting,—the most extraordinary horsemen whom Catlin had seen,—together with the Pawnee Picts whose wigwams were built of grass and looked for all the world like beehives of straw. The expedition went to the edge of the Rockies to hold council with the leaders of the Pawnee Picts, and Catlin painted more portraits and Indian scenes before disaster overtook them all. The frightful heat, the contaminated food and the foul water of the buffalo wallows brought scores of dragoons down with fever. General Leavenworth himself died, with a third of his officers, and finally only two hundred men were left. Catlin was again desperately ill by the time they returned to Fort Gibson, but nevertheless he set out alone for Booneville on the Missouri, five hundred and forty miles over the prairie. He had bought a cream-coloured mustang that was called Charley, with a long black tail that swept the ground, and, keeping his course in a straight line by the sun or by his compass, he cantered over the prairie hills and flats. Charley pranced and gallopped over the sea of waving grass, and Catlin occasionally lay down for an hour or so until the chattering of an ague chill passed off. He had started against the advice of all the officers at the fort, but he made the journey in twenty-five days, with a bear-skin spread over Charley's back, a coffee-pot tied to it and a few pounds of hard biscuits in his portmanteau. He carried the sketch-book strapped on his back and a fowling-piece and pistols in his belt. He halted by a little stream at sunset, got water for the coffee and wood for the fire, spread out his iron spoon, his cup and his bowie knife with his salt, sugar and a slice or two of ham. Or he had a prairie hen or a venison steak, falling asleep finally on his bear-skin with a buffalo robe for covering and with his saddle for a pillow. Charley, a wild horse of the Comanches, was picketed near by. Catlin woke up in the morning undisturbed by the wolves that stood a few feet away, gazing at him.

At Alton he rejoined his wife, and then, for a year or two, with or without her, he visited other frontier forts in the

Western country. From Camp des Moines he went to a village
of the Sacs and Foxes, sixty miles up the Des Moines river,
where he painted at full length on horseback the proud chief
Keokuk who was excessively vain but very graceful: he appeared in all his gear and trappings mounted on a black horse,
supposed to be the finest on the frontier. There Catlin saw
again Black Hawk, the deposed chief, who had been released
from prison, in an old frock coat and brown hat, whom Catlin
looked upon with pity. He visited Pigs' Eye, the trading-post,
the site of St. Paul, Minnesota, with its great stone fortress
on a bluff over the river, and Fort Snelling, on the Falls of
St. Anthony, where Mrs. Catlin, Clara, was with him for a
time. It was a camp of the Ojibways, or Chippewas, with their
birch-bark canoes, whom he visited and painted every day,
celebrating the Fourth of July with several hundred wild
Indians, Ojibways and Sioux. He placed his wife on a
steamer for Prairie du Chien, and set out in a canoe for St.
Louis, nine hundred miles, with ducks, deer and bass for game
and food; and, back at headquarters, where he joined his wife
again, he introduced her for the first time to General Clark.
After a winter there, he set out for New Madrid, three or
four hundred miles south, trudging through the snow with a
tough little pony and a pack-horse, cooking his own meat
and with his own gun. He ascended the Platte river to Fort
Laramie in the later Wyoming, where he painted the Buffalo
Bull of the Grand Pawnees. At one time or another he met
the French hunter and guide of Washington Irving, who
was making his tour of the prairies at about this time, as well
as the Honourable Charles Murray, the son of the Earl of
Dunmore, who had also visited the Pawnees. Murray was to
see much of Catlin later. At Buffalo, in a building that had

once been a church, Catlin exhibited his pictures and Indian collection.

First or last, he visited almost every part of the great river valley, viewing men, as he wrote, in the "artless and innocent simplicity of nature, happier than kings or princes *can* be." He had set out to acquaint the world with the real character of the Indians of the West, and he had travelled through the later Dakotas, along the borders of Nebraska, Iowa, Kansas and Missouri. He had painted the chief of the Puncahs, who described for him the poverty and distress of his nation and predicted the certain and rapid extinction of the tribe, which he had not the power to avert, and Catlin had witnessed the degradation and the misery of the frontier, where the Indians acquired the vices of the whites. Among his subjects were the brother of Tecumseh and the chief of the Shawnees,— He Who Goes Up the River,—together with the Foremost Man, the chief of the Kickapoos, a small remnant of a once powerful tribe that had been wrecked by whiskey and small-pox. Then there was the Shawnee prophet, a devoted Christian, painted in an attitude of prayer, while he begged the tribe to give up whiskey drinking. The Peorias and the Delawares who had moved West wore dresses of civilized manufacture. Catlin had painted the Whirling Thunder, the Driving Cloud, the Walking Rain, the Hard Hickory, the Earth Standing and the Mouse-Coloured Feather, and he represented Indian ceremonies like Looking at the Sun, in which the neophyte, with skewers run through the flesh of both breasts, hung back, facing the sun all day. Above all, he invariably attended a ballgame, sometimes riding thirty miles to do so, straddling his horse, looking on or dropping with laughter off the horse's back at the succession of kicks and scuffles. For all sorts of droll tricks ensued in the almost superhuman struggles for the ball.

Finally, with an English friend whom he had met on the way, he visited the famous Red Pipe Stone Quarry, west of Lake Superior and the Falls of St. Anthony, setting out from Green Bay, Wisconsin. He had left his wife for the moment and deposited his collection at the little town of Buffalo on Lake Erie, and, travelling to Detroit and Mackinaw, he had stopped at Sault de Ste. Marie, where he found Indians he had not seen before. He painted a view of Mackinaw, seen from the distance. All the tribes visited the Red Pipe Stone Quarry to obtain the claystone that was used in Indian pipes, sacramental and common, including the calumet, the symbol of peace, smoked when they supplicated the gods to protect them. From the Mississippi to the Rocky Mountains, and from Canada to Mexico, smoking was a ritual at council meetings, and the bowls were always made of the same red stone that came from the same quarry in the Sioux country. Catlin was forbidden to go there. "No white man shall go!" the chiefs of the Sioux had said to him, but he replied that he must and would and he and his friend rode off at the risk of their lives. He had ridden to the Coteau des Prairies, in the southwestern corner of Minnesota. There were thousands of inscriptions and paintings on the rocks of the quarry, left when the tribes made pilgrimages there. It was twenty miles from the Thunderer's Nest, where the thunder was hatched out on the hottest days by a small bird that sat on its eggs in a thicket. The red stone was called Catlinite by mineralogists later.

IV

Far more real to Catlin's ear were the Indian yells and war-whoops than the groans one heard in civilization about banks and deposits, and he was bent on presenting the case of these simple people who seemed to be so rapidly fading away. It had been the passion of his soul to seek out nature's wildest haunts and give his hand to nature's men, who had filled the earliest page of his juvenile impressions, when the ploughmen in his father's fields had turned up Indian skulls and Indian tomahawks, arrowheads and beads. His mother as a child had been captured by the Indians, but they had treated her very well. Now he had visited forty-eight tribes, all speaking different languages, and had brought back three hundred and ten portraits in oil, painted of chiefs and their wigwams, with two hundred other paintings, views of their villages, dances and games: he had been the first artist to visit the further West. Few people knew how the Indians lived, or how they dressed and worshipped, and he had travelled not to trade but to record for posterity the customs that were destined to die in all the tribes. He dreamed of a great national park that would perpetuate man and beast in all the wild freshness of their native beauty; and he had made an Indian collection of headdresses, robes, bows, drums and shields, and pipes designed and carved with taste and skill. There were also specimens of spinning and weaving, by which they converted dogs' hair and the wool of the mountain sheep into robes that were durable and splendid. He took to Washington his Indian gallery, hoping that Congress would buy it, and Daniel Webster said he had been blind to the injustice of the government and all this Indian majesty and beauty. But, although Henry Clay and Seward were also in favour of the bill that would have acquired Catlin's collection, it was defeated by Jefferson Davis's vote. Besides, Catlin was on the wrong side, practically speaking; for the fur companies and the distillers discredited his statements condemning the system of rum and whiskey selling. He had attacked the sins of the government, which constantly made treaties that only the Indians respected.

In 1837, Catlin exhibited his Wild West show in New York, lecturing on the manners and customs of the Indians. One evening, at the Stuyvesant Institute on Broadway, Keokuk appeared at the lecture, with a delegation of Sioux and of Sacs and Foxes, and one of the Sioux corroborated Catlin's statement that an arrow could be shot through a buffalo and come out on the other side. Keokuk rose and said that in his tribe this had happened repeatedly; he had seen it often. The show was immesely popular, but Catlin closed it suddenly when he heard of the capture of Osceola, who was imprisoned with four chiefs near Charleston. Osceola had fled to the Everglades in Florida, where for six years he kept a large army at bay, and he had been taken under a flag of truce, a stratagem that was condemned by every officer except the one who was responsible for it. Indignant over this treachery, Catlin went to Fort Moultrie, fifteen hundred miles from New York, with canvas and brushes to paint Osceola's portrait; and he found this warrior, who was not a chief but a man of great influence in his tribe, with a turban, three ostrich feathers and a rifle in his hand. He painted two fine portraits of Osceola, who died a day after Catlin left. Osceola arrayed himself in full dress, shook the hands of the officers and chiefs and then lay down and died in silence.

Presently, in 1839, Catlin decided to go to England, taking his great Indian collection with him. He had a letter, advising

him to come, from Charles Murray, his old fellow-travel-
ler on the Mississippi, who was now Master of the Household at Buckingham Palace and in charge of Queen Victoria's
private affairs. Catlin set out with eight tons of freight and
two grizzly bears which he had reared since they were cubs
and which, weighing another ton, were kept in an iron cage
that was like a small house lashed on the deck. The bears were
to cause trouble until Catlin finally sold them to the zoo at
Regent's Park. Murray had hired for him the Egyptian Hall
on Piccadilly, and Catlin erected a wigwam in the middle of
the room, with twenty or more buffalo skins that were curiously ornamented and embroidered with porcupine quills.
His Irish helper Daniel and his nephew, Theodore Burr Catlin, had accompanied the collection to England with him, and,
thanks largely to Murray, the exhibition was a success, with
ten dukes and five earls and their ladies on the opening day.
Among them were the Duke of Wellington and the Duke of
Cambridge. For three years the show went on, and then
Catlin took it to other cities, among them Edinburgh and
Dublin. Meanwhile, he showed the Queen at Windsor Castle
the model of the Falls of Niagara he had made years before.
She asked him to point out the principal features of the
scene, and the Prince Consort wished to hear all about the
Indians.

Then a group of nine Ojibways were also brought to England, followed by a party of fourteen Ioways, and Catlin included them in his exhibition, erecting a platform in the
hall for the Indians to use in their dances. They were
all invited to lunch at Disraeli's in his great house facing
Hyde Park, where they sat at a table that was splendidly appointed, and the Queen received them at Buckingham Palace,
where the Indians sat in a circle on the floor. They danced

their Pipe Dance and their War Dance, each warrior stepping forward, as their custom was, and relating in a boasting
manner the exploits of his life. They sounded their war-whoop
at the end, to the amusement of the servants in the gallery
who remained after the Queen and the Prince Consort had
left. The Queen later sent them twenty pounds to be divided
among them, together with a piece of plaid of her own
colours. The Indians were taken on omnibus drives to the
Thames Tunnel, London Bridge, St. Paul's Cathedral and
Westminster Abbey. Hyde Park reminded them of the
prairies and the shores of the Skunk and Cedar rivers, and they
were amused by some of the great chiefs who did not know
how to ride, for they had a man riding behind to pick them
up if they fell from their saddles. The Indians had brought
three wigwams which their squaws erected on Lord's Cricket
Ground, where they danced and exhibited their archery and
ball-play. Mrs. Catlin had come to England, and she and her
husband, and their nephew Burr, went to a ball at the Man-
sion House, dressed in Indian costumes from the collection,
passing for real Indians, for they refused to speak or answer
questions. Mrs. Catlin begged her husband to go home, for
he was an artist, she said, not a showman. In fact, he had
stayed there too long; the interest in the show was running
out, and he was approaching the end of his tether. He had
published in London his great book in two volumes, *Letters
and Notes* on the North American tribes, with a list of sub-
scribers headed by the Queen. He had filled thousands of
pages of his journal with details of tribal life, and, while
his writing was occasionally clumsy and repetitive, this was
to remain a standard work.

But Catlin had made up his mind to visit Paris also, and, in
1845, hiring a hall in the Rue St. Honoré, he took his wife,

his four children and the Indians over. The Indians had promised not to drink any spirituous liquors, but they had been permitted to drink the Queen's champagne, which they called "chickabobboo"; and, after that, ale and beer were also "chicka-bobboo," a great joke for Catlin and the Indians also. The King had arranged for Catlin to set up his exhibition in one of the large halls of the Louvre, and Victor Hugo and George Sand went to see it. Baudelaire described two of Catlin's portraits that were shown at the Salon of 1846, saying that when the showman of savages first appeared in Paris it was said that he could not paint and could not draw: if he had made a few passable sketches, it was thanks to his courage and his patience. But it was affirmed now that Catlin knew very well both how to paint and how to draw, and these two portraits were enough to prove it to Baudelaire, even if his memory did not recall many other pieces that were equally beautiful. The skies especially struck him because of their transparency and lightness. "Catlin has rendered superlatively well," Baudelaire wrote, "the proud free character of these brave men, and, as for the colour, there is something myste-rious in it that pleases me more than I can say." The Indians were driven about in an omnibus with four horses, and they amused themselves counting the women they passed who were leading little dogs in the street. They were saddened at the Jardin des Plantes by the poor old buffalo, which seemed to be desolate and jaded.

When the King and Queen of the Belgians came on a visit to Paris, Louis Philippe invited the Indians to appear before him, and they decked themselves out in a full blaze of colour with necklaces of grizzly bear's claws, shields, bows and arrows, tomahawks, war-clubs and lances. For the King they painted the stem of a beautiful pipe, bright blue, orna-

mented with blue ribbons. On the floor of the palace they
prepared for their Eagle Dance, singing and beating their
drum for the kings and queens. The Belgian King had
visited America as a guest of George Washington, long years
before, and Louis Philippe had visited George Washington also, at Mount Vernon, during his exile of 1797-1800:
Washington had given him directions to follow in his horseback journey over the Alleghany Mountains. Louis Philippe
told the story of his rambling life in the American backwoods.
He had descended, with his two brothers, the Ohio and the
Mississippi in an old Mackinaw boat, purchased at Pittsburgh,
making their way six hundred miles to the mouth of the Ohio
and then travelling to New Orleans, a thousand miles further. They had lived on game and fish, killed by themselves
or bought from the Indians, sleeping in their leaky boat or
among the canebrakes with the alligators and rattlesnakes
on the shore. Louis Philippe had visited Lake Erie and Niagara,
paddled his canoe to Ithaca through Seneca Lake and then,
on foot, with a knapsack, he had tramped to Philadephia
through the Pocano mountains. His horse had been mired in
Buffalo creek, but he had slept, near Buffalo, in the wigwams
of the Senecas, and he had even passed through a village
called Wilkes-Barre, when Catlin was a few months old in
his mother's arms there. Louis Philippe had stayed with the
Delawares on the Ohio and with the Cherokees and Creeks
in Georgia and Tennessee, all of fifty-two years before, and
he had seen many other tribes. From Catlin he ordered fifteen paintings for the palace at Versailles and then twenty-
seven more depicting the story of La Salle. The two men
selected the episodes together. The King saw Catlin's collection in the Louvre and invited the artist to a royal break-

fast at St. Cloud, together with the King and Queen of the
Belgians.

v

But then misfortune fell upon Catlin. His wife died in Paris,
and his little son George died also. Three of the Indians died
and six more were in a hospital. The French Revolution of
1848 broke out and Louis Philippe was spirited away. Catlin's association with the King had not been good for him,
for the mob invaded his studio and destroyed some of his
pictures; and when, with his three daughters, he escaped to
England, he was in a tragic plight. The bodies of Mrs. Catlin and the dead child had been sent home, and the remaining
Indians were sent home also; and his wife's family, in whose
eyes Catlin was a failure, took his three daughters back to
New York. His friend at court, Charles Murray, had been
sent to Egypt on a diplomatic mission, and at this time he
received the news that Congress in Washington had finally
decided not to buy his pictures. Schoolcraft had come to London hoping to obtain them to illustrate his encyclopædia of
the Indian tribes, and, when Catlin refused to give him the
pictures, Schoolcraft, angered by the rebuff, said his account
of O-Kee-Pa was a cock-and-bull story. Catlin had mortgaged
the pictures, and finally his creditors had seized them, intending to sell them piece by piece, when an American who had
lent Catlin money bought up all the claims and shipped the
collection to Philadelphia. There it was stowed away in the
basement of his warehouse.

After a year or two, Catlin returned to Paris. He seemed to
be defeated and he was alone. He had come back to paint
the pictures which the king had commissioned but for which
he was never to be paid, and he wandered about the boule-

vards, solitary and unknown. The studio, with the few pictures he had brought back from London, had lost all its
charm for him, and he haunted the public reading-room of
the Bibliothèque Imperiale, where he read Humboldt's South
American Travels. He had met years before in the Louvre the
great Baron von Humboldt, who had been impressed by his
work in ethnology and who questioned him about the northern
Indian tribes. Later he was to write to Catlin, telling him
about Schoolcraft's accusations and saying he must take steps
to counteract them, and it was owing to this that Prince Maximilian of Neuwied came, at Humboldt's suggestion, to Catlin's defence. But, meanwhile, in the library, Catlin fell in with
an habitue who told him about the gold mines in the Crystal
Mountains of northern Brazil,—mines which the Spaniards
had worked and abandoned to the Indians,—and Catlin pored
over maps of Central America, Brazil and Peru, eager for gold
and dreaming of equatorial volcanoes and jungles. He saw
himself paddling up tropical rivers in a dugout canoe, painting the Indians in these little-known countries; for Latin
America was full of Indians and he could start afresh and
redeem the apparent failure of his first explorations. Destitute
and deaf, he was fifty-seven when he sold his few possessions
and slipped out of Paris with a bundle of old portraits, Bristol
board and maps. For he knew that in the humidity of South
and Central America the paint would dry too slowly for him
to use the canvas he had rolled up in his former expeditions,
and, besides, Bristol board was easy to carry. It was 1853. He
sailed to Caracas, in Venezuela, the best approach, he knew,
to the pampas tribes and the Crystal Mountains. He had
somehow obtained a British passport.

VI

Thus began the further travels of this idomitable man who was to spend six years exploring South America, ascending the west coast as far as the Aleutians, travelling and painting even at Kamchatka. Twice he set out from Paris and twice he returned there, laden on each journey with new Indian pictures. At Caracas he was joined by a German botanist, Dr. Hentz, who gathered plants and flowers while Catlin painted portraits. Their progress was slow, for they were impeded by vines that twisted about their legs and the mass of fallen leaves was also fatiguing. They tramped over the plains to Angostura on the Orinoco, a hundred and fifty miles,—but that was "nothing,"—among acres of geraniums and wild roses and at least fifty varieties of flowering plants. Catlin was almost as happy, he said, as Dr. Hentz, putting these beautiful scenes into his portfolio, painting the pampas Indians and their Handsome Dance in which three young women joined, entirely naked. The Indians threw their raw-hide bolas, tipped with balls of lead, killing the wild horses for their skins and hair, and the monkeys chattered as they leapt from branch to branch in the dark forests overlooking the Orinoco. Alligators basked in the sun and plunged off their slimy logs, turtles paced out of the woods and sought shelter in the waves, and there were hundreds of wild swans and pelicans, while sticks that were floating in the river turned into snakes. Catlin and Dr. Hentz passed hungry jaguars and harmless sloths, hanging all day without moving from the limbs of trees, and they descended the Orinoco to Georgetown, with their faces burnt almost to the colour of the Indians. There, in the capital of British Guiana, they encountered a young Englishman who had seen Catlin's show in London and who recognized the old painter at once, working on the portrait of an Indian chief who stood in front of him. The young man, Smythe, hearing that they were going to the Crystal Mountains, attached himself, as a good shot, to the expedition.

Catlin painted in the neighbourhood and at Parimaribo in Dutch Guiana. Then they all set out in a big canoe up the Essequibo and, leaving the canoe, took to the land, struggling through swamps to an Arowak village where Catlin showed his pictures to the chief. He astonished the Indians with his marksmanship. Stretching an old cowskin over a hoop, and standing at sixty or seventy yards, he fired six shots, with "Sam," into the bull's-eye. ("Sam" was the carbine that had been made expressly for him by his old friend, Colonel Colt.) At this village they left Dr. Hentz, and Catlin and Smythe went on together, about a hundred miles, to the Crystal Mountains where Catlin soon lost his "nugget fever," happy to be at his old vocation, stopping among the tribes along the way. "Fortune has given me," he wrote, "life, health and wisdom, —my only wealth, my portfolio." He was almost overcome with the sickening odour of a rattlesnake that was lying underneath his cowskin rug and that was soon ready for battle when he got up; and once, when Symthe was roasting a wild pig over the fire, he shot a large tiger that visited the camp. "Smythe," he said, "be perfectly calm and cool. Don't move. There's a splendid tiger just behind you." Symthe, slowly turning round, saw the tiger, stretched out, playing with the feet of their sleeping Indian guide. Catlin whistled, the tiger raised his head, Catlin fired point-blank, and the tiger, killed at once, leaped into the air. Crossing the mountains to the Trombetas river, they descended in a dugout loaded with hides. At Para, Catlin procured leggings of strong buckskin, with knives, beads and fishhooks to distribute among the Indians. There Smythe left him, and Catlin sailed up the Amazon on the first steamer that had ever ascended the river.

Catlin had picked up at Para, as a bodyguard and porter, a gigantic escaped slave from Cuba, Cæsar Bolla, a good-natured Negro whose back served Catlin as an easel, for Cæsar carried the portfolio with its waterproof covering. For five years they were to remain together, wandering through the wilderness for thousands of miles, visiting many primitive tribes whom no white man had seen before, beginning with the tribes on the Amazon river. These tribes were the nakedest and ugliest but the least warlike and hostile, for there were no buffaloes or beavers in this country to excite the white man's cupidity, and the Indians were all friendly to the whites. There were the Muras, on both sides of the river, the Iguitos, the Ticunas and the Conibos who made pottery and were experts with the blowgun, and others who killed monkeys and sent their skins to Paris to be used in the manufacture of gloves for ladies. The forest was alive with peccaries and the vines twisted to the tops of the trees and hung suspended in the air like huge serpents. Beautiful parasitic flowers grew from the stems that strangled the palms. Catlin and Cæsar slept in hammocks, slung between two trees, building fires to protect them from animals and reptiles, and once Catlin was overcome from the heat and clung for a week to his hammock; but they had provisions enough and a variety of fish. They were sixty-nine days on the river, and Catlin sketched thirty tribes in their canoes or fishing or in groups on the banks; and he painted the unknown grandeurs of the stupendous forest. One chief refused to give his name to be put on the back of the portrait, for then he would be a man without a name. Sometimes when the Indians objected to being painted, for they were full of superstitious fears, Catlin worked behind the bulwark that served as a screen.

From the headwaters of the Amazon, they tramped or rode westward, working their way over the Andes through snows and ravines, until they came to Lima, the most beautiful city in the world, as it seemed to Catlin at the moment. Thence, by steamer, they sailed to Panama, to San Diego and San Francisco, and then by sailing vessel to Nootka Sound, the Aleutians, Queen Charlotte Island and Kamchatka. The captain of the ship was a Spaniard who was planning to return with a cargo of dried fish, sheepskin and wool, and Catlin finished several sketches on the slow sail up. He painted the Hydas Indians, the Stickeens and the Nayas, whose women wore in their underlips circular blocks of wood, but to Catlin all fashions were the same, rings in the ears and rings in the nose, crinoline of the waist and crinoline of the lip. Off the west coast of Vancouver, among the pines and rocky peaks, he painted the Klah-o-quats on Nootka Sound, and the Indians brought oysters and fish to barter for their rum. Catlin and Cæsar walked through the woods to the Fraser river, which was all in confusion, the new El Dorado; but Catlin was indifferent to the gold-rush, wary of gold as he was, having just recovered from the nugget fever. He and Cæsar took ship for Astoria and ascended the Columbia to the Dalles, where Catlin learned that a band of Crows were encamped in the Salmon river valley, and, opening his portfolio in the lodge of the chief, he heard a sudden piercing yelp: one of the Indian group recognized a Crow whom Catlin had painted twenty years before at Fort Union, at the mouth of the Yellowstone river. A moment later this Very Sweet Man himself walked into the lodge and, saying "How! How!" gave Catlin a hearty handshake. He said he had seen Catlin also paint a portrait of the Jumper.

There Catlin bought a horse for himself, with a mule for Cæsar and a pack-mule, and they both set out for the Rocky Mountains, for Catlin's interest in geology had been growing and he was bent on examining the gneiss and granite there. The two of them crossed the Rockies by the Santa Fe pass, the later route of the Pony Express, known already to Kit Carson, while they slept in pioneer cabins or on the rough ground, advancing by means of Catlin's pocket compass. They went through the country of the Apaches, with whom the government was at open war. Once they were seated by a rousing fire when two grizzly bears appeared and one of them, seizing a firebrand with both paws, dropped it and began to cry in the most piteous manner. He wiped his nose and paws on the grass and both the bears galloped away, whining. Catlin and Cæsar crossed the Colorado and paddled down the Rio Grande eight hundred miles to Matamoros, and from there they sailed to Sisal, in Yucatan, where Cæsar bade farewell to Catlin. He could not wait to confide his adventures to Sally Bool, the mulatto girl who sold oranges at the head of the quay at Para, at the mouth of the Amazon river in Brazil. Catlin lingered for a while at Sisal, for he had read John Lloyd Stephens, and, painting some of the Mayans, he visited Palenque and Uxmal and the coast of Campeachy.

Then, returning to Paris, Catlin went to see Humboldt at Potsdam and told him about his discoveries in geology and ethnology. It was 1855, and Humboldt, now a very old man, remembered him and welcomed him kindly. He even presented Catlin to the King of Prussia. Catlin, at Humboldt's suggestion, showed the king some of his new Indian pictures, and the king bought several of these that were later owned by the gallery in Berlin. Humboldt told Catlin that he must go back to South America and collect more data, and he gave Catlin a list of places he must visit and a letter to his fellow-explorer, the botanist Aimé Bonpland. Catlin was to find this old man, who had left science far behind, living on the right bank of the Uruguay river, with a squaw and half-caste children, in a dilapidated cottage. For, in 1856, Catlin sailed again from Le Havre to Cuba and later the West Indies, finding in his cabin a letter from Humboldt ending with the words, "If I were a younger man, I would join you in the expedition at once." Exploring Jamaica, Antigua, Trinidad and the Gulf of Maracaibo, he went on to Rio de Janeiro, where he once more delighted in the great forests and the rivers and swamps that lay to the south of the city. Then, going to Buenos Aires, he hired a half-Indian guide and servant who belonged to the Auca tribe on the Salado river, and together they paddled to Corrientes, a big town on the Parana where groups of Indian tents lined the shore. They had started up the river in a sort of barge that was like the keel-boats of the Mississippi, five hundred miles to the mouth of the Iguau, whence they crossed through the woods to the upper waters of the Uruguay. The banks of these rivers were covered with dense and magnificent forests, abounding with monkeys, parrots, ant-eaters and tigers that lived on the peccaries and soft-shelled turtles on the shore, and they slept in their strong, dry canoe, ready, at a moment's notice, to push off into the current of the stream. Catlin did many portraits of the Indians on the banks, among them those who used blocks of wood in their under-lips, like the Nayas tribe of the Northwest. There were the Payaguas, the Tobos and the Linguas; there were also the anacondas and the rattle-snakes that were common in all the forests and on all the rivers. Catlin ate a tiger's tail, wrapped in leaves of the wild cabbage and roasted in a camp-fire under the embers, and once he shot an ant-eater that was twelve feet long to the tip of its tail and that had its long nose almost in the fire. On another occasion a jaguar leapt upon him and flung him to the water's edge, where his servant and the boatman rescued him. He had picked up a first-rate paddler who worked his passage to Buenos Aires, down the Uruguay river, seven hundred miles. Catlin had known nothing more delightful than to travel down stream in such a river, with plenty of powder, ball and fishing-tackle.

Recuperating from his wounds in a Buenos Aires boarding-house, he completed some of the sketches he had made on the rivers, and then he visited an Indian family who lived on the pampas, riding a silver-grey stallion with a black mane and tail. Although he was now nearly sixty, he kept his seat as of old, and this unsaddled stallion could not throw him. He took part in a flamingo chase, of which he made a picture, and a chase after ostriches, one half the size of the African ostrich, which ran in all directions away from their nests. Then, on board the "Gladiator," a sailing packet bound for Chile on the west coast, he passed down the hilly coast of Patagonia, going ashore to paint the Patagons with one of the cabin-boys to carry the portfolio which he showed the chief. He explained that he had visited the Indian villages in North America, pointing them out on a map that he had brought with him; and he sketched some of the people who crowded into the tent and went ashore again on the third day. Through an interpreter he drew up a vocabulary of Patagon words in a village of the Fuegians, a branch of the Patagons, and, passing through the Straits of Magellan, he went on to Panama, where for a few months he dropped out of sight. But he was still painting when he received the news that Humboldt was dead.

Altogether, he had painted a hundred and twenty tribes in North, Central and South America. He had visited more tribes than any other man, and he was everywhere treated with hospitality and kindness.

Catlin was nearly sixty-two when he returned to Europe. Going first to England, he retired to Brussels, where he was to live for several years. He had a studio in an obscure street near the Antwerp railway station, in the northern part of the city. He lived frugally, taking his meals at a little restaurant near by, and the American consul remembered that he never spoke of his family or gave any reason why the "friend of the Indians" lived there. In his retired life he finished many paintings of the South American Indians and the northwest coast, and he wrote in Brussels three books. *O-Kee-Pa, Last Rambles* and *Life Amongst the Indians*. The last book had a large sale when it was published in England.

VII

Then, in 1870, when he was seventy-four, Catlin returned to New York. He had been out of the country for thirty-one years, and he brought with him a new collection of more than a hundred and fifty paintings. His three daughters met him on the pier. They had grown up in affluence and offered him a home, but, saying, "I have twenty years' work to do still," he went off to live in Washington. His loyal old friend Joseph Henry, who was now secretary of the Smithsonian, asked him to exhibit his new pictures there. He gave Catlin a painting-room, with a bed, high up in a tower of the Institution, and there he remained until he became ill with Bright's disease and was too weak even to get up. He was taken back to his daughters and their uncle in Jersey City, where he died in

1872. He was then seventy-six years old, and he was buried beside his wife and son in an unmarked grave at Greenwood Cemetery in Brooklyn, near the graves of Beecher, Morse and Greeley. He had constantly asked, "What will happen to my gallery?" the great collection that Congress had refused to buy; and finally, but not until after his death, it was given to the Smithsonian, and the hope of his life came true. Upon these paintings and drawings of Catlin were to be based all the Indian pictures since his time, all the Wild West shows and the "Western" movies, and countless tales of ethnologists and writers. He had given his whole life to the painting of the Indians of whom he had once said, "I love the people who have made me welcome to the best they had, and how I love a people who don't live for the sake of money!"

CHARLES WILKES

THE first Exploring Expedition of the United States Navy sailed from Hampton Roads in the summer of 1838. There were six vessels in the squadron that cruised for nearly four years, two sloops of war, a gun-brig, a store-ship and two tenders, and the commander was Charles Wilkes, a lieutenant from New York who was already a master of navigation. The objects of the expedition were to advance American commerce, determine the existence of shoals, doubtful on the charts, make treaties with Polynesian chiefs, reconcile factions in the South Seas, protect missionaries and find the best ways for whalers, the whaling fleet that, as Wilkes said, "at this very day whitens the Pacific ocean with its canvas." But to Wilkes the advancement of science was the main object of the expedition. He had refused to be a "money-changer" and, although he was to bring back the first global whaling chart, he despised the ships of the whaling captains, the vessels that were dirty and greasy with the blood of the whales. He took with him a corps of artists and scientific men that outnumbered those in any other expedition, except perhaps the French expedition to Egypt. There were nine of these "clam-diggers," as the naval officers called them at first, who were socially accepted only as time went on, while Wilkes himself shared many of the tastes of the artists, botanists and mineralogists, the philologists and ethnographers of the expedition.

Charles Wilkes, who was forty years old at the time, was the son of the banker in New York who had been a friend of Fanny Wright. The father had come from London after the Revolution, himself a nephew of John Wilkes, the English politician who had taken the side of the colonists in the House of Commons. After him and Isaac Barre, his fellow-Parliamentarian, the town of Wilkes-Barre had been named. Charles Wilkes, after his mother's death, had been largely brought up by Elizabeth Seton, the aunt who was later well-known in Roman Catholic history, and, taking lessons in navigation, he had drawn a map of the English channel for a captain who had left his charts at home. At seventeen, in Washington, at the house of the French minister, a friend of his family with whom he was visiting, President Monroe gave him a midshipman's warrant; and, in a Mediterranean cruise that lasted three years, he had gained a practical knowledge of nautical science. Then, marrying Jane Renwick, the daughter of Robert Burns's "Jeanie," he had gone on a two years' cruise in the South Pacific. He made surveys of Narragansett Bay and the harbours of Beaufort and Wilmington, while the great Bowditch, examining his charts, told each and everybody that Charles Wilkes was a first-rate surveyor. When John Quincy Adams, the President, urged Congress to fit out ships to expand the country's fisheries and for scientific knowledge, Wilkes had already erected, at his own expense, a tower for astronomical observations. This pleased Adams, who encouraged the scientific Wilkes and hoped he might command an expedition that would rival the expeditions of James Cook for England, La Pérouse for France and the Russian Admiral Bellingshausen.

The expedition was postponed until Martin Van Buren was President, with Joel R. Poinsett as Secretary of War, the discoverer of the poinsettia who hoped that Wilkes would bring back plants, shells, birds and minerals for a national museum. In 1838, James K. Paulding, the old friend of Washington Irving, was Secretary of the Navy; and the President and these two aides went to Hampton Roads to bid farewell to the adventurous squadron. Wilkes had been sent abroad to buy instruments and charts in London, Paris and Berlin, and he had visited well-known geographers and purchased books on meteorology and terrestrial magnetism. Nathaniel Hawthorne, according to his son, would have liked to join the expedition as the official historian of the long cruise. As the voyage went on, most of the officers were excited by the work of the "scientifics" who studied the habits of whales and seals, observed birds, animals, fishes and shells, studied fossil remains and found useful plants. The artists were Joseph Drayton and A. T. Agate, later well-known as a miniature-painter, who made charming and accurate drawings of the flora and fauna, while Wilkes himself was a draughtsman of unusual talent, as one saw in his sketches of icebergs and rock-lined harbours. There was the picture, for instance, in Wilkes's *Narrative*, of the sloop "Vincennes" in Disappointment Bay. Asa Gray, the botanist, who had been chosen, resigned in favour of James Dwight Dana, famous as a mineralogist in after years, and Horatio Hale, the son of the editor of *Godey's Lady's Book*, was to fit himself as a Polynesian linguist. Charles Pickering was the zoologist of the expedition; and his assistant was W. D. Brackenridge, who was especially a student of ferns and mosses. Brackenridge was to bring back plants and seeds from the South Seas that became the nucleus of the Botanical Garden in Washington, and, as a landscape architect, he laid out the grounds of the Smithsonian Institution. There were others besides Titian Peale who had "not come on board to be comfortable" and contented himself with a cabin as small as a bedstead. Over and beneath the berth were packed his clothes, guns, boxes and books, and he ate his meals in the wardroom with the officers, by candle-light, under the surface of the sea.

In some respects, Titian Peale might have stood for all these naturalists at a moment when the type was dying out, when the explorers were giving place to the classifiers who were to be superseded by the scientific specialists. The youngest son of Charles Willson Peale and the brother of Rembrandt and Raphaelle Peale,—not to speak of Angelica, Rubens and Rosalba,—he had been born in Philadelphia, at Philosophical Hall, where his family had been installed as caretakers. He said he had "imbibed a taste for nature" in the Peale Museum where he had grown up among students of science and his father's artist friends: Thomas Sully rented rooms from the Peales and Thomas Jefferson's grandson lived with them. It was already a family project, managed by the brothers and sisters, when they all moved to Independence Hall with two small grizzly bears kept in a cage in the yard, monkeys from Africa and alligators from Carolina. There were the Indian artifacts from the Lewis and Clark expedition, the leggings, tobacco-pouches and beaver-skin mantles, and the children, learning to paint from their father, learned also how to label the minerals, birds, insects, butterflies and shells. In their circle were Alexander Wilson, Audubon and Charles Lucien Bonaparte, the ornithologist who was Napoleon's nephew and for whose extension of Wilson's *American Ornithology* Titian Peale was to draw most of the plates. Titian Peale had joined Long's Yellowstone Expedition, travelling from St. Louis up the Missouri, reporting the existence of the Great American Desert, the unmapped territory of the Louisiana Purchase; and he had studied the Indian mounds, measuring them and taking notes, while he once killed two deer with a single shot. He had sketched insects, butterflies and birds, Indian scenes and landscapes, and then he had taken part in a South American expedition, travelling four hundred miles up the Magdalena river. An expert taxidermist, proud of his ability as a collector and observer, he sent back from this "glorious field for the Lepidopterist" large boxes of fishes, birds and shells.

Titian Peale was the only member of the scientific corps who was to go into the antarctic regions. He had joined the expedition on the understanding that its main object was natural science rather than national glory or commercial prestige, and he was to describe and draw sea-fowl, mollusks and animals, at the same time keeping his journal along with the others. He was "very proud and difficult to manage," Wilkes wrote in a letter, though Wilkes placed great confidence in Peale as a guide and helper at difficult moments. For the commander liked his buoyancy of spirit, the trait he described as "so truly characteristic of our countrymen." Wilkes enjoyed jovial company, and, a superb commander himself, he constantly felt on the verge of some overwhelming calamity to the ships and the crews. But he was extremely emotional and overbearing at a time when naval officers rode the high horse, —owing in part to the exploits of the Navy,—when the captain of a warship, at anchor in Sicily, kidnapped a military band to make music on his return across the Atlantic. (He sent the band back when the "Chesapeake" sailed for the Mediterranean.) Peale referred to Wilkes in his journal as a "petty tyrant" whose "quarterdeck insolence" annoyed the scientists, —they were all, at one moment or another, at odds with the commander,—for he was not only peppery, he was a hard master, unyielding in his insistence on efficiency and order. He had a seaman flogged because he had dressed so hurriedly that he left one of his buttons out of its hole, and at his court-martial at the end of the voyage he was publicly reprimanded for illegally punishing men under his command. He said he had given only one-tenth of the lashes that a court-martial would have inflicted. But those were the days of Billy Budd when striking a petty officer was reason enough for hanging a man at the yard-arm.

The first year of the cruise was rather unproductive, and the ships entered the antarctic circle only after visiting South America, and then merely for a brief attempt. It was too late in the season, and they had to postpone for another year their real exploration of the zone of icebergs. First sailing to Madeira, where they spent nine days, enabling the scientists to make observations on bats, hawks, canaries, mollusks and insects, they went on to the Cape Verde islands, with a half-African population, where Horatio Hale obtained a vocabulary of the Mandingo language. The others added to their collections of plants, shells and zoophytes before the ships sailed on to Rio de Janeiro, where Brackenridge and Pickering, who spoke Portuguese, took notes about the trees on an expedition to the Organ mountains. Wilkes wrote historical accounts of Brazil, Argentina, Chile and Peru, describing all varieties of Negroes on the continent, including the free Negroes of Brazil who were on an equal footing with the whites; and Dana found many minerals, gypsum and fossils, both in Brazil and Argentina. In the convict settlement of El Carmen, an American from Rhode Island claimed the protection of the expedition. He said he had been impressed for the Argentine army, but actually he had been engaged in a riot at Buenos

Aires and was known to have killed two or three men. At Valparaiso, Peale went in search of guanacoes, which were said to frequent only inaccessible heights, and killed one that was nine feet long and four feet tall, while two of the other men measured Tupongati, several hundred feet higher than Chimborazo. An American who had made and lost fortunes in revolutions was working the silver-mines in the vicinity of Santiago. Near the temple of Pachacamac, on the summit of a Peruvian hill, the explorers discovered artifacts that were buried before the Spaniards came, wooden needles, cotton seeds, pottery and plated stirrups, and four of them went to the cordilleras to make botanical collections, dangerous because of the bandits frequenting the route to the mines of Pasco. Brackenridge gathered seeds of a species of cactus that grew in dense tufts all over the mountains.

Then from Callao they sailed to the Tuamotu islands, where a petty chief, half naked and tattooed, stood in the bow of his skiff brandishing a boat-hook. The natives were hostile because they had been fired upon by trading vessels that were engaged in the pearl fishery. On the island of Clermont de Tonnerre the birds were so tame that they suffered Peale to climb the trees and take them by hand. In several cases one had to push them off the nest in order to see their eggs. One little fellow alighted on Wilkes's cap, as he was sitting under a tree, and sang melodiously and long. The explorers were welcomed at Tahiti, whose steep cliffs were a contrast to the barren coast of Peru. The high peaks there were covered with vines and creeping plants, delightful to the botanists of the expedition, and there at Papeete the crew of the "Peacock," having leisure on their hands, performed a play to amuse the natives and themselves. They had chosen Schiller's *The Robbers,* the parts of which they had rehearsed in afternoons at sea, and the

acting, which the officers thought was at least tolerable, gave
great pleasure to the Tahitians. They breakfasted together on
taro, pig and breadfruit, the standard dishes of the islands,
where about a hundred whaling ships annually came from American ports, and Wilkes established an observatory in a shed on
Point Venus and formed parties to survey the four principal
harbours. His main object was to obtain accurate charts for
the whaling ships, and indeed Wilkes's charts were so exact
that they were still in use in the second world war.

Wilkes sent out a party of naturalists from Papeete to cross
the island, and the officers were given a feast by one of the
chiefs; but there were less than two hundred present in the
Protestant church of the missionaries and Wilkes questioned
the wisdom of the missionaries in dealing with these gay and
cheerful people. The women were dressed unbecomingly in
flaring chip bonnets and loose silk frocks with showy kerchiefs
tied about their necks, and, passionately fond as they were of
flowers, their use in dress was discouraged by the teachers as
vanities inappropriate for Christians. Wilkes had been disgusted by the sight of the chiefs, large and noble-looking, passing from ship to ship soliciting soiled linen to wash and
performing other services that were not in keeping with their
rank. The washing of the soiled linen of the crews was one of
the prerogatives of the Queen. It happened, however, that the
Queen, Pomare IV, was pregnant and unable to visit the ships,
so they had to choose a less distinguished laundress; but when
she asked for soap, in great request in Tahiti, they were happy
to oblige her. On a second visit there, Wilkes saw something
of the domestic broils of the royal family when the Queen,
with her followers, rushed into the house of foreigners to
escape from her consort who pursued her with threats. He had
struck her in the street and attempted to strangle her, then,

thwarted, he had gone to the palace, broken her boxes and trunks, torn her clothes to pieces and smashed the windows. But this was less surprising because the Queen had been in the habit of giving him a sound cudgelling, even in the high-way.

In the Tuamotu archipelago, Wilkes surveyed fifteen islands and discovered two islands that had not been charted. Then at Pago-Pago in Samoa, the ships were surrounded by a large number of canoes. The chief, admitted on board, an athletic-looking man, studied Wilkes from head to foot, and, when he was asked why, he said he had on shore a coat that was too tight for him. He thought the coat would fit Wilkes,— could they exchange? Wilkes, instead, gave the chief a small hatchet. A native named Tuvai had killed an American and the chiefs tried to save his life. Wilkes decided to transport him to some other island. Horrified, Tuvai said that he would rather be put to death on his native island than be banished elsewhere, and, when the chiefs asked anxiously if there would be any cocoanuts on the island where he was to be banished, Wilkes, wishing to make the punishment severe, said there would be none whatever. He finally landed Tuvai on Wallis Island where his fate would remain a mystery to his country-men.

The great antarctic cruise began after a visit to New South Wales where, at Sydney, the ships were put in order for it. The convicts there were a quarter of the population, and Wilkes visited a convict ship, expressly prepared for the pur-pose, with narrow boxes on deck where the convicts stood upright for punishment. But most of them were ruddy enough and healthy looking after the long voyage of transportation, and Wilkes wrote a detailed account of the customs of the aborigines, including the boomerang, their special weapon.

He described the crimps who kidnapped sailors from their ships, concealed them when they were drunk and rented or sold them to other ships. Then the squadron set out for Macquarie Island, south of New Zealand, where myriads of penguins covered the rugged hills. One of the party, ascending a crag, could not hear himself speak because of the din of squalling and gabbling, while the penguins snapped at him, caught hold of his trousers and pinched his flesh until he kicked them down the precipice. The birds stood in rows, like Lilliputian soldiers, and the invader knocked some of them on the head while he collected a few of the penguins' eggs. He captured a king penguin of enormous size, forty-five inches from tip to tail, stunning him first with a blow from a boat-hook. The crews witnessed a sea-fight between a whale and one of its many enemies, in this case a killer orca. The sea was quite smooth and offered the best possible view of the whole battle. First, at a distance, they saw a whale floundering, lashing the sea into a perfect foam. As he approached the ships, they saw that a great fish, apparently about twenty feet long, held him by the jaw, while the contortions and throes of the whale betokened the agony of the huge monster. The whale then threw himself at full length upon the surface, with his mouth wide open, his pursuer still hanging to the jaw, while the blood that issued from the wound dyed the sea to a distance roundabout. At last the orca worried him to death.

They entered the region of blizzards and fogs where albatrosses hovered about with cormorants, grey snow petrels and cape pigeons, and they began to encounter all kinds of icebergs, some huge and quadrangular, others deceptively sunken. There were vast ice-islands, in one place eighty icebergs, and the foresheets were covered with ice while water froze on the decks. A gale set in, the snow fell, and there were many birds about, one of them a sheath-bill; and at midnight came a display of the aurora australis. It centered in a bright spot that changed into a crescent, and, from this, feathery-edged rays of pale orange-colour branched off in every direction, while over them the prismatic colours seemed to flit in rapid succession. The whole southern hemisphere was covered with straw-coloured arches from which streamers radiated of almost a lustrous white, with the stars visible among them. Then massive cumulus clouds formed that were tinged with pale yellow against a background of red, orange and purple. The sailors lay on the deck, face upward, to watch this wonderful spread of beauty.

At times the weather was so thick that they could see only a few yards ahead and the snow might have been armed with sharp icicles or needles. The spray that struck the ships was at once converted into ice, and a seaman who got on the lee yard-arm was almost frozen to death when the sail blew over the yard so that he could not get back. The cry rang out, "Ice ahead!", then "Ice on all sides!", and all hope of escape seemed to vanish. Some of the icebergs were three miles long and two hundred feet above the surface of the water, some forming obelisks, some towers and Gothic arches, others exhibiting lofty columns with a natural bridge resting on them of a lightness and beauty that was inconceivable in any other material. Their sides had been excavated by the waves and the arches often extended to a considerable distance into the body of the ice, and the sea, rushing in, produced loud and distant thunderings. The flight of birds, passing in and out, recalled ruined abbeys and castles, while here and there a bold projecting bluff, crowned with pinnacles and turrets, resembled a mediæval keep. In some cases the sides were perfectly smooth, as though they had been chiselled, while sometimes the tabular bergs were like masses of beautiful alabaster of every variety of shape and tint. If one could imagine an immense city of ruined alabaster palaces, composed of huge piles of buildings grouped together, with long lanes winding irregularly through them, some faint idea might be formed of the grandeur and beauty of the spectacle of these icy and desolate regions. Every sound on board the ships, even the sound of voices, reverberated from the massive and pure white walls.

In *The Sea-Lions,* James Fenimore Cooper, a friend of Wilkes's father, reflected some of these descriptions that appeared in the captain's *Narrative,* just as one found there a picture of the setting of Cooper's other novel that was called *The Crater.* For Wilkes's five-volumed account of the cruise found no more eager reader than this novelist who had also served in the United States Navy. The schooner, "The Sea-Gull," was eventually lost: it disappeared off Cape Horn, supposedly swamped, with all hands on board. For the rest, the sloop "Peacock" had the narrowest escape when the bergs closed in and the ship was caught fast in the ice. The gunwales were pressed together so that the ship was almost crushed, wedged in between masses of ice before the icebergs retreated; she laboured in the swell, with ice grinding and thumping against her, and every moment something either fore or aft was carried away, chains, bolts, bob-stays, bowsprit, shrouds and anchors. The "Peacock" was drawn at first stern foremost against an iceberg that chewed up the rudder and the keel, so that she barely escaped for repairs; and a great pillar of ice had fallen in the wake that would have crushed the vessel a few seconds earlier. Most of the icebergs were covered with eighteen inches of snow, and on the oldest there were ponds of fresh water that enabled the ships to replenish their supply. They put in for repairs at Orange Harbour in Tierra del Fuego, the "far and lonely bay" of *Thulia,* the poem that was written by the surgeon, James Croxall Palmer, who was later the medical director of the Navy. Palmer had said that "The Flying Fish," the other schooner of the expedition, would at least serve its commandant as "an honourable coffin."

The great achievement of this far-southern cruise was the discovery of the seventh continent, although Wilkes's claim was not generally accepted until Shackelton's expedition proved, in 1908-1909, that Wilkes was right. He was not the first to find antarctic land there, but he had followed the coast-line for sixteen hundred miles, enough to show that it had a continental character. One day the sun and moon appeared at the same time, the moon nearly full and each throwing its light abroad. The moon tinged with silver the clouds in its neighbourhood, while the sun illuminated the distant continent with deep golden rays. For, while, owing to mirages, Wilkes was mistaken in reporting distances, he distinctly saw a lofty mountain range that showed many ridges and indentations. It was easy to mistake piles of snow and ice for mountain summits, but, steering among the icebergs that were sometimes eight hundred feet high, he had begun to realize that this coast was indeed a continent. He had sometimes sailed for more than fifty miles together along a straight and perpendicular wall of ice, two hundred feet, more or less, in height; and he made a sketch of one harbour with dark volcanic rocks a few miles away. The commander of the French expedition, Dumont d'Urville, believed he had found the antarctic continent earlier on the same day, and Jules Verne, describing d'Urville's voyage, said that Wilkes had only pretended to see it. But d'Urville had made a miscalculation: he found the continent ten hours later than Wilkes.

The squadron sailed on to the Fiji islands where the eating of human flesh was still a common and general practice. Three or four canoes came out, and portions of the cooked body of a Fiji of another tribe were brought for sale on board the "Peacock." There were human bones with flesh adhering, and, taking up a skull, one fellow picked out an eye while he bit off a piece of the cheek. There had been much discussion in the wardroom as to whether or not the Fijis were cannibals, but one of the missionaries had seen twenty men cooked; their bodies were green from putrescence, the flesh dropping from the bones. In fact, the bodies of enemies, bound and placed in the oven, covered with leaves and roasted, were always eaten. This missionary had stood in the yard and seen an enemy chief cooked, with perfect insensibility and no indication of revenge, and he said that the missionaries closed their windows to keep out the sight and the smell, and that the king's son had given them a warning: if this happened again, he said, he would knock them on the head and eat them. They averred that during their residence there had been only one natural death; all the natives who were dead had been strangled or buried alive, for children usually strangled their feeble aged parents, the deformed and maimed were commonly destroyed, and when they had lingering diseases their heads were wrung off. Another of the missionaries pointed out to Wilkes a chief of high rank who had strangled his mother. He had witnessed the procession to the grave, with the mother dressed in her best attire; a rope of twisted tapa had been placed around the old woman's neck, and a number of natives, besides the son, taking hold of each end, strangled her and buried her forthwith. On an August day in 1839, seventeen of the wives of one of the chiefs had been strangled, considering it a privilege to be so; and, in fact, by their own request, wives were often put to death or buried alive at the funerals of their husbands. Titian Peale wrote in his journal that he was shown five pits in which five persons had been recently roasted, having been first laid on their sides along with the spears and clubs that had been captured with them. Peale collected tapa mats, pottery jugs and bowls, a wooden idol and models of boats. He obtained a few plants in the mountains that were not found near the coast, and he had taken the idol from the consecrated grove after the natives sold it for a paper of vermilion.

On the island of Ovalau, Wilkes chose a site for an observatory; with room for tents, houses and instruments, it was thirty feet above the beach. He wrote down many observations on Polynesian mythology; and, in the case of a bloodthirsty chief who had murdered the crew of a brig from Salem, he decided, instead of hanging the man, to bring him in irons to the United States. This Vendovi, who said that American sailors walked like Muscovy ducks, was to die in New York in the naval hospital, and his skull was stored later in the Smithsonian among the ethnological collections. On Ovalau, Wilkes encountered a wrinkled old man with a long beard who spoke with a broad Milesian accent. The natives called him Berry but his real name was Paddy Connell,—he had been born in County Clare,—and, taking part in the first Irish rebellion, he had been sent to Cork and placed on a convict ship for New South Wales. There set at liberty, he had sailed on a vessel for Tonga and had lived for forty years among the savages. He knew the Fiji character very well. He said he had had a hundred wives and he had forty-eight children, and, begging for a hatchet for his little boy, he could only give a few hens in exchange.

Wilkes named several islands which the squadron visited: Bowditch Island, Hudson Island, named after his second in command, and Speiden Island, the name of the purser of the "Peacock," one of the most valuable officers in the squadron. Wake Island was a discovery of the expedition. On Pitts Island a Scotsman appeared in one of the canoes of the natives: he had been left by an English whaler seven years before and he was incoherent with excitement, talking to Wilkes in the native tongue and with the natives in English. On Drummond Island they made a large collection, eighteen bales, including about forty pounds of necklaces and belts. Budd Island, composed of scoriae and large blocks of lava, no doubt suggested the setting of Fenimore Cooper's *The Crater*, for the centre was an almost perfect volcanic bowl which, with its rim, formed the island. At last they reached Honolulu on the island of Oahu with churches and dwellings in the European style that brought back civilization. There, on the summit of Mauna Loa, Wilkes established a pendulum house for his scientific observations: it contained, besides store compartments, an observatory and a magnetic room where he conducted technical experiments. The crater of the volcano was so vast that the New York City of 1840 would not have been noticed if it had been placed there. The naturalists were divided into three parties to explore the island, the botanists and the geologists going in different directions. Peale made a drawing of the stump of the cocoanut tree near which Captain Cook breathed his last.

Later, the squadron returned to Hawaii on its way to the Philippines, but it turned first to the Northwest American coast to explore the Columbia river at the mouth of which the "Peacock" was beaten to pieces; although the crew was saved, the ship was abandoned on the rocks and many of the collections were lost with her. The expedition surveyed the river, camping on an island in the bay, for there were few harbours on the rocky coast of Oregon that could be entered at all times with safety. Astoria, which had once had forts, gardens and banqueting halls, was now an assemblage of log cabins, pigsties and sheds. Within the town there was a half-breed Canadian, still hale and hearty, who had served under Burgoyne in the Revolution and who had been in Oregon fifty years, and there was another settler in the Willamette valley who had been one of the party of Lewis and Clark. The widow of an Indian chief whose time of mourning had expired arranged herself every half hour with her seven maids in a row, informing the bystanders in a chant that she had given her grief to the winds and was now ready to espouse another. Later Wilkes wrote a book, *Western America,* that was published in 1849, at the time of the gold rush in California, containing the first accurate map that had been made of Oregon, together with a map of the Columbia river. Meanwhile, Peale rode on horseback from Vancouver to Yerba Buena where the buildings of San Francisco were easily counted, a few frame houses, a blacksmith's shop and a billiard room, an old dilapidated adobe, a store and a bar. Peale visited Captain Sutter on his domain at Sacramento where the Mexican government had given him a grant of thirty leagues square. At New Helvetia, with his distillery and his corrals and adobes, Sutter kept forty Indians at work along with the hunters and trappers. He had bought the Russian fur settlement of Bodega where he had a thousand horses and three thousand cattle.

The ships returned to Honolulu partly to procure clothes for those who had lost everything in the sinking of the "Peacock"; there was little to be obtained on the coast of California.

Then they sailed on to the Zulu archipelago, and, beyond, to Manila and Singapore. Wilkes and Captain Hudson went ashore at Soung to make a treaty with the Sultan of Zulu for the sake of trade with the United States and to put an end to the pirates who infested the inlets and islets. These pirates were supposed to possess two hundred ships that were usually manned by forty or fifty men, and, along with the Malay pirates, they had been as cruel and troublesome as the Barbary pirates had been years before. The beautiful archipelago swarmed with birds and monkeys, and the plants and corals and minerals interested the scientists, while Wilkes made magnetical observations on the great beach and Peale shot several birds, among them a Nicobar pigeon. Agate made a portrait drawing of the Sultan's son. Following the example of Thomas Jefferson in northern Italy, Wilkes sent home from Manila samples of different kinds of rice, and he described the interior of a Chinese junk and the two thousand sampans that filled the harbour of Singapore. In this great mart of Oriental commerce, frequented by twenty-four nations, one saw tiny cockboats and stately and well-found Indiamen. The squadron sailed home by way of Capetown and St. Helena, a barren rock rising abruptly from the sea. Longwood, Napoleon's house, neglected, was little better than a barn, with the outer walls disfigured and the glass broken, and the dining-room where Napoleon died was strewn with chaff and straw and occupied by a patent threshing machine: his tomb was near the house, for his body had not yet been returned to France. The master's mate, Benjamin Vanderfore, who had died in the Far East, was the only man with whom the Polynesian prisoner Vendovi had been able to talk. Vendovi could not be persuaded to look at the corpse of his only friend and his spirits flagged from that time on. His illness made rapid strides and he died in the naval hospital soon after the ship reached Sandy Hook.

It was June 10th, 1842, but the aftermath of the expedition was a shocking anticlimax. Wilkes went at once to Washington, only to be received there by "a cold and insulting silence," as John Quincy Adams said. The first proposer of the expedition, Adams supported and praised Wilkes, and Joel R. Poinsett praised him also, but the new President, John Tyler, together with Congress, ignored the commander who had expected to be welcomed with some kind words of the government. The expedition had surveyed two hundred and eighty islands and constructed one hundred and eighty charts, and it had brought back a thousand species of birds, five hundred insects and two hundred and fifty fishes. More than two hundred of the ten thousand species of plants which the botanists had carried home were still living in a greenhouse; and there were countless minerals and native tools and artifacts. Moreover, Wilkes and his assistants had abolished piracy in Far Eastern waters and gathered a mass of information of immense value to whalers. But Wilkes was court-martialed, mainly for trumped-up reasons, and reprimanded for an excess of severity in dealing with his men. Although there was justice in this, no doubt, it should simply have qualified instead of replacing altogether the praise that Wilkes deserved. The scientists, after what Audubon called their "four years of constant toil and privation," were totally ignored: their treasures had been unpacked by an ignorant man who removed all the tags, so that many of them could not be identified, and Peale found that the legs of one bird had been placed on the body of another, while the ends had been sawed off several arrows in order to make them fit into stands. Naturalists had ceased to interest the public in a day of railroad-building, and, although two German geographers placed Wilkes Land on their maps, Wilkes was accused of fabricating his discovery of a new continent. The Whig administration was bent on condemning all the enterprises of Martin Van Buren, and the Secretary of the Navy, when Wilkes called upon him, did not offer him a handclasp or a chair.

That republics are ungrateful had been known before the times of Wilkes, but at least the government splendidly published Wilkes's *Narrative* in five volumes, together with a long series of books that were written by the scientists. As the "Hero of the Trent," during the Civil War, Wilkes became popular later, when, stopping a British packet, near the coast of Cuba, he took off the Confederate Commissioners, Mason and Slidell. For this he was remembered by many who had never heard of the expedition that discovered a continent, abolished the pirates who molested ships in the Far East and filled American museums with its treasures.

CHARLES GODFREY LELAND

I

WHEN Charles Godfrey Leland was born in Philadelphia, he had for a nurse an old Dutch woman who was supposed to be a witch and was at least familiar with occult matters. One day the baby and the cradle were missing, but they were presently found in the attic, surrounded with candles, a Bible and a knife to secure the future success of the infant and its rise in life. This was the old nurse's explanation. Going upstairs was a symbol of ascent; moreover, a person who was carried in this way was destined to become an adept in sorcery and magic.

The son of a rich commission merchant, a master of folklore in later years, a friend and student of Gypsies and Italian witches, Leland, with his patrician air, was to spend much of his life among tinkers, tramps and fortune-tellers. He was drawn, he said, to the "outside class of creation." He had a proclivity toward low society and ways that are dark, and he possessed a talent for the marvellous that came out more and more as he advanced in life. The mysterious for him was the savour of existence; his pockets were always full of amulets and charms, and, in short, one might have said that his guardian angel was Poe's Angel of the Odd.

As a boy in Philadelphia, he studied occult literature, devouring dark lore from Agrippa to Zadkiel. He made a copy, at fifteen, of the *Pimander* of Hermes Trismegistus, and he collected Alduses and Elzivirs and black-letter editions of Paracelsus, Baptista Porta and the Rosicrucian writers. At the same time he worked at Provençal, Icelandic, High German and Old Swedish. He could not learn the multiplication table, but he had a passion for linguistics. At the Germantown school of Bronson Alcott,—"the worst and best teacher I ever had,"—he cultivated the European boys for the sake of their strange languages, dividing his pocket-money between black-letter folios and the comic almanacs of David Crockett. The almanacs aroused in him another passion for wild Western life that he was to taste years later, but Rabelais was "like an apocalypse [to him] . . . like the light that flowed upon Saul journeying to Damascus." After this revelation of fun and wisdom, he never again felt like the same person, and he argued in one of his early books for the Rabelaisian point of view as opposed to the "diseased pathos" of many romantic writers. He was to found in London the Rabelais Club of which Thomas Hardy and Bret Harte were members.

The old Irish servants said there was something uncanny in this young man who grew gigantically tall. He undoubtedly knew a good deal about the Voodoo sorcerers who flourished secretly in Philadelphia. Silent and unseen, they conjured and worked among the coloured people, while the white people knew nothing whatever about them. Leland remembered a lecture, at Princeton, of Professor Joseph Henry: he said that people would not believe him when he explained to them how the tricks of a conjuror were executed. They did not wish to be disillusioned, and there were times when Leland seemed to feel the same way. He took long and lonely walks in the

wild New Jersey woods, charmed by the magic of the knots
on the ancient forest trees, and he could imagine that they
were the heads of witches buried near by and trying to get
back into life again. For the rest, he made a serious study of
interlaced patterns, in Ireland, Norway, Sweden, Denmark
and England, copying literally thousands of them, many of
which were to appear in the bizarre illustrations of some of
his books. He believed that through them ran a mystic meaning,—whether Scandinavian serpents or Gothic ribbons,—that
they were all mysterious hieroglyphics to which one could get
the key by inspiration and study.

In 1845, when he was twenty-one years old, Leland went
from Princeton to the university of Heidelberg, and there he
fell in with students and artists who were devoted to the revival of the Middle Ages. There too he met Captain Medwin,
full of stories about Byron and Shelley, and an old German
poetess who had known Madame de Staël. With a knapsack
and a pipe, he tramped along the Rhine, then, walking to
Munich, where he studied aesthetics, he called upon Lola
Montez, who was, or was soon to be, mistress of the king.
Later, in New York, Lola proposed to him to make a bolt with
her to Europe, whereupon a friend who was in the room said,
"But, Madame, by what means could you two live?" To this
she replied, "Oh, people like us can get a living anywhere,"
and she rolled a cigarette for him and another for herself. Leland said he was the only friend she had at whom she had
not thrown a plate or a book or attacked with a dagger or a
poker. Later he went to Paris to study at the Sorbonne, staying in the Hotel du Luxembourg, a fragment of an old palace
where lived other students who were plotting the revolution
of 1848. When this broke out, Leland, dressed as a Dumas
hero, went out with a dirk and pistols and a red sash tied about

his waist. Towering over the others, with a single eye-glass and a rakish cap on the side of his head, he fought at one of the barricades, at a time when the mob was invading the studio of George Catlin, who had been befriended by the King.

Before he went home again, he had been to Italy, he had been to Russia, and, becoming a lawyer in Philadelphia, he drifted into journalism and was soon associated with P. T. Barnum. The great showman had established an illustrated weekly magazine, and Leland, moving to New York, became the assistant editor under Rufus Griswold, the enemy of Poe. One day he found in Griswold's desk, which had been turned over to him, a great mass of papers to the discredit of Poe, and, burning them all at once, he told Griswold he had done so and gave him at the same time a good scolding. Barnum, he thought, was a genius like Rabelais, and years later Leland remembered his coming into the room like a harvest moon, smiling, big with some new joke. Leland himself turned out articles for the *Knickerbocker Magazine,* writing *Meister Karl's Sketch-Book,* for which Washington Irving praised him, with various translations of German poetry and prose. He translated several volumes of Heine, who is not known to have read this work but referred to it in a letter to the publisher Calmann-Levy. Above all, he wrote the *Hans Breitmann* ballads, with a forty-eighter as a prototype, popular in a day of dialect in novels and verse, a series that had a "humble little sixpenny immortality," as Leland said when he was seventy-eight. But, soon tiring of New York, he began to tire of Philadelphia,— "I had been in Arcadia. I was now in a pleasant sunny Philistia, but I could not forget the past"; and he went off to Tennessee, where there were more bears and deer than men, and where he looked for oil and for Indian legends.

During the next few years, in fact, Leland saw much of frontier life, buffalo-hunting and living with the Indians; and he could understand Jim Beckwourth, the semi-outlaw chief of the Crows, whose "life and adventures" he introduced in England. Leland had a gift of getting on with Indians, as he was to get on with Gypsies and the witches in Tuscany; and on the coast of Maine, in the tents of the Passamaquoddies, he would sit over the fire by the hour listening to the Algonquin legends. With their love of bright colours, their dark faces and their out-of-doors life, they seemed to Leland much like Gypsies, and in their wigwams under the pines, in the cool fragrant shade, they welcomed him on many a long afternoon. The original stock of the Algonquin myths still existed in Maine and New Brunswick among the Passamaquoddies, Penobscots and Micmacs, and their folklore seemed to Leland grander than the Chippewa and Iroquois Hiawatha legends. It assigned to every rock, river and hill in New England a fairy, elf, naiad or hero, and in it spirits existed for the terrible winters of the North, for the drifting icebergs and frozen Arctic wastes. The legends were mostly taken down from the memories of old squaws, and in combination they formed an epic, the only real Indian epic, with many weird monsters of Eskimo mythology. There were traces of the Norse legends of Greenland in them: the mischief-maker Lox was probably derived from the Norwegian Loki. There was also the terrible Chinoo, a human being with a heart of stone, while the gentlemanly Glooskap seemed to Leland congenial to the reader of Rabelais and Shakespeare. Years later he published *The Algonquin Legends of New England.*

II

In 1869, soon after the end of the Civil War, Leland went to England, where he spent nine years, and there he began the study of the Gypsies that was to take him to Egypt and all over Europe. He fell in with Thomas Carlyle, who seemed to have "vinegared" on himself, the result of knocking people down and meeting with no resistance; victory had palled upon him and he needed someone to put on the gloves and box with him, metaphorically, once a day. Nothing could have been better for him than a few thumping blows, and Leland thought Carlyle would not have shrunk from a tussle à la Choctaw, with biting, gouging, tomahawk and scalping-knife. One day, at the British Museum, Leland was introduced to George Borrow, the Nestor of Gypsyism, who was seated at a table, reading a book in Old Irish, and he discussed horses and Gypsies with the grand old Romany rye who was more than six feet tall and eighty at the moment. Borrow was at that time living in Brompton Square, and he had the air of an old-fashioned Gypsy bruiser, full of craft and merry tricks. Leland had already written a book on the English Gypsies and their language, and, before publishing this, he had asked Borrow's permission to dedicate his book to the old master. Borrow, who had not replied, immediately announced in the newspapers his own *Wordbook of the Romany Language,* with many illustrations of the Gypsy ways of speaking and thinking and an account of various things relating to Gypsy life in England. This was exactly what Leland had told him his own book was to contain, but, inasmuch as he owed to Borrow all his own love of gypsying, he had no ill feeling about it: in fact, he would gladly have burned his book if it would have pleased the grand old man. He knew that a part of Borrow's book had lain in manuscript for thirty years and that it might never have appeared except for this provocation. Borrow asserted that the English Gypsy speech probably did not amount to more than fourteen hundred words, whereas Leland's own collection contained nearly four thousand words of which he was constantly verifying those that were doubtful. But Borrow's faults were trifling, and his vigorous originality had been schooled by the study of natural simple writers like Defoe and Smollett.

It seemed to Leland that Borrow's sympathy for Gypsies was not so much a result of their dramatic character, but rather because they were a part of out-of-doors nature, associated with sheltered nooks among rocks and trees. Hedgerows, river-sides and wild roads appealed to Leland in the same way, and, like Borrow, he got easily into the good graces of the Gypsies, who told him without reserve their tricks and secrets. In gypsydom and the wandering life there was a strange charm for him, something of green leaves and silent nights that was somehow commingled with the forbidden, a witch-aura and a fierce spirit of social exile from the world that surrounded the Gypsies. There was a piquancy for him in their love of lonely places, under old chestnut trees, near towering cliffs, wood-paths and deep ravines among the rocks, together with their secret language and superstitions, a joyous consciousness of their own hidden ways. They had what seemed to him a goblin or elfin state of mind, and he could not resist the blue smoke rising from a Gypsy camp, with its caravans, tents, donkeys and smouldering fires. The young people fishing in the stream, the busy basket-makers, the dark forms of the children frolicking about seemed akin to the foxes and the hares and birds, free and at home only with nature. In Epping Forest, at Oatlands Park, at the Hampton races, he had been drawn to the Gypsies from the first in England, and in the southern counties he had become intimate with all who camped in the woods and roamed the roads.

In Brighton, at the Devil's Dyke, six miles out of town, a large old Roman encampment, he fell in with the Coopers, old Gentilla Cooper, the famous fortune-teller, and Matty who gave him lessons in Romany two or three times a week. Neither had ever slept in a house or under a fixed roof, unless perhaps in a stable at some fair. Matty Cooper, in his knee breeches, with his red and yellow neckerchief, came to Leland's room to give him lessons, and they went together through a Hindi and a Persian dictionary while Leland wrote down every word that Matty remembered or recognized. When Leland asked Matty the word for poet, he replied that such a man was generally called *givellengro*, but he thought the word *shereokero-mush* was more elegant and deeper than this other word, which meant song-master. For it signified headman, and poets made songs out of their heads and were also better in head-work than all other men. One day Matty proposed that they should set out "on the drum" together; he himself would buy a donkey and borrow a cart and a tent, and Leland would brown his face and hands in order to be dark enough. Then Matty would provide a nut-brown maid to do the cooking for them and earn money to support them by fortune-telling. By the use of his newly acquired language, Leland could soon scarcely walk two miles without making the acquaintance of some wanderer on the highways. He would take his staff and sketch-book and set out on a day's pilgrimage, and as he strolled by some grassy nook he would see the gleam of a red garment and find a man of the roads with dusky wife and child. He would sit in the gypsy camp, hearing some of their secrets, and talking familiarly in their strangely softly flowing language.

Wandering afoot with the Windsor Froggie,—another of Matty Cooper's names,—Leland would often stop at inns and order lunch in a private room, observing the neat-handed Phyllis awed into bewilderment as the two communed in mystic words. Red and yellow were the favourite colours of the Gypsies; they loved a bright yellow neckerchief and a red waistcoat and perhaps a frightfully dilapidated old white hat, with a striped corduroy coat and leather breeches, and the long red cloak was dear to the heart of the Gypsy fortune-teller. Leland had known two fortune-telling sisters who spent a considerable sum on new red cloaks; for there was luck in a red cloak, and to wanderers whose home was the roads and whose living was precarious luck became naturally a real deity. One day he met an old woman who told him her sad story: she said she was a Methodist and for forty years a washerwoman, and she had walked sixty miles to see her daughter who was dying. But as she turned toward the sunlight, he saw in her the witch eye, the wildcat eye of the old sorceress, though, dumbfounded when he spoke to her in Romany, she pretended not to understand him. He gave her a penny, saying there was a pocketful where this came from if she would talk in Gypsy to him, whereupon the Romany devil flashed up in her and she said, "I'll have you know, when you talk to me, you talk to a reg'lar shrewd old female thief." In fact, she turned out to be old Moll of the Roads, and she went dancing away in the sunshine, capering backwards along the road, merrily shaking the pennies in her hand for music. A witch to the last, she sang a song in Romany and vanished as only witches can. Leland published, with two friends, one a professor at Cambridge, a collection of English-Gypsy songs, which seemed to him like the songs of the American Indians, with no perceptible form and without rhythm or metre. They contained many Hindustani, Sanskrit and Persian words, and a military friend of his from India, visiting a Gypsy camp, had tried to talk with the Gypsies in Hindustani. Later one of them said to Leland that his friend spoke "very bad Romany, but it *was* Romany and the gentleman was a Romany rye." The Gypsies made a mystery of their speech, from which came words like *shindy, pal* and *slang,* and, only after drinking a pot of beer, would they confirm the rumour that the Gypsies had a queer language of their own.

Witches could be found everywhere, Mrs. Petulengo said, —the wife of the master of the horse-shoe,—and she added, "There's a many witches as knows clever things. I learned from one of them how to cure the rheumatiz. Suppose you've got the rheumatiz. Well, just you carry a potato in your pocket. As the potato dries up, your rheumatiz will go away . . . You may know a natural witch by certain signs. One of these is straight hair that curls at the ends. Such women have it in them." Leland had met the Petulengos near the bridge at Walton-on-Thames, where he had seen a tent and a wagon by the hedge. He knew by the curling smoke that Gypsies were near, so he went over the bridge, and, sure enough, there on the ground Mr. Petulengo lay at ease, while his brown wife tended the pot. When Leland addressed her in Romany, she burst out in amazement as each new sentence struck her ear, and she exclaimed, "Well, well, that ever I should live to hear this! Why, the gentleman talks just like one of us!" Mrs. Petulengo trudged about from one farm-house to another, loaded with baskets and household utensils, selling them with wily art and wheedling tones. Leland spent eight months in this neighbourhood, wandering to every old church and every tower, manorhouse or ruin, finding at Oat-lands Park a lodging-house for "travellers," those who dwelt upon the roads and earned their living in the open air. Above the high fence one could always see the tops of two or three Gypsy vans, and there hung about the establishment the general air of mystery that goes with places haunted by people whose ways are not as our ways. There was a spot on the river-bank, under an old willow-tree, where one seldom failed to see a lightly rising smoke, a tent and a van, as the evening shadows blended with the mist from the river. In spring and summer the Gypsies attended fairs and races, cock-shying, fortune-telling and trading in horses. At the Derby there were always innumerable Gypsy tents. In the hopping season they gathered in Kent, but they wandered all over England, selling baskets less and less because the French basketware had become so cheap.

Leland had found in the Gypsies a natural politeness that always showed itself when they were treated properly, a cheerfulness, a gratefulness and an instinctive refinement that spoke for the Oriental in them. Setting out in his velveteen coat and his corduroy pantaloons, he filled his pockets with chestnuts and oranges for the children, the small black-eyed umber-coloured elves who tumbled about the little tents and vans; and he was used to the whispered warning, "Don't talk Romany, sir,—there comes a policeman," that obstacle to the Gypsies in their search for a living. For their whole life was simply a hunt for enough food to sustain life in their warfare with the world. They could never disguise their origin. Forty centuries of association with civilized races had not succeeded in obliterating a sign of it, and skill in begging implied the possession of every talent they most esteemed, artfulness, cool effrontery, the power of arousing pity and provoking generosity by figure or by humour. One day, in Epping Forest, Leland met a young Gypsy woman with whom he held a

conversation chiefly about toads, that emblem of productive-
ness of which he possessed amulets, an old silver ring, for
instance, with a toad carved in blood-stone. An old Gypsy
woman named Lizzie Buckland told him that in the old time
Gypsy girls made a special kind of cake which they threw
over the hedge by night for their lovers. Their language was
rapidly vanishing, but it seemed to Leland that people who
lived in wild places, watching waving grass and falling waters,
believed in their inspirations and felt there was the same mysterious presence in all people who lived and moved as well as
themselves. When George Eliot, speaking of her *Spanish
Gypsy,* told him that she had seen Gypsies only once or twice,
he felt that, for all her genius, she should have known something of Gypsy life before she attempted to make pictures of
it. The spell of the Romany especially lurked, it seemed to
him, in the paintings of Ruysdael and Salvator Rosa.

In Wales, the Gypsies struck him as more archaic than in
England. There existed deep ravines, rocky corners and roadside nooks and thousands of acres of the wildest lands, and
there one could boil the kettle and pitch the tent, entirely undisturbed by the rural policeman. Once, on a Welsh road, Leland fell in with a party of Gypsies, and they seemed to be
delighted when he addressed in Romany a young man in the
party who carried a fiddle. They drove to a little wayside inn,
where they alighted and rested, and Leland said, "Now, if
you will, let us have a real frolic." After a quart of ale, the
fiddle was set going. Leland sang in Romany, and the rustic
landlord and his household wondered what sort of guests they
might be, a real swell and dusky vagabonds of the road. Mat
Woods played well and his sister touched the harp and sang,
dancing by herself to her brother's fiddling, while the villagers
gathered and gazed into the hall, and Leland felt that there

survived among the Welsh Gypsies some of the spirit of their
old Eastern music. It was in Wales that he discovered Shelta,
once the common language of all the old tinkers and still
spoken by the Irish who were on the roads. He happened on
this "tinkers' talk" in 1876, a kind of slang and rhyming cant
that was based on old preaspirated Irish Gaelic. It was a secret
jargon, descended from the ancient bards, spoken by knife-
grinders and Irish horse-dealers, and once at the Marlborough
Road station he met two little boys who were selling ground-
sel and chattering in Shelta. No English writer but Shakespeare had ever mentioned this Celtic language, but he had
found that all who spoke it were also acquainted with Romany.

III

While he was writing on the English Gypsies in 1872, Leland went to Egypt to spend the winter, the land they originally came from, as many supposed, where he sailed up the
Nile in company with a Persian prince of whom he asked the
meaning of certain Gypsy words. The Persian gave him in
most cases the correct meaning, speaking himself in his native
language, only asking why he wanted to know those old words
which were spoken solely by peasant women. Leland delighted
in the long strings of camels, in the choruses of the boatmen,
in a Coptic wedding that he attended in Cairo, in the picturesque lattice windows that made one feel one should go to
the East not to teach art but to learn it. For with tools of a
singular rudeness the Egyptians excelled in jewelry, in embroidery, leather work and engraved metal. He observed the
annual marching forth of the pilgrims for Mecca, with a splendidly canopied camel at the head of the procession, its pyramidal top surmounted by a ball and crescent of silver gilt and

with gold and crimson, green and black brocade. Emerson, who was also at Shepheard's Hotel, exclaimed when he saw in the garden the banyan tree of which he had heard so much, and Leland jumped up and picked a leaf from the tree which he brought back to the sage of Concord. Together they went to see the howling dervishes whose exhibition Emerson did not greatly enjoy, for he did not like anything that showed man in a ridiculous light or seemed to lower him to the brute. But Emerson recalled a remark that Leland had made to him twenty-five years before, at an earlier meeting, that a vase in a room had the effect of a bridge in a landscape as a point on which the eye involuntarily rested. On a platform in front of the hotel, the Egyptians stood begging all day long, peddling and offering their services to tourists, and there a Gypsy boy, a snake-charmer of sixteen, offered to eat alive a cobra if he were paid a rupee for it. Sinuous and tawny, with unmistakably wild Gypsy eyes, he kissed the cobra that he held in his hand, and he presently exhibited the other snakes that he kept under his shirt by his bare skin. He stowed under his cap the live scorpions and the small serpents that he could not trust to dwell with the larger ones. In Cairo, Leland examined books of the African sorcerers, the black Takrooni who drew their magic largely from Arabic cabalists. He found there a great deal of mediæval Europe, the harpers, for instance, with one-stringed harps, singing metrical romances like those of thirteenth-century Italy and France.

One who spoke Romany, Leland thought, need be a stranger in few lands, for one could meet Gypsies on every road in Europe and America and even in northern Africa and western Asia. He encountered Greek Gypsies in Liverpool, French Gypsies at Geneva, a Gypsy family in a beer garden at Homburg, Piedmontese Gypsies at Bagni di Lucca, a van full at

Innsbruck, and German Gypsies at Dinan, under the ramparts. By moonlight, near Budapest, in an old Roman amphitheatre, he fell in with a whole camp of wild Gypsies, a picturesque sight, with the blazing fire, the strangely dressed men, the tempestuous singing and dancing women. When he asked them what they wore for luck they showed him small sea-shells, saying they were powerful against everyday misfortunes. Around the necks of babies they hung three Maria Theresa silver dollars,—a dollar that was held in high esteem for magical purposes in many lands, even, Leland found, in the heart of Africa. He liked to address the Gypsies in Romany and watch their astonishment as he towered over them with his long flowing beard, telling their fortunes and their own stories and singing to them their own songs, the myths they had brought from the East and that still clung to them. G. H. Lewes, whom he met later, said that to tell fortunes to Gypsies struck him as the last word in cheek.

The winter of 1876 Leland spent in Russia, where the Gypsies of Moscow seemed to him the most interesting he had ever encountered. He remarked that they received him as a brother, and the Austrian gypsies who were there said they played for him as they had never played for any other man. At a café outside the town, surrounded with young and comely faces, he read the hands of the Gypsy girls, who crowded round him with serpentine smiles and pantherine eyes, saying, "Tell my fortune, rya! Tell mine! and mine!" It would have made, Leland thought, a good subject for a picture, but this time he spoke in French, which was translated into Russian. The Russian Gypsies succeeded in their songs in combining the maddening charm of the true wild Eastern music with a regular and simple melody that was intelligible to the Western ear. From St. Petersburg he went to another café in the country, half an hour's sleigh-ride from the town, where there were six or eight girls and two Gypsy men and every pair of great wild eyes was fixed upon him. A young man who looked like a light Hindu stepped up and addressed him in Russian, and Leland, staring at him for a long time steadily, at last replied in the Gypsy language. They were all surprised: what new species of Gypsy might this very tall bearded man be? The two prettiest girls sat on either side of him and plied him with questions about Gypsy life in other lands, while the young lady at his left said, "We are going to sing only Romany for you. You will hear our real Gypsy airs." Then he listened to the strangest sweetest singing he had ever heard, the singing of Lorelei, sirens and witches. He in turn sang them a ballad taken from Borrow's *Lavengro*, and the Gypsy girl, with her black eyes sparkling, cried, "I know that song!" She sang him a ballad that was much the same, in which a damsel described her fall, her Gorgio lover and her final expulsion from the tent. Strange, after so many centuries, to find English and Russian Gypsies, parted from the parent stock, singing the same song. Where had they all come from? He told the Russian Gypsies what he knew of their origin, how their fathers had wandered from India, the fatherland of divination, and appeared in Europe in 1417. Their travels could be traced by the words in their language, Persian, Rumanian and Greek. In this last wave of the primitive Aryan-Indian ocean, the words were virtually the same in India, Germany, Russia and England, geographical allusions which the men, at least, understood. When Leland went to Paris, for the exposition of 1878, he was in the Orangerie when a procession of men and women came in dressed in gaily coloured Oriental garments. They were the Gypsies from Moscow, and one of the girls recognized Leland and called out, "O Romany Rye!"

IV

One of Leland's Gypsy friends in England said he would like to go to America "because you know, sir, as America lays along into France, we would get our French baskets cheaper there." Most of them, in fact, had gone to America, their true Canaan, where there was room for roaming and where they grew more vigorously and soon ceased to beg like their brothers in Europe. Leland himself returned to Philadelphia in 1879, and there for four years he conducted an evening school for the teaching of the minor arts, embroidery, wood-carving, decorative design, porcelain painting and leather-work, with two hundred children as pupils, and a few women. He had always amused himself carving and working at the minor arts, and, watching the boy-jewellers in the bazaars at Cairo, he had hoped that Americans might become like the mediæval craftsmen, who made every pot a thing of beauty. He fell in with Walt Whitman who was eager for news of the Gypsies. There were Gypsies camping, in fact, about a mile from his house in Camden. Walt sat in a big chair by a fruit-stall at the foot of Market Street, gossiping with the Italian dealer while he ate peanuts and shaking hands with the horse-car drivers. He admired the wooden Indian, a tobacconist's sign, near by, which he thought was a bit of true folk-lore.

One day, in Chestnut Street, Leland met three dark young men with hair in black ringlets down their shoulders, and with silver buttons as large as hen's eggs, to whom he spoke in Italian, changing to Illyrian and to Serb, of which he knew a few phrases. They spoke fluently all these languages and told him how they were getting on, where they camped and how they sold horses; Leland had always found that the feelings of Gypsies were easily aroused by kindness and especially by sympathy and interest. On another day, at the corner of Liberty and Fourth Streets, he met a Gypsy barker who was selling a Gypsy elixir and who had been born in a tent on Battersea Common. Was this the corner?—it might well have been, like the turn of a rapid river, so great was the crowd of busy men that flowed past,—which Henry Charles Lea passed on his afternoon walks, deducing the principle that the number of persons passing any given point would be a logical index to its relative value. Working on this principle, Lea bought real estate until he became one of the largest property-owners in Philadelphia. Lea shared certain of Charles Godfrey Leland's interests, although, as an active publisher, he had scarcely begun in the eighteen-seventies a half-finished history of magic, or the control that men have assumed to possess over supernatural forces. The subject of witchcraft had always fascinated Lea, just as it had always fascinated Leland, and his work on the Inquisition had been, he said, in some sort an outgrowth of this other interest. For three years before his death he devoted all his time to gathering the "materials toward a history of witchcraft" that was published in three volumes thirty years later. This was at the moment when Leland was living in Florence, in daily contact with Tuscan witches and wizards.

Meanwhile, in walks about Philadelphia, Leland encountered vagabonds, unknown in 1860, from every part of Europe, Italians of the most bohemian type who swarmed as fruit-dealers and bootblacks and who were wonderfully common in 1880. There were Czechs and Croats with whom he could practise the Slavonian languages; and one morning, in the garden of his house, he heard the tap-tap-tap of a hammer and the clang of tin and knew there was a tinker near with whom he could speak Shelta. The Voodooism in Philadelphia was exactly like the pre-Aryan magic practised by so many Gypsies, the Shamanic spells and charms of the most primitive Tartar tribes that had been preserved from prehistoric times. Leland was in correspondence with a Missouri folk-lorist, Miss Mary Owen of St. Joseph, deeply instructed in Voodooism, who was recording her knowledge of the vast stock of traditions she had been brought up with. Leland had never known anyone so at home in her subject except one of the Indians, a Passamaquoddy, who knew all the folk-lore of her tribe and who had told him, as a thing unknown, that the three hills of Boston had been split apart by Glooskap, the Algonquin god. The Rabbit of the Voodoos of whom Miss Owen had heard as a child was an altogether different creature from the Brer Rabbit of Uncle Remus.

Outside Philadelphia the Gypsies pitched their little brown tents, and they would come to one's door, sharpening knives and scissors, wearing strange garments and with flashing eyes and long black hair. Among them were Val Stanley and Rosanna Lovell. With his note-books and sketch-books, Leland would join them, getting off a Romany joke or perhaps singing a Romany song, or he would go with Britannia Lee over the river into New Jersey, stopping to talk with Walt Whitman at the Camden ferry. Then Britannia would say, "I see a smoke and a tent and a wagon," and they would find the real witch-aura in the Rembrandtesque half-darkness where three or four Gypsy sorceresses sat on the straw. Their black eyes flashed together at Leland, like those of a row of eagles in a cage, while the young men, with three or four girls, were eating their four o'clock dinner on a bit of canvas spread over the ground. Sometimes Leland went off alone, walking until he came to a place where he knew the Gypsies must be camping, one of those picturesque spots, not to be seen from the road, that artists loved and Leland especially rejoiced in; for these green haunts were the best links to bind one to the people who dwelt by wood and wold. Once, turning a corner, he saw before him the low round tents, with smoke rising from the tops, and the gaily painted vans near by and he wished that Plato Buckland were with him to share the fun he was, as ever, sure to have. There was no sign of life as he drew near the first tent, for as usual all was silent at the sound of a stranger's footfall. But, knowing the tent was packed with inhabitants, he called a greeting in Romany and was immediately invited to enter. He found himself in a scene that would have charmed Callot or Goya.

Leland knew the day was coming when there would be no wild wanderers, no more wild nature and certainly no Gypsies. But meanwhile, he found nothing to keep him in Philadelphia, nothing to engage his ambitions, such as they were. Regarding the city, at that time, "there was not one in the world," he wrote, "of which so little evil could be said, or so much good, yet of which so few ever spoke with enthusiasm. Its inhabitants were all well-bathed, well-clad, well-behaved, all with exactly the same ideas and the same ideals. When a Philadelphian gave a dinner or supper, his great care was to see that everything on the table was as good or perfect as possible. I had been accustomed to first considering what should be placed *around* it on the chairs as the main item." So Leland once more betook himself to Europe, and there he became the chairman of the first European folk-lore congress that was held in Paris in 1889. He had organized a folk-lore society in Hungary and he set about organizing one in Italy after he went to live in Florence. He felt that folk-lore was "the last great development of the art of learning and writing history, and a timely provision for future social science. It sets forth the most intimate inner life of people as they were, and the origins of our life as it is." Everywhere honoured as a Gypsy scholar and a friend of the Gypsies, he was to become a master of Italian folklore also, and he said, "There is a great difference between collecting folk-lore and *living it in truth*. I do not believe that in all the folklore societies there is one person who lives in it in reality as I do . . . Real folk-lorists like us live in a separate occult hidden wonderful fairyland. We see elves and listen to music in dropping waterfalls and hear voices in the wind." At Nuremburg and in Vienna, he was to read papers at congresses of Orientalists and folk-lorists.

v

In Florence, forty years earlier, he had lived in the Palazzo Feroni, at that time the best hotel in the town, one of the most picturesque of mediæval palaces, though it had suffered a little from restoration. Its first inhabitant, "Big Iron" Feroni, had fought with an iron table and broken it with his giant arm, one of the legends that Leland collected when he dwelt in other hotels in one of which he was to die in 1903. He stayed for a while in a hotel from which he could see the castle of Bellosguardo across the Arno. He lived, as it were, in witchcraft as he had lived in Romany, finding that the Tuscan peasants retained their primitive Shamanism more than any other people in Europe except the Sicilians and the Gypsies. Anything, he said, to take him out "of this neat-handed five o'clock tea Philistia of a common *comm' on dit* world!" Collecting songs, spells and stories of necromancy, he found that the witch-lore in Florence was stranger even than Gypsyism and altogether an unexplored field. Prowling about the town, in his soft wide-brimmed hat, he met by chance a woman whom he called Maddalena, a young woman who would have been taken in England for a Gypsy but in whom he learned to know the antique Etruscan. She had in addition the mysterious glance of the witch. Maddalena had grown up in a witch family of the Romagna Toscana, among cliffs, forests and legendary castles, a family that had, from time immemorial, told fortunes, repeated legends and gathered enchanted herbs, philtres and spells. Her witch grandmother and stepmother had brought her up to believe she was destined to be a sorceress also, and they had taught her, in the forest, to chant incantations and to invoke the ancient Italian gods. For in this region that lay between Forli and Ravenna, *stregeria,* witchcraft, existed to an astonishing degree; something more than sorcery, something less than a faith, it consisted of the remains of a mythology of spirits, preserving the names of the old Etruscan gods. Tinia had been Jupiter, Terano had been Mercury, and with these there still existed the most ancient rural deities, Silvanus and Pan, to whom prayers were addressed. Leland had made the acquaintance of Maddalena in 1886, and she began to communicate to him the traditions of the older time that were known to her sisters of the hidden spell. Her brain was a veritable library of folk-lore. It was curious how he found such characters, for he did not seek them. They came to him as in a dream.

Leland, who saw Maddalena constantly, met her in old parts of the town, amid buildings bearing shields of the Middle Ages, and, when he asked her what she was doing, she would reply, for instance, "There's an old woman here who knows a story." Then a long colloquy in dialect would follow ending with some legend, perhaps of the bronze imp of Giovanni di Bologna. But Maddalena led a wandering life, and, leaving

Florence, she would send him incantations and odd news of her friends in Arezzo or Siena or Volterra. Once she found for him the manuscript of *Aradia, or the Gospel of the Witches*. She introduced him to women endowed with strange powers, one of whom was an old woman living with a magnificent cat who fixed his eyes on Leland as if he recognized a friend. Sitting among her herbs and bottles, the old woman said, "You come to *me* to learn, Maestro, but it is fitter for me to take lessons from you," and she asked for the wizard's blessing, which he gave her in Romany.

Another was Marietta whom he found installed in an ancient palace from which the splendour was sadly departed. The vast and desolate rooms were unfurnished, the stone floors were bare, and the walls were frescoed with scenes from Tasso. There was a single window in one grim apartment, and from this Leland sketched the fourteenth-century statue of a rain-worn saint on the opposite wall. He asked Marietta if she knew the name of Aplu and found that it awoke in her some shadowy reminiscences. Aplu turned out to be the Etruscan Apollo, and Leland gradually came upon a mass of obscure old legendary names that poured down upon him like the Arno from the mountains of the Romagna Toscana. Divinities who had been supposedly extinct for fifteen hundred years lived on as real *folletti* among old witches, and in the mountains all the names of the old Etruscan gods were still remembered by the peasants. One of these was Faflon, the Etruscan Bacchus, the spirit of the vineyards and of wine, and there was Tituno, the spirit of thunder, Bovo, who always did good to people, and a spirit called Ra, much talked of in Volterra. To a shoemaker Leland owed his knowledge of Bovo and Ra, who was especially the protector of children. Attilio was a merry devil, like the jolly Brownies of English folk-lore, a great tease of servant-girls who shared their couches and made them no end of presents. Then there was Tana, the old Etruscan name for Diana, the queen of the fairies and the moon; and there were red-caps and house-goblins, familiar to the early people of Italy before German or Celtic beliefs were ever heard of. The peasants of the Romagna Toscana had lived since prehistoric times with very little change, and they had preserved, under Etruscan, Latin and Christian rule, their primitive Shamanism or animism. Jupiter, Venus and Mercury still lived under Etruscan names among the old women of the Tuscan mountains, some of whom could astonish the learned by their legends of the Roman gods, mingled with lore one found in Theocritus and Cato. The "gods in exile" were still alive in Tuscany to a degree that would have astonished Heine.

An Italian had told Gladstone once that in rural Tuscany there was ten times as much heathenism as Christianity. This seemed to be true, Leland found, although even the learned Italians were indifferent to the strange lore of the witches: they left it to him, a foreigner, to collect and preserve it. There seemed to be no interest in the fact that this lore contained a quantity of old Roman minor myths and legends of the sort that Ovid had recorded, though it was rapidly vanishing before the newspapers and the railroads. Leland was assured that what he had recorded, in his *Etruscan-Roman Remains* and his other books of Tuscan folk-lore, could no longer be collected, since it had only existed in the memory of a few old women who were disappearing every day. Twenty years earlier still, a vast collection might have been made. But while the country people had recourse to priests and saints on great occasions, they used magic all the time in secret,—assuming that one religion was good if the other failed,—mortally afraid of the priests as they were and concealing from the educated everything that related to the "old religion." For the priests taught that all spirits not sanctioned by the Church were devils. The educated Italians said that they who knew the people had never heard of witches or met with any of this old lore. They were like the respectable Philadelphians who knew nothing of the Voodoo sorcerers. Yet Leland discovered that hymns were still sung, even in Florence, to Jupiter and Bacchus by *strege* who had often come from families that went back to Roman times.

Leland himself was once in a conventicle of witches at which Satan was believed to be present and ceremonies were performed that were described as damnable by great authorities of the Church. For the people understood the old religion of nature and were deeply devoted to the poor old forbidden gods. They performed strange rites in which the deities were invoked, while they made and sold amulets and good-luck emblems. Rebels, outlaws and the discontented adopted witchcraft as their religion, especially the worship of Laverna, the goddess of pickpockets and thieves, and Diana, the protectress of all outcasts. There were many who knew nothing of Diana as a Roman goddess but who were familiar with her as the queen of the witches, and this Diana, with her daughter Aradia, the female Messiah, was invoked in hymns that had been handed down. Diana was the good genius of those to whom night is their day, while Aradia had established witchcraft and witches, and the worship of Aradia and Diana by witches had been condemned in the sixth century by one of the councils of the Church. However, it was still carried on at secret meetings in desert places or among old ruins that were accursed by the priests, though no doubt the ancient hymns had been much garbled and deformed in transmission.

The peasants met in winter around a fire, first reciting a rosary
and *aves* and other prayers and then beginning to relate tales
of *folletti*. There were incantations and benedictions of honey,
meal and salt, evidently a relic of the Roman mysteries, and
love-philtres were compounded with curses upon enemies
over whom the witches muttered spells. The spirits of rock
and river, forest and cavern were invoked as in the earliest
Tuscan time, and offerings were made to them, perhaps three
sunflowers that were laid on a window-sill. To Abel the
sorceresses preferred Cain, the first murderer, to whom they
also sang invocations, taking pains to intone or accent them
accurately, in a manner like that of Church chanting or Arab
recitations. They always took the side of the sinner and the
heretic, while most of their stories comforted the poor, for they
taught the delusive but cheering lesson that good luck and fortune might turn up some day, even for the most unhappy.

VI

Mystery and secrecy surrounded the *vecchia religione*, and
the peasants were averse to communicating tales to anyone
who was not a fellow-heathen. While pursuing his researches,
Leland had a sense of the police hovering over him like a
dark shadow, and he often felt, moreover, that he was lost in
a kind of elf-land. But there was a wondrous poetry of thought
in the witch traditions that had much in common with the
sorcery of the Gypsies. He remembered a day in London when
two pretty young Italian model-girls were posing for one of
his friends, an artist, while a droll old Gypsy, a venerable
wanderer, sat in the studio imparting to him the lore of the
Romany. Till the Gypsy appeared the girls behaved like moral
statues, but for the rest of the sitting they were like devilettes,

for some of the wild and weird in the Italian mountain life seemed to awake in them like unholy fire. They responded sympathetically to the gypsy wizard-spell. Over mountain and sea, and through forests dark with legends, these semi-outlaws of society recognized each other, for Gypsy and Italian sorcery went back to the same root, the old faith of the devil-worshipping pre-Aryans. Occult remedies had been preserved from remote antiquity with other relics of pure classic heathenism. For instance, as a cure for headache, earthworms should be gathered with the left hand and powdered with earth from the threshold of a house. For pains in the bladder, the fresh skin of a hare should be burned, reducing it to the finest powder of which three spoonfuls should be given to the patient. For the spleen, a green lizard should be hung alive in the door before the bed of the sufferer, and for toothache one should give a grain of salt, a crumb of bread and a dead coal tied together in a bit of red cloth. To have a dream that would come true one had to sleep in a pig-pen, and to learn the future in a dream one must sleep on one's face. Curses for the devils of fever and gout were "awful," Leland said, enough to frighten a cowboy or stir an impenitent mule to move. Orange was always the fruit of the sun and lemon the fruit of the moon in all these spells and conjurations.

From Maddalena and many others Leland gathered the *Legends of Florence* and the *Legends of Virgil* that he also collected, the first consisting of old stories of the Duomo, the Campanile, the city gates and the palaces and bridges of the town, tales over which often hung a dim air of sorcery,— how the Street of the Fly, for instance, got its name. There were legends of the Cascine and the Boboli Gardens, the story of the lanterns of the Palazzo Strozzi that were shaped like onions and the tale of the egg-woman of the Mercato

Vecchio. Virgil had first appeared as a magician in the twelfth century, and he appeared in the legends as a magus who was always on the side of the suffering, the lowly and the weak. The fame of the humorous sage, who was benevolent and genial, spread all over Europe, and some of the legends owed their existence to the Virgil of Dante, commonly known among the people. He brought back to life the dead oxen of the poor peasants, he changed a bird into a flageolet, he created beautiful women out of statues and he drove the flies away from Rome. Virtually all the stories of mediæval magicians were in the end attributed to Virgil.

A few of the legends Leland drew from an old vellum-bound history of Florence that he bought from a book-hawker for about four cents. Far beyond the picture-galleries, cheapened by the raptures of the tourists, he prized the old barrows about the Signoria, and from them he picked up battered mediæval relics, early copies of Dante, Roman lamps and ancient classics in parchment. There was a girl with a small hand-cart from whom he constantly bought all sorts of relics for a few soldi, a paper, for instance, of bronze medals of Julius Caesar and Pietro Aretino, knowing that the girl had already realized several hundred percent profit from them. The dealers in antiques were supposed to be shrewd, but he had to explain to one of them the value of a portrait of Charles I with the name of Van Dyck which he found on the back. He would buy a gold-background madonna that was fearfully dilapidated and restore it with gesso and gouache, gum and gold, so that it looked all of its four hundred years; and there were two small folio volumes, beautifully bound, in black letter, that he rescued from their total dilapidation. He moistened the ragged surface, applied gum-arabic in solution and smoothed it down with an agate burnisher, then, painting it

over with strong liquid India ink, he varnished it lightly
and rubbed it with his hand. He found that relics of saints
sometimes lost value. He saw for sale once a large silver casket, stuffed full of the remains of the holiest saints, together
with certificates of their authenticity, a mass of old bones,
nails, rags with blood and dried-up eyes, offered for the value
of the silver in the casket, the relics being thrown in. He
liked to patch and restore antiquated objects, while at the
same time he wrote manuals of leather-work, metal-work,
carving and repairing. In England he had been one of the
founders of the Cottage Arts Association, a parallel of his
Philadelphia School of Industrial Design.

In his hotel rooms in Florence, Leland was always restoring
madonnas, binding books and making frames with gesso. He
went on working at languages, learning low-German Hebrew
and talking Czech, mixed with Russian, Gypsy and Italian,
with a Ruthenian Slovak from the Turkish border. The old
man in his seventies, six feet four inches tall, with his long
white palmer's beard, worked all day, more assiduously, and
without any sense of weariness, than at any earlier period of
his life. He wrote a book called *Have You a Strong Will?*
that led him to reflect on the subliminal self, and he found
that by willing to be free from vanity, envy and irritability,
he eliminated from his mind a vast mass of folly. A master
of auto-suggestion, he found that he could effect marvels if
he resolved to be vigorous, calm and collected. Meanwhile, he
wrote in Florence a ballad that became a broadside, sold at
street-stands by old women, appearing with a ship and a flying
bird to grace the head and tail of the sheet, an arrangement
that he owed to Marietta; and he who had once written a
book that Abraham Lincoln heavily marked, occasionally
had prophetic ideas about the twentieth century. "How long,"

he wrote in *Gypsy Sorcery*, "before the discovery of cheap and perfect aerial navigation will change all society and annihilate national distinctions. These and a thousand strange discoveries will during the ensuing century burst upon the world, changing it utterly."

But, amid all his activities and the many books Leland wrote, the study of folk-lore remained his ruling passion, an ungrateful task for a pioneer struggling with ignorant country-people who were endowed with a gift for improvising. The old were very inaccurate and the ignorant younger people had only half learned the half-forgotten traditions, so that the feeblest critic could point out no end of errors in the work of the most careful student and collector. Leland said he had worked under circumstances "when I had, so to speak, to feel my way in the lurid fog of a sorcerers' Sabbat, in a bewildering, strangely scented witch-aura, misled ever and anon by a goblin's mocking cries, the tittering cheeping of bats on the wing, the hoots of owls, blindly feeling my way from the corner of one ruined conjecture to another, ever apprehending that I have found a mare's-nest, or, more properly, a nightmare of the most evasive kind." Admitting all possible imperfections, he begged other scholars to use civil language when they corrected him and not accuse him of recklessness or of untruthfulness or carelessness; and his friend Frederick York Powell, the professor of modern history at Oxford, said in his obituary of Charles Godfrey Leland, "He could and did make careful and exact notes, but when he put the results before the public he liked to give them the seal of his own personality and to allow his fancy to play about the stories and poems he was publishing, so that those who were not able to distinguish between what was folk-lore and what was Leland were shocked and grumbled (much to his astonishment and disgust), and belittled his real achievement. He thought clearly, and many of his 'guesses' have been and are being confirmed," both in the world of the Gypsies and of Tuscan folk-lore.

ANECDOTES OF MAURICE PRENDERGAST *

THE artist Maurice Prendergast was born in St. John's, Newfoundland, in 1859. When he was two years old, his family settled in Boston, and there, or in the suburbs round about, he lived until he had passed the age of fifty. As a boy, he went to work in the drygoods shop of Loring and Waterhouse, where his task was to tie up packages. He always had a pencil in his hand, and, whenever he could spare a moment from the paper and string, he sketched the women's dresses that hung about the shop. Nothing amused his eye more than a pretty dress, blue, green, yellow or old rose, as one saw in all his pictures to the end of his life, the beach parties and fairy-tale picnics with their charming wind-blown figures and little girls with parasols and flying skirts.

His family lived at the South End, and every Sunday and holiday morning he set out early for the country, with his lunch and his box of water-colours. He would leave his coat in Day's Woods and wander all over the meadows after the cows, and when he came home in the evening his sketch-book was full of cows, heads, feet, tails and cows all over. He was apprenticed to a painter of show-cards and began by washing out the other men's brushes. Then he drew show-cards himself for a living, while his brother Charles carved and

* As related to me by his brother, Charles Prendergast.

gilded picture-frames. Maurice had made up his mind to be an artist, and he planned to go to Paris to study as soon as he had saved a thousand dollars. When he had his thousand dollars, the question rose, did he really have enough talent to be an artist? One of his friends was Mrs. Waterbury, the wife of the minister in Boston. He framed some of his sketches and hung them up and asked for Mrs. Waterbury's opinion. Should he go to Paris? "I decidedly should," she said. Ten days later he sailed for France.

This was in 1886, and Prendergast was twenty-seven. It was May when he arrived in Paris. He first took a room in the Place Montparnasse, and presently he settled in an artists' lodging-house in the Rue Campagne Première. The house had a beautiful court-yard, with a balcony on the second floor. On this balcony opened the rooms of a dozen poor souls who were trying to keep alive while they studied art. As one walked along the balcony in the morning, one saw these young men with their doors open, some of them still in bed, some washing and shaving themselves, some pulling on their boots and cooking breakfast. At least, it was warm and often sunny.

Prendergast put down his name at Colarossi's school. He had never seen students working together, and all with such an air of serious effort. After a while, he went to Julien's and entered the life-class there. He had never tried to draw a nude figure. When the master, Jean Paul Laurens, glanced at his first sketch, he said, "You should go down-stairs and study from the casts." Prendergast took this as a challenge. He made up his mind to stick to the model until he had made a good drawing, and soon he made a number that were hung in the Concours. In the summer he went to Tréport and Dinan, where he stayed for two or three months; and when, on his return, he showed Jean Paul Laurens some of his sketches, the master asked what part of the world he came from. "Boston? Ah, yes, Boston baked beans. Boston baked beans." But Jean Paul no longer advised his pupil to go to work in a shoe-shop. He always stopped to look at the young man's pictures.

For more than three years, Prendergast lived on his thousand dollars. Once he even sold a picture. He was sketching on one of the boulevards when a Frenchman stopped to look at his work and asked him how soon it would be finished. When the sketch was done, the Frenchman reappeared and paid for it and carried it away. At this time, Prendergast was living with a fellow-student, a young English sculptor named Stark, and one day a friend of Stark's, the son of a British general who had fought in the Soudan, dropped in to see them. Prendergast's sketch-books were lying about, and this young man put one in his pocket. Later, in London, he showed the sketches to Whistler, saying that he himself had done them. Whistler, struck by the talent they revealed, arranged with *The Studio* to publish a group of them. When Stark saw the magazine, with the falsely attributed pictures, he wished to call down fire on the swindler's head. But Prendergast, a man of peace, preferred to let the matter go unnoticed.

At the end of his years in Paris, he returned to Boston. He went back to drawing show-cards, and then for a while he found work with the publishers. He illustrated various books, Barrie's *Lady Nicotine* among them. He also drew poster-advertisements; and once, when he sold a water-colour, his father said, when he saw the cheque, "Well, all the fools are not dead yet." He exhibited some of his monotypes, for, in order to see how a sketch would look in a painting, he sometimes put it down in this form first. He could not afford a regular press, and his quarters in Huntington Avenue were so cramped that he had no room for a work-bench. So he made his monotypes on the floor, using a large spoon to rub the back of the paper against the plate and thus transfer the paint from the plate to the paper. As he rubbed with the spoon, he would grow more and more excited, lifting up the paper at one of the corners to see what effects the paint was making. The clattering of the big spoon made a great noise on the floor; and soon he and Charles would hear the sound of a broom-stick pounding on the ceiling below. That meant the end of the day's work.

He often went for excursions into the country. Once, at Westfield, he was spending the day at the house of a cousin. It looked as if it was going to rain, so his cousin gave him a silk umbrella to take into the fields while he sketched. He soon caught sight of a little scene that pleased him, and, laying the umbrella on the grass, became absorbed in his work. In about an hour, the rain came on. Gathering up his brushes, he opened the umbrella. But what had happened? The grass-hoppers had collected all over the silk and eaten the umbrella to shreds.

One of his friends in Malden, a good-natured business man, arranged to have an auction of some of his pictures with others by his fellow-painter, George Noyes. It was a summer day, and the auction was to take place in an open barn. After they had hung the pictures, Prendergast and Noyes gathered greens and wild flowers to make the barn attractive. Then they lay down in the grass, outside the window, to listen while the connoisseurs of Malden made bids for their pictures. What they half expected to hear was "Five thousand dollars," and they were going to celebrate at Tomford's. But what they heard was this, drifting out of the window, "One dollar fifty,—is that all I am offered for this picture?"

When Prendergast had his exhibition, a lady who admired his work offered to send him to Venice. This was in 1898. He was very happy in Venice. He liked to spend his afternoons at the Café Oriental, sketching the boats that came in from the Lido and the girls at the neighbouring tables. Often Gedney Bunce would sit down with him, sharing one of those Toscano cigars that were meant to be broken in two, while he pounded on the table for his coffee. Sometimes Bunce brought a lettuce that he had picked up in the market and pounded for a bowl to make a salad. In the evening, Prendergast joined the other artists, French, Italian, Russian or whatever, and gathered in the latest news from Paris. They usually met at Florian's which had not closed its doors for three hundred years. Few of them spoke the language of the others, but they all gestured so much that it made little difference. Prendergast felt that Venice had been made for him, and he was deeply influenced by Carpaccio's work. In later years, it was sometimes said that Sisley and Monticelli had affected his painting, though he never mentioned either of these artists. Actually, he cared for neither, but Carpaccio really influenced him. He was always talking about Carpaccio, his gondolas darting over the water, his figures on the steps of the canals and his spots of colour. Once he sent this line to his brother, "The work of the grand Venetians makes me ashamed to call myself an artist."

He had a commission in Venice to paint the old clock-tower. He went there two or three times for preliminary sketches. Each time, as he began to work, a little boy who was passing stopped to watch him. The little boy stood motionless and silent until he closed his box and went away. The next day, there was the boy again, waiting for him, following all his movements. Prendergast was frantic. He packed up his box and walked over to Florian's, and he kept peeping round the corner to see if the boy was there. Not a soul in sight! He went back and unfolded his stool. Presto! There was the boy again; he seemed to have sprung from the ground. There he stood watching and never said a word.

Prendergast loved beautiful frames. He carved the frames for most of his pictures, and he was always making notes of the frames he saw in museums. In the evening, at home, after supper, when he had smoked his cigar, he would set to work copying these frames. He never designed original frames, but, walking through museums, he studied the frames as much as he studied the pictures. While he was in Venice, he bought eight or nine fine old frames. They were of no great value, but he had them carefully boxed, and setting out for home, he sent them to the inspector's office where works of art had to be examined before they were permitted to leave the country. He waited in the office, and presently two men came in with long beards and elegant uniforms and an air of great importance. They told the porter to take off the cover and show them the contents of the box. Then they looked at one another gravely and, pointing to the frames, shook their heads. They frowned and gesticulated and poured out a flood of words, as if they were two gendarmes who had caught a thief; then, finally, shaking their heads, they left the room. Prendergast felt as if his last hour had come. In any case, he had certainly lost the frames, though he had not understood what the men had said. What else could they have meant by all those frowns? He went to see the consul, who looked into the matter. There seemed to be no objection to his taking the frames. Then why were the officials so excited? They had merely said that Prendergast had come on the wrong day. Next Wednesday was the day for examining frames.

One afternoon in Venice, passing an antique-shop, he noticed a sampler in the window. He bought it for two or three lire from the old woman in charge. Then, stepping outside, he saw the old soul bestirring herself to put up the shutters of the shop. He watched her for a moment through the window, as she took off her apron and threw it on the counter, brushed back her hair and went out in the street. She walked a hundred yards and opened the door of the shoemaker's shop and called to the old man at his bench. The shoemaker took off his apron and tossed it over the bench, then he joined the old woman at the door. Arm in arm, the two sauntered down the street and entered the nearest café, to celebrate the sale of the little sampler.

While he was in Venice, Prendergast was taken ill. He was obliged to have two operations. From the Cosmopolitan Hospital, where he spent two months, he wrote to his brother Charles, "It is too bad for your sake I am sick. It would be so fine to be home in the old studio, helping you along with the frames. We together were such a fine team. I am feeling strong and healthy and with dutiful trust in God am ready for the second operation." He came through safely and left for home soon afterwards, having had, as he said, the visit of his life. He brought a great number of pictures with him, mostly water-colours, together with what remained of his letter of credit. When he returned the letter of credit to the husband of his patroness, "What have you been living on?" the latter asked. "Straw?"

He exhibited his pictures at the Boston Water-Colour Club, and six or seven were sold. He sometimes had to sell a picture he would have liked to keep. The wife of a Boston broker was bent on having a large painting, one of his best oils. Prendergast hoped he would not have to lose this picture, but one evening he went to dinner with Mr. and Mrs. B., together with his brother Charles, at an Italian restaurant. Prendergast and the broker walked in the rear, and his brother heard the broker's voice boom out, "Well, how much do you want for it?" Prendergast kept answering, "Well, it isn't finished yet." He had never done anything so good, and he was very unwilling to part with this picture. But the broker repeated, "How much do you want for it?" until Prendergast had to surrender. He was cornered, and he was obliged to sell the picture.

At this time, he and Charles were living at Winchester. Every summer morning, when it was fair, he walked the four miles to Malden, and there he caught the car for Revere Beach; for he never lost a chance to paint a beach, covered with bright dresses and bathing-suits, with ships and sails in the distance. As he worked, he often sang,—

> Tell me, young maiden, whither are you going?
> The bark spreads its sails and the breeze is blowing.

He often went to Marblehead, where many of his water-colours were painted. Once he decided to stay there, and he found a fine painting-room in a beautiful old-fashioned house. He did not stay there very long, however. He sketched and painted away, and everything seemed to be going well, but, when his brother Charles came to see him, Maurice met him with the words, "I've got to get out."

"Why, what's the matter?"

"She's begun to make love to me."

He was fond of quoting Kipling's lines,

> If a man would be successful in his art, art, art,
> He must keep the girls away from his heart, heart, heart.

He had many good friends in Boston. Once, Mrs. Bartol gave him an order for a picture of her husband's church in Cambridge Street. The colour of the church doors had turned to a beautiful green-blue faded tone. He took pains to paint the rest of the church first, saving these fine doors till the end. Just as he was ready for the doors, two housepainters came along the street. They stopped in front of the church and set their pots of paint on the steps. Then, right before his eyes, they painted the beautiful doors a cold, raw blue.

While he had friends in Boston, there were other Boston people whom he did not like quite so well. In Venice, he had stayed on the Giudecca, in a pension-palace owned by an impoverished countess. A number of other artists stayed there, and every afternoon several priests and monks arrived to take their coffee with the countess. One day, an American family came, a disagreeable-looking Boston man with his wife and two daughters. The artists were greatly disturbed. They had taken refuge on the Giudecca, and the Philistines were pursuing them even there. The following year, in Boston, the head nurse of the hospital where Prendergast had had his operations came to see him. He was glad to take any amount of trouble, in the way of dressing up, to meet some friends of hers in Marlborough Street. He and Charles called at the house; but, when the door opened, who did the lady's friends turn out to be? The disagreeable-looking Boston man and his wife and two daughters.

Just the same, he liked Boston. He wrote in one of his notebooks, "I never imagined the summers in Boston could be so beautiful." He often painted on the Common, for he liked parks and scenes of holiday-making, ponds and flashing fountains and paths chequered with sunlight and flickering leaves. On the backs of some of his Boston sketches, he jotted down remarks,—for instance, he wrote these in 1905:

> She's not got a beautiful face from an artist's point of view,—that is, a stimulating face, but she has a splendid figure and mahogany-coloured hair. She comes to the studio and poses one evening a week when I make pencil drawings of her and I take her out on Saturday and Sunday afternoons.

> Very blue this afternoon. I suppose it comes from abstaining from the customary afternoon cup of coffee. You must make yourself a strong man. You are on the threshold as an artist. Be firm and determined.

> Accustom yourself to master things which you seem to despair of.

> The love you liberate in your work is the only love you keep.

> There is nothing like the good old red wine for making the blood run.

After 1901, he made occasional trips to New York, and in 1914 he and his brother moved there. They settled on the top floor at 50 Washington Square. The Prendergasts had had a stroke of luck. Several years before, Thomas W. Lawson, the financier, had ordered some of Charles's frames, one to surround a picture, four or five yards long, that represented Mr. Lawson's dogs. This had enabled the brothers to move from Winchester into Boston, where they had taken a studio in Mount Vernon Street. It was another order for eighteen frames that enabled them to go to New York. There Prendergast became one of the well-known "Eight," with Sloan, Henri,

Luks, Ernest Lawson, Glackens, Shinn and Arthur B. Davies.

Every day until he grew too feeble,—he died in 1924,—he took his daily stroll through Washington Square. Then he climbed upstairs again and picked up his brushes and lost himself in his work. He had grown very deaf, so deaf that he could not hear the knock on the door when Charles was out and people came to see him. So his friends took to thrusting a newspaper under the door, which they rattled back and forth till he saw it. Prendergast did not greatly regret his deafness. He said he was glad to find that people did not shout the disagreeable things they had to say. Besides, he was never too deaf to hear good news from the art-world. When he was told that some young painter had received a deserved recognition, he would always say, "Well, there's still hope for the country."

When short skirts came into fashion, after he had settled in New York, he spoke of the beautiful movement that women had made when, at a street-corner, they turned round to lift up their skirts before they scurried across the street. "That's a lost art," he said. It was one of the scenes he had always loved to paint ever since the days when, as a boy, he had sketched the dresses in the shop in Boston.

RANDOLPH BOURNE

I

I KNEW Randolph Bourne. In my house in Connecticut, he spent much of the summer before he died, writing his autobiographical novel and typewriting *Jacquou the Rebel,* a French novel that my wife was translating. During the previous summer of 1917, he walked out with me to Provincetown, where we had rooms high up over the water, facing the harbour. The Provincetown Players were flourishing and Greenwich Villagers were as thick as the mosquitoes, Randolph wrote, among them Susan Glaspell and Mary Heaton Vorse; and we went to see Eugene O'Neill who had written a story for *The Seven Arts,* the magazine with which we were both connected. O'Neill, in a bathing-suit, sat silent in the window, trembling all over, for he was already a victim of Parkinson's disease. Then we walked back most of the way to Boston. With Randolph's feeling for style, he delighted in the old squares and the fine red-brick houses on Beacon Hill. "The eye is constantly charmed," he wrote to Alyse Gregory, "by noble old houses and gracious expanses and wonderful white steeples." This was my real introduction to the New England capital to which I had been largely indifferent during my years at Harvard.

Randolph had gone to Columbia, but in a roundabout way: he had entered college when he was twenty-three. He had passed with high marks the entrance examinations for Princeton, but a change in the family fortunes prevented him from going there. He had grown up in Bloomfield, New Jersey, where he was born in 1886, the nephew and grandson of ministers and lawyers. One of his grandfathers had been the pastor of the church at Sleepy Hollow, where Washington Irving was buried, and he was given the middle name Silliman after his uncle, Colonel Silliman, a Union officer killed in the Civil War. He had had what he called once a "terribly messy birth." The doctor had been incompetent and had caused his facial disfigurement; and this, with tuberculosis of the spine, which he developed when he was four, caused him to be deformed, dwarfed and hunchbacked. His face was badly twisted, he had a misshapen ear and his breathing was audible and hard. He grew up in what he remembered as a tall white house, belonging to his grandmother, to which he was taken at the age of six; and, joining the Presbyterian church, he later became a Unitarian after reading *The Sympathy of Religions* by Thomas Wentworth Higginson. The Bible to him was a "magical book that you must not drop on the floor," and he made a New Year's resolution to learn one Bible verse a day "and," as he wrote in a diary, "to be more cordial."

It is recorded that at school he took part in a debate on the question of whether China would benefit by Russian control, a prophetic question in 1900. He was a "very dutiful child," he said in *Education and Living*, governed by his moral rather than his intellectual sense. "The French and Italian which I picked up later I can read more easily than the German upon which I spent three school years," and this was prophetic, too, for Germany was to repel him while he was instinctively drawn to the Latin countries. He said that the *New York Tribune,* lying on the doorstep every morning, was "gathered in like intellectual manna by my small and grateful self": it told him every day of a wide and fascinating world, and to it he reacted with never-failing curiosity. But he revolted against "that silent 'sect-pressure', ceaselessly trying to mould you to ways of thinking and acting." He discovered socialism in which he saw applied Christianity "moving towards an ever more perfect socialized human life on earth." Later, for the *Atlantic Monthly,* he made a study of Bloomfield, which had become a suburb of Newark and New York. Called *The Social Order in an American Town,* it was a case-history of urbanization.

Meanwhile, music was his ruling passion. An aunt had taken him to various operas and to concerts at Carnegie Hall, and the piano was his great consolation. "We are scarcely out of that period," he said in one of his later books, "when it was a moral obligation upon every child to learn to play the piano." Deformed as he was, he suffered tortures in trying to learn to skate, climb trees, play ball and conform in general to the ways of the world, but he never resigned himself to the inevitable: he over-exerted himself constantly in a grim determination to succeed. On the other hand, he said, "one can get at grips with one's piano and feel the resistance and the response of the music one plays." He wrote to a friend, "Music is a real inner sanctuary to which one retires alone . . . I thump and pound my piano until the dejection passes and the blood flows again and my spirits are righted. I have just been playing the third act of 'Meistersinger' almost entirely through and the divine music warms me like wine." He played Bach, Ravel, Scriabine and César Franck, together with the Brahms rhapsodies and "my ever-beloved MacDowell, one of my first musical loves and one who never fails." One of his friends at Columbia said, "I remember my astonishment when I found how beautifully this strange misshapen gnome could make a piano sing and talk," and Paul Rosenfeld, one of his good friends, spoke of his "long, sensitive Gothic face, and the fine musician's hands with their delightful language, the joyous, youthful, certain dance of the mind." Later a lady whom he met in England wrote to him, "Do you know that the first time you came to this house your music seemed to me to transfigure everyone in the room. I had never had such an experience in my life before."

In his early twenties, before he entered college, Randolph was employed as a proof-reader in a pianola-record factory at Newark. Then he worked for a composer who owned a newly-invented machine on which could be cut perforated music-rolls for "player pianos." He was paid five cents for every foot of roll he cut while the owner received fifteen, composing symphonies meanwhile in the next room. Later, Randolph took this as an example of the exploitation he was to fight all his life: it was "one of those rudimentary patterns of life which remain to fix the terms in which we interpret the world." He gave a few music lessons, and during his college years he played accompaniments in a vocal studio at Carnegie Hall.

Randolph, who had applied for a university scholarship, entered Columbia in 1909, and there he found his "spiritual home," he said, and the "talkative people without whom I starve." There were, among the professors, James Harvey Robinson and Charles A. Beard, Giddings, Franz Boas, Shotwell, Woodbridge, and, above all, John Dewey, whose hopeful and intelligent imagination made him, from Randolph's point of view, "the most significant thinker in America." Dewey's enemies were routine, the ready-made in ideas and the decline of life into a state of passivity, and Randolph was to remain an ardent disciple of Dewey until he broke with his old teacher at the beginning of the first world war. "Columbia appeals to me especially," he wrote to a friend, "because the teachers are, a few of them, not the cloistered kind that one finds in some of the older country colleges, but rather men of affairs in whom philosophy and science are not mere games, but real aids in understanding the world and living a worthy part in it." He went in mainly for history and philosophy. He said later that he was "to put literature in its proper place, making all 'culture' serve its apprenticeship for him as interpreting things larger than itself." He found that Robinson's course in history was "considered *the* great course." Later Randolph said that he must have absorbed the Francophile atmosphere of the history department, for he found in Paris that he liked "nearly everything French, whereas England was always exasperating me and shocking my instincts."

On the other hand, the teachers of literature seemed to him curiously narrow and childish, and he spoke of the "pernicious high priests of bad morality and bad psychology, the professors of English literature in colleges." In *The Professor* he was to present a satirical portrait of one who was "laying out a career for himself as a poet—or 'modern singer,' as he expressed it," one for whom scholarly criticism could scarcely be too cautious, yet who had "dared unutterable things with Shelley. . . . One of his most beautiful poems pictures his poignant sensations as he comes from a quiet hour within the dim organ-haunted shadows [of the chapel] out into the sunlight, where the careless athletes are running bare-leggedly past him, unmindful of the eternal things." The last consecrated saint of the literary canon was Robert Louis Stevenson, and the most popular of the English professors had never heard of Galsworthy. Another was creating a flurry of scandal in the department by recommending Chesterton to his classes. Emerson, Whitman and Thoreau, to whom the professors seldom referred, "have delighted me," Randolph said, "infinitely more than all my English official reading. Why can't we get patriotic and recognize our great men?" A chance lecture in his native town by William Lyon Phelps led him to study the modern novel. Irony, humour, tragedy, sensuality suddenly appeared to Randolph as literary qualities in forms that he could understand. They were like oxygen to his soul. The lecturer, who talked about Hardy, Turgenev and Tolstoy, might have been a heretic or a boy playing out of school. There was an air of illicit adventure about him, and Randolph returned to college a cultural revolutionist, applying pick and dynamite to the whole structure of the canon. While he was reading *Resurrection,* his class in literature was making an "intensive" study of Tennyson. It was too much; he rose in revolt, and he forswore literary courses forever. He "did not know that to naughtier critics even Mr. Phelps might eventually seem," he said, "a pale and timid Gideon." In history and philosophy, Randolph was a first-rate student. Charles A. Beard directed his reading, and when Arnold Bennett visited Columbia in 1911 Randolph was one of the first to meet him. However, he had his doubts about "Dr. Alexander Mackintosh Butcher," whom he described in *One of Our Conquerors.* This was Nicholas Murray Butler, who, in presenting the degrees, emphatically warned the graduates against everything new, untried, untested.

Randolph lived in Hartley Hall, and there he and his

friends formed a discussion club that was called the Academy, made up largely of what were described at that time as radicals. "Our reactions are swift and immediate," he wrote in *Youth and Life*. "Our minds are made up instantly, 'friend or no-friend.' By some subtle intuition we know and have measured at first words all the possibilities which their friendship has in store for us. If I am to like a man, I like him at once." Among these friends were Arthur MacMahon, later the political scientist, and Carl Zigrosser, who became the curator of black and white art in Philadelphia and who was a follower of Prince Kropotkin. Another was Roderick Seidenberg, the author of *Post-Historic Man*, and Randolph dined with Joyce Kilmer and Rockwell Kent, who was "quite mystical and very fervent." He visited the farm of Carl Zigrosser's father in beautiful rolling country at the foot of the Catskills, "a really charming place, with rocky, Norwegian-looking scenes, a comfortable old house, beautiful woods, a piano and lots of books." At this farm he wrote the final essays of *Youth and Life*, papers that appeared in the *Atlantic Monthly*.

An essay had been published previously denouncing the younger generation, and Professor Woodbridge, the philosopher, suggested to Randolph in his junior year to write an article in reply to this one. Woodbridge sent his essay, *The Younger Generation*, to Ellery Sedgwick, the editor, who became from that time on another friend of Randolph's. The older generation, the essay said, tolerated shams, observed social distress with equanimity and discouraged youthful aspirations, and Randolph objected to the guarded defences and discreet apologies for it that kept filtering through the papers in the *Atlantic*. The older generation seemed to him to lead intellectually far too vegetative a life, and it was misled by the fact that the young did not talk about self-sacrifice and concluded that they did not know what this meant. It believed that social ills could be cured by personal virtue. But these ideals of sacrifice and service were utterly selfish because they took account only of the satisfaction and moral consolidation of the doer. How well one knew the type of man in the older generation who had been doing good all his life! How he had ceaselessly been storing away moral fat in every cranny of his soul! The need and depression of other people had been the air he breathed. Without their compensating misfortune and sin, his goodness would have wilted and died. If good people would earnestly set to work to make the world uniformly healthy, beautiful and prosperous, the field of their vocation would be destroyed. That they so stoutly resisted all philosophies and movements which had these ends primarily in view was convincing evidence of the fierce and jealous egoism that animated their so plausibly altruistic spirit.

In this way Randolph attacked the older generation which had had a religion and a philosophy that reigned practically undisputed until the appearance of his own generation. It had never felt called upon to justify itself, he said, it had never been directly challenged, as it was today. It believed in extracting all the luxury from the virtue of goodness, while obtaining the advantages of living in a vicious society. Those dry channels of duty and obligation through which no living waters of emotion flowed should be broken up. The young would have no network of emotional channels that were not brimming, no duties that did not equally include love. The elders were always optimistic in their views of the present, pessimistic in their views of the future, while youth was pessimistic toward the present and gloriously hopeful for the future.

Randolph defended the young with their irreverence for the

old conventions and their delight in the novel and the star-
tling. He admonished youth to be proud of its destiny and
impatient of social pressures that might distort its true per-
spectives. To keep one's reactions warm and true was to have
found the secret of perpetual youth, and perpetual youth was
salvation. One of the qualifications of youth, he wrote to a
friend, is "a sense that the world has just begun with you,
that it is in a dreadful condition but will speedily be set right,
mostly through your own efforts." Randolph became a spokes-
man for his generation. Meanwhile, he was editor-in-chief of
the Columbia *Monthly,* and his predecessor later said it would
have been stupid to compare Randolph's with any other undergraduate contributions, for "his ideas and their expression
were even then . . . quite the equal of those of our foremost
professors." Randolph's classmate Alfred Knopf remarked that
"undergraduate writers were somewhat awed by a fellow who
had made the *Atlantic.*"

With Maeterlinck's *The Blue Bird* Randolph was delighted,
and he saw in Maeterlinck "the best of modern mystics": he
told us that "the valid mystery does not begin at the threshold
of knowledge but only after we have exhausted our resources
of knowing." As for the members of Randolph's conversation
club, they talked about William James, H. G. Wells, G.
Lowes Dickinson and Bergson. "Tolstoy was their god, Wells
their high priest, and Chesterton infuriated them," Randolph
said. He himself had the pleasure of introducing to Bergson,
who lectured at Columbia, the old philosopher-naturalist,
John Burroughs. He had had the good luck to spend a few
days with Burroughs at Woodchuck Lodge at Esopus on the
Hudson, a "noble old man, very simple and modest, who likes
simple childish people best. He looks at the world," Randolph
wrote, "with the eye of the artist, and uses his science to il-

lumine his artistic insight, which I believe is the eternally right way and attitude of the intellectual life." John Burroughs himself was pleased with Bergson. Randolph said, "We are all instrumentalists here at Columbia. Thought is a practical organ of adaptation to environment, knowledge is a tool to encompass this adaptation rather than a picture of reality." So spoke the disciple of John Dewey, the pragmatist, though he was to change his tune in later days. Randolph had a cult of friendship. "A friend," he said, "becomes the indispensable means of discovering one's own personality. One only exists, so to speak, with friends"; and again, "My friends, I can say with truth, since I have no other treasure, are my fortune. I really live only when I am with my friends. I am a battery that needs to be often recharged. I do not spark automatically, but must have other minds to rub up against and strike from them by friction the spark that will kindle my thoughts . . . The doors of the handicapped man are always locked and the key is on the outside. He may have treasures of charm inside but they will never be revealed unless the person outside coöperates with him in unlocking the door . . . One comes from much reading with a sense of depression and a vague feeling of something unsatisfied; from friends or music one comes with a high sense of elation and of the brimming adequacy of life."

Often, at Columbia, Randolph appeared with girls in tow, sometimes at lectures, sometimes at tea. "I am keen on girls' friendships," he wrote to one he had never seen. "A charming girl, if by any miracle she has a mind of the same texture as yours, is simply a heaven-sent companion and the blessedest gift of the gods." To another he wrote, "Have you not observed when you confront me with your valued friends that I have a weakness for charm, yes, even beauty? A mere mind is apt to chill me. I hate to be crude, but I was rather shocked at the way I did not rise to the mental lure of your last brilliant galaxy." He was not drawn to the "serious puckered women" whom he had known as teachers of children, but he had found the friendship of attractive young women the most delightful and satisfying of all, though in his case the social convention that every friendship between young men and women must be on a romantic basis was naturally irrelevant. He spoke of himself as "a man cruelly blasted by the powers that brought him into the world, in a way that makes him both impossible to be desired and yet—bleak irony that wise Montaigne knew about—doubly endowed with desire." Alyse Gregory later wrote, "In Randolph's life, girls beckoned or they eluded. He could charm them to him at any moment by his audacious thought and his power of revealing them to themselves, but he had only to venture an inch over a forbidden line to have them fly from him like shy birds startled from their leafy bower." He was to write delightful character sketches of some of them. His understanding of them was almost uncanny.

II

"At twenty-five," Randolph said, "I find myself full of the wildest radicalisms and look with dismay at my childhood friends who are already settled down and have achieved babies and responsibilities." He had written a letter to the Columbia daily protesting against the unfair treatment of the scrub-women at the university. Like other universities it professed a high standard of social ethics while at the same time it prac-tised a low one. Later he addressed the trustees, objecting to their dismissal of Professors Cattell and Dana, capable teachers who held unpopular opinions, and he wrote an article explain-

ing what "trustee control" meant for a university. He said
that the American university had been degraded from its old
noble ideal of a community of scholars to a private commercial
corporation in which professors were employees who could be
dismissed for lowering its prestige in the public mind.

Randolph supposed that he had destroyed his chances for
preferment at Columbia. But, nevertheless, he had won the
Gilder Fellowship, which enabled him to spend a year in
Europe; and he sailed in 1913 on the "Rochambeau." There
was a grand piano in the saloon at which he improvised on
the first day out, and this served as an introduction to the
other passengers. They got up a little concert, and Randolph
played at that and for a few singers who were on board, but
some of the American tourists upset him with their inane remarks and their hazy knowledge of where they were going.
"I sometimes shudder," he wrote, "for my country that sends
such brainless people round the world." He himself went first
to England where he had introductions, one to William Archer
that Brander Matthews had given him. Then an English author, one of whose books he had reviewed invited him to spend
a fortnight in Wales. This writer's letters had given him high
expectations, and Randolph was under the delusion that he
was a sympathetic amateur psychologist who might become a
congenial friend.

What he found was anything but a shy, retiring student of
psychology, for the writer turned out to be a ruthless man of
affairs, who listened with stupefied incredulity to Randolph's
preachments of socialism and gave him in return a creed of
business success. The stupid and the rotters, this man said,
had to work for their living while the shrewd could make
money by buying Canadian real estate. The house was full
of visitors; there was much riding and fishing and the talk was

in favour of militarism, imperialism and the preservation of all the old English snobberies. Randolph had fallen into the midst of a sophisticated literary set, not the big people but various little novelists, art-critics, journalists and reactionary barristers, and before him paraded the best nearly brilliant talk he had heard, shot through with all the illusions of the age. He was shown up in this society as a prophet of absurd ideals and the possessor of a hazy muddled mind. His host could hardly conceal his disgust and amazement, and Randolph was left stranded like a young Hosea or Amos at the court of a wicked worldly king. At the end of four days, his host's wife turned him away on the plea that his room was needed for her old father and mother. Of course, this clever writer had been in a difficult position. He had been horrified by Randolph's deformity, and his other guests had threatened to leave, irritated as they were by Randolph's talk.

But, after that, in England, everything turned out well enough, though at the end of three months he went away almost cured of all that went under the head of Anglo-Saxon civilization. He had assumed that a writer's letters and books were a part of himself instead of a quite detachable hobby, and he found that Englishmen were gifted in running an insulated current quite separate from the main stream of their personality. The impression he got from the newspapers was of an exuberant irrelevance, a vivacity of interest about matters that seemed alien to personal and social issues. There seemed to be in London no significant discussion, while a continuous fire of ideational badinage took its place. One could never discover whether or how much an Englishman "cared" about anything, and in no country was so large a proportion of the literary production a mere hobby of leisurely gentlemen whose real interests were quite elsewhere. In fact, one felt that the intellectual life of the country was "hobbyized," that ideas were taken as sport and sports were taken for serious issues. A sort of fatuous cheerfulness seemed to reign everywhere, and Randolph became convinced that the good things in the American temperament were not English. Rather, they were the fruit of a superior cosmopolitanism, which made one more *au courant* with the world in New York than in the most enlightened circle in London.

Meanwhile, Randolph followed his usual practice of flying about here and there, picking up samples of every kind of phenomenon, supper with a lower middle-class family, a week at Oxford with a middle-class family, lunch with a Tory leader-writer for the *Times,* lunch with the Bohemians of the *New Statesman.* He spent an evening with a club of journalists and one at the house of a classical professor, and he lunched with Jewish barristers, took tea with the Webbs and had an evening with a surgeon in Harley Street; then he talked with Graham Wallas, J. A. Hobson, Alfred Zimmern, George Lansbury, Jane Harrison and Havelock Ellis. Moreover, he went to lectures by Gilbert Murray, Bernard Shaw, Chesterton and Sidney Webb. He heard Winston Churchill speak at a great liberal demonstration, interrupted constantly by suffragettes who were thrown out with the greatest violence. The militant suffrage movement, he wrote to a friend, "is the only live thing that I can discover in England." Later Professor Woodbridge took him to task for underrating England, which had "done more for sound politics and government than any other modern country." Randolph undoubtedly shared the prejudice of many others of his time, who were turning away from their inherited pro-English culture.

The Fabian Society seemed to Randolph to retain the allegiance of its members rather than to enlist the enthusiasm of the younger generation; and Sidney Webb lectured, as he talked, with the patient air of a man expounding arithmetic to backward children. Randolph was present when Mrs. Webb swept into the *New Statesman* office, producing a sudden panic of reverent awe among the editorial staff. Mr. Webb talked to him informingly and pleasantly, while Mrs. Webb went to sleep; and he seemed to think they both enjoyed their unpopularity outside their circle of radical politicians and writers. Shaw struck him as clear, straight, and fine as an upland wind and summer sun, and he wrote to a friend of "the clean strokes he makes down through the binding cords of convention and professionalism and hypocrisy and shows the possibilities of fearless, straightforward personal human intercourse." On the other hand, he found Chesterton gluttonous and thick, with something tricky and unsavoury about him. To Carl Zigrosser, now at Keppel's on the way to his later career, he wrote that Shaw was certainly "one of the great prophets of the day. His prestige and influence here are enormous. He is undoubtedly the most influential man in England, and there is a sort of earthquake in the prevailing order every time he opens his mouth." To H. G. Wells, Randolph sent a note, asking if he might see him, and Wells replied inviting Randolph to his flat at 9:30 that evening. Randolph enjoyed the party very much. It consisted of a dozen or so, including William Archer and H. W. Nevinson, and they were all grouped about an Indian gentleman, discussing art and religion, the caste system and East and West. The Indian supplied the facts, while Wells played about them with his most luminous and beautiful mind. Nothing, Randolph said, could have been more genial than his manner towards everyone that night. Later the name of Randolph Bourne appeared in the book that Wells called *Boon*. He was one of the writers of whom Boon spoke when he organized his conference on the mind of the race.

At the Cheshire Cheese, Randolph fell in with Walter Lippmann, who was on his way back to New York. He had met Lippmann the previous spring, and he said of *Drift and Mastery*, "There is a book one would have given one's soul to have written." They walked along the embankment to Chelsea, where they saw Carlyle's house and Whistler's studio and had tea at a tea-room by the river. Lippmann must have told him, as he told me in London, about the *New Republic* which was just being started. "We have the opportunity," Lippmann wrote to me, "of focussing the young men in America, and if we succeed we ought to do something that America needs very badly. We may be able to define the issues on the robust middle plane." This was a project that concerned us all; it was the project of the moment. A few months later Randolph was to be connected with the *New Republic*. As for England, he wrote to Carl Zigrosser, "The whole country seems very old and weary, as if the demands of the twentieth century were proving entirely too much for its powers and it was waiting half cynically and half apathetically for some great cataclysm."

From London he went over to Paris, where he spent another three months, "a new world," he wrote, "where the values and the issues of life got reinstated for me into something of the relatively proper emphasis." He was thinking still of England where "you did not know anything about anybody but your own class. In France everybody assumed an intelligent interest in everything," with "a solid robust air of equality which one felt in no other country, certainly not our own . . . I soon felt an intellectual vivacity, a sincerity and candour, a tendency to think emotions and feel ideas that wiped out those irrelevancies and facetiousnesses and puzzle-interests and sporting attitudes towards life that so got on one's nerves in England." To a friend he wrote, "The irony and vivacity of the French temperament delight me," and "I look with envy on the parks and cafés and benches along the boulevards, such admirable places for interminable talks and walks." Although he missed very much his vivid circle at home, he found France incomparably the most enlightening country for a curious American to visit. Brownell's *French Traits* was the only American book he could find that dealt with a foreign country adequately; but he discovered among the Americans there little curiosity about the French mind and French culture as a whole. The travelling Americans, in short, were a great trial to him. They were all concerned with the horrible immorality, contrasting it with the purity and beauty of the American home. He could never discover why they so unanimously left that American home and came over to expose themselves to the dangers here, or why so many of them "lived permanently among a people whose faithlessness they abhorred, whose political corruption they shuddered at, whose abused femininity they shuddered over, whose inefficiency enraged them and whose literature they would sooner think of burning than of reading." This attitude amazed him, and he wished there were some forum, when he got back to America, from which he could preach a few disagreeable truths to his countrymen.

He seemed to have learned to speak French but only after he had given up trying to learn. At the Bibliothèque Ste. Geneviève he read sociology; he went to a socialist school and he left his name at the Sorbonne as one who would like to engage in French conversation with some or any French person. In consequence he fell in with a girl whose name was Madeleine and of whom he wrote in his essay *Mon Amie*. A model, he said, of sparkling youth, she belonged to that France which Jean-Christophe, in Rolland's novel, found in his friend Olivier, a golden world of ideals, a world of flashing enthusiasms and ideas. She was nineteen and had just completed her studies, and their first walk was through the dusky richness of the Museé de Cluny. She had gone to a convent school where the nuns did not care for the theatre or for books, which she adored; and her dark, lithe, inscrutable personality showed him how hard was the gem-like flame with which she burned. None of the social currents of the day seemed to have passed her by, and she was a symbol of luminous youth, a glowing militant of the younger generation who by her courage could have shrivelled up the dangers that so beset the timorous. With her blazing frankness, she summed up the lucid intelligence with which the French mind cut through layers of equivocation. The French language, Randolph felt, was made for illumination and clear expression, and to have crossed the sea and come upon his own ideals and enthusiasms vibrating with so intense a fervour seemed to him an astonishing fortune. This girl's charm took in all that rare spiritual climate in which one absorbs ideas and ideals as the earth drinks in rain. They carried on their walks in museums and gardens and along the quays.

Randolph was struck by the soul of modern France which pervaded even the walls of convents with its spirit of free criticism and its play of the intelligence, which examined and ruthlessly cast aside, just as his vibrant, dark-haired, fragile friend was casting aside, whatever ideas did not seem to embrace the clear life to be lived. He found the feminist movement inspiring, for it was going, he hoped, to assert the feminine point of view, the more personal, social, emotional attitude, and so soften the conditions of the hard, hierarchical civilization which masculine domination had created in Anglo-Saxondom. Meanwhile, he poked about the various quarters of Paris and talked with as many people as he could meet. Seeing "Down with the Republic" posted on the government's official bulletin-board, he was impressed by the political tolerance of the country. It was cheaper to see Molière at the national theatres than it was to go to a moving-picture show, and at Loie Fuller's Ecole de Danse at the Odéon he heard Debussy's *Sirens* and Mussorgsky's *Thousand and One Nights*,—"genuine fresh eternal youth, the Arcadia of nymphs and fauns." The French workingman was a rather distinguished-looking person in his suit of corduroy, while he talked with an unquenchable vivacity that showed the intellectual verve behind it. Randolph, who was interested in the "Unanimistes," went to see Jules Romains and found that Romains revered Walt Whitman. The Unanimiste school would have seemed bizarre to most Americans who were not used to feeling so keenly social reverberations, the power of the group or the intoxication of camaraderie.

The French professors of English at the Sorbonne arranged for him a *soirée* at a Society of French Students of English and he held forth from the tribunal of one of the amphitheatres on the ideals of French and American youth. Then, in reply to questions, he sailed off into an exposition of the philosophy of James and the poetry of Whitman. There were about forty in the audience, very polite and attentive. To a philosophic Brahmin who had studied at Edinburgh, he expounded American philosophy, and they became very enthusiastic about the similarity of Eastern and Western ideas. When the Brahmin left for India, Randolph presented him with a copy of *Leaves of Grass* to read on the way, so that he could see the rapprochement of thought of the very oldest

Eastern country and the newest Western. The university was inspiring just as a spectacle,—the big amphitheatres with paintings by Puvis de Chavannes, the crowds of eager people waiting at the doors and rushing in for seats half an hour before the lecture, the concourse of students of all nationalities, men and women, wonderful types, in the courts and corridors, the distinction and elegant diction of the professors, the tremendous list of courses and the strong psychological and sociological bias of the thinking. Paris, he thought, must be the greatest university in the world, and the treasures of libraries and special schools and museums were colossal there. This incomparable university was free to everyone, while Oxford was a luxury, and even the University of London, with its poor equipment, was costly to the student.

To the Anglo-Saxon, Randolph thought, life was what people were doing; to the Latin, rather the stream of consciousness, what individuals and groups were thinking and feeling. He sketched out a whole book every other day, but the feeling that he ought to study sociology took hold of him and he did not even begin to write. The reading of Rousseau's *Confessions* was a genuine event for him after the rather low opinion of Rousseau he had got from the English biographers and critics. Morley's book, in the light of Rousseau's own story, was certainly a literary curiosity. What arrogance these great English critics had, he thought, to attempt the biography of men whose inner life they were quite incapable of imagining! Reading Rousseau, so frank, human, sensitive, sincere, he found himself saying at nearly every page, "Yes, that is what I would have felt, done, said! I could not judge him and his work by those standards that the hopelessly moral and complacent English have imposed upon our American mind. It was a sort of moral bath; it cleared up for me a whole new democratic morality, and put the last touch upon the old English way of looking at the world in which I was brought up and which I had such a struggle to get rid of." To another friend he wrote, "There is an intellectuality here, a grip and clear-headedness far superior to anything we have in Anglo-Saxondom, it seems to me. When I read the *Independent* or *Harper's Weekly* after a long period of French reading of magazines and newspapers, I seem to be suddenly plunged into a less real and relevant world, a world whose ideas and principles are not very clear or well thought out."

On his way to Italy, Randolph went to Nîmes, a town of white-grey stone, red roofs and yellowish facades, quite modern, yet as charming as one could wish with its quiet provincial life and French mellowness and culture. His early morning walk about the town and its terraced environs with their olives and vineyards under the deepest of blue skies represented, he felt, the high mark of his travels for charm and satisfaction with life. Meanwhile, he and his travelling companion had parted company, the curious bespectacled youth who thought Randolph was the height of sentimentality because he responded frankly to everything and went about sniffing in his delight. Tall, lanky, lugubrious and red-haired, this young man prided himself on his stoicism and he was enthusiastic about nothing; he followed Randolph grudgingly, unhappy unless he was talking about religion or a girl whom he expected to meet in Munich. Their parting was mutually happy.

Randolph himself enjoyed roaming through a little hidden village as much as some busy city square, but in Rome he found the one city where the ancient and the ultra-modern lived side by side, both brimming over with vitality. He spoke of "the professional tourist fashion I hate so much . . . I really haven't the sightseer's instinct, for I prefer to go sauntering about the streets, looking at all sorts of charming and obscure scenes, than to dash madly about from one celebrated monument to another." But Rome had for him a peculiar fascination because it was so entirely alive in a modern way and yet had all the materials for an imaginative reconstruction of the successive layers of its ancient life. He would have given for one little orange-coloured piazza there most of the dark brown streets of Florence, which he found over-touristized and hopelessly artificialized: it exploited, he thought, its old life and had no genuine throbbing modern life of its own. There, however, he encountered Futurism, the crude and glaring artistic expression that arose from the intellectual ennui of the antique with which the young Italians were surrounded, the swarms of uncritical foreigners, the dead museums. Nietzsche was raging through the young Italian mind. In Switzerland he attended the Berne Exposition, moved by the ideas of social planning evidenced by the exhibits he saw there. He had taken at Chamonix a long walk at 7500 feet without any ill effects. He wrote to a friend at home, "Tell me anything of socialistic or literary importance, what happened to the Paterson strike and anything about the I. W. W.; socialistic people over here are keen about it. We must keep our eyes open for social art of any kind." He had seen the fine Meunier bronzes in Brussels.

Randolph found the atmosphere of Germany unsympathetic, though he liked the clean and massive lines of the new German architecture and the boldness and versatility of the household art there. With their instinct for order, the Germans made their factories and workshops look almost like hospitals or laboratories. He liked their town-planning charts and their municipally-owned apartments and workingmen's cottages in Ulm, and it was dramatic to sweep up through the endless billowing fields and carefully tended forests to the imposing factory towns. But there was something in the soul of the people which he knew he did not like, a sort of opaqueness and sentimentality and a lack of critical sense that put them poles apart from the ever-delightful and expressive French. When he went on to Sweden, after a midnight flight, he found the most advanced civilization, yet without sophistication. A luminous modern intelligence selected and controlled there, never overwhelmed by the chaos of twentieth-century possibility. He had got in Europe exactly what he wanted, impressions of the qualities and superficial aspects of town and countryside of the chief countries, the way in which the physical body of each country clothed itself, the social psychology of the different peoples and their characteristic ways of living. He had read contemporary novels and plays, read the newspapers, talked with people, gone to church and court-house, schools and universities. The tendency, he found, was to conserve the old styles in civic art and to make radical revolutions in ideas and institutions. Moreover, he had gained a new feeling of the toughness and homogeneity of the cultural fabric in the different countries, England, France, Italy, Germany and Sweden. The distinct languages embodied, not different sounds for the same meanings, but actually different meanings that spoke for the distinct temperaments and psychologies.

While he was in Germany, the first world war broke out. He had been there on July 13th, 1914, with H. W. L. Dana, Longfellow's grandson, and the two had stood in the crowd under the balcony when the Kaiser declared war. Then he had flown to Sweden with a motley horde of scared Scandinavians and Russians. He had an interview with the socialist leader Branting, and he listened to the moving eloquence with which this great man mourned over the wreck of socialistic and humanitarian hopes. It struck him that most of the tendencies of international understanding, democracy and social reform had been snapped off like threads, perhaps never to be pieced together again. He had spent his year of observation in the last breathless hush before the explosion. The wheels of the clock had completely stopped in Europe. The civilization he had been admiring seemed about to be torn to shreds, and he no longer wished to think about Europe until the war was over and life was running there again.

III

When Randolph returned from Europe, he had only four years to live, but these years were to be packed with living, thinking and writing. He appeared in New York in the long black student's cape that he was to wear for the rest of his life, and as a "prophet of the younger generation," the name that someone bestowed on him, he was to play a lively part in the new American renaissance. While the clock of Europe seemed to have stopped, the clock of America seemed to have resumed the rhythm of the eighteen-fifties, with new writers appearing, new magazines, experimental schools, new picture-galleries, clubs and little theatres. *Poetry: a Magazine of Verse* emerged with the *Little Review, The Smart Set, The New Republic* and *The Masses;* new publishers appeared for the new books and psychoanalysis flourished, with movements for birth control and women's rights. Meanwhile, Randolph was obliged to tackle some real problems of livelihood that loomed, after a year of ease, threateningly ahead of him.

There had been in Europe no encouraging signs from home for him. His good friends ignored his delicate suggestions for a humble place at Columbia, and his bad friends told him that he had as much chance of obtaining a post there as Voltaire would have had of obtaining a bishopric. "The hand," one of them wrote, "does not instinctively feed the mouth that bites it." He felt that he could not give himself whole-heartedly to the scholarly labour that would win academic preferment, "for I get restless over details," he wrote to Alyse Gregory, "and indignant with academic attitudes and ideals." But he had previously written from Zermatt, "There is an interesting prospect in the way of a new radical paper dangling tantalizingly before my eyes," a reference to *The New Republic* that was to materialize soon, for Randolph had an article in the very first issue. This appeared on November 7th, 1914, and the article, called *In a Schoolroom,* was a reminiscence of his old school at Bloomfield. It prefigured Randolph as a writer on education.

His well-wishers, Ellery Sedgwick and Charles A. Beard, who had published the previous year his *Economic Interpretation of the Constitution,* had persuaded Herbert Croly to take Randolph as a contributor and guarantee him at least $1000 a year. Croly had himself written *The Promise of American Life,* and, as Randolph said, "The conservation of American promise is the present task for this generation of malcontents and aloof men and women." While Randolph called his position an "ornamental role," he was glad enough to have it and to keep it. "I feel," he wrote, "as if I were attending an incomparable school of journalism. I get in an occasional article and editorial and more frequent book reviews. I spend almost my whole time writing for them, but produce much more than they use." Croly believed in having editors go away and write books on full salary outside the office. "I thank God," Randolph said, "every day for Croly and wonder how soon the burdens of his office will make him lay down the sceptre in favour of Philip Littell." Randolph was not at ease with this literary editor. "I am irresistibly led to put Philip Littell in a class" that Wells wrote about in *The Research Magnificent,*— "those who have given up as priggish and unnatural the expectation to lead a noble life." Randolph surmised this both from Littell's writing and from "that suave and discreet disapproval which I feel him to be shedding around the more fervent things which I send to the office of *The New Republic.*" With Francis Hackett, on the other hand, he was on cordial terms.

A reformer by instinct, as Randolph called himself, he saw it as one of his goals to revitalize American education, and *The New Republic* presently sent him to Gary, Indiana, to write a series of articles on the "Gary System." This was the day of Madame Montessori, of Ellen Key's *Century of the Child* and of Mrs. Maritta Johnson's "organic education" at Fairhope, Alabama. It was the day especially of John Dewey's theories, which were embodied in the schools at Gary. The United States Steel Corporation had founded the town in 1906 as the site for its new plant: it was a waste of sand-dunes and scrub-oak swamps at the southern end of Lake Michigan, thirty miles from Chicago. There, under the direction of William Wirt, the Froebel, Pestalozzi and Emerson schools undertook to educate the "whole child," physically, artistically and manually as well as intellectually. These "work-study-and-play schools" were a development of the time, envisaging education not as a preparation for life but as identical with living, based on the cultivation of interest rather than discipline, play rather than drudgery and the scientific rather than the cultural emphasis. There were gymnasiums, swimming-pools, drawing and music studios, science laboratories, machine

shops, playgrounds and gardens, even museums and zoos;
and the system tried to take the place of the old household
community life that provided the practical education of which
city children were deprived today. In these "schools of to-
morrow," the children cared for flowers, plants and gardens;
they studied the habits of animals in the zoo, beginning the
study of the sciences while their minds were still plastic and
their interest in natural phenomena was still keen. The old
schools assumed that children were empty vessels to be filled
by knowledge, whereas, in fact, they were not empty vessels
at all, nor were they automatic machines that could be wound
up and set running on a track by a teacher. They lived as
wholes far more than older people did, and they could not
be made to become minds and minds alone for four or five
hours a day without stultification. In *Ernest, or Parent for
a Day,* Randolph wrote a charming character-sketch of a little
boy who had been committed to him for twenty-four hours.
"I always find it almost impossible," he said, "to resist the offer
of a new experience," and "I could always maintain the
amused aloofness which is my usual attitude towards children. The lively, spontaneous Ernest was a case in point of
what a little boy is and ought to be."

To Randolph, an ardent disciple of Dewey, the Gary schools
seemed for a while what he called "the biggest thing in the
country today." He remembered the restless pushing curiosity
that characterized his own childhood in a world where every
passing train was a marvel or a delight, when a walk down-
town meant casting himself adrift into an adventurous country
where anything might happen. When he became familiar
with the town, the fairies were banished to remoter regions
until they finally disappeared altogether. But to keep alive the
wonder of childhood and its flexibility appeared to him the

great goal in education, not to think of oneself as a cupboard in which were stored bundles of knowledge or to be one of those "good" children who grow up as bigoted conventional men. For the "bad" children were those who had more initiative than the rest, and to them the careful network of discipline and order was simply a direct and irresistible challenge. In the old-fashioned school the prizes went to the docile and unquestioning, and it seemed to him that "progressive education" and John Dewey's teachings were one of the most reassuring signs of the moment. They were all concerned with the future, and "concern for the future," Randolph wrote, "is so new a thing in human history that we are hardly yet at home with the feeling." But, arranging the articles for his book, *The Gary Schools,* saddened him with the banality of the undertaking. He had tried to make them inoffensive to teachers and to quench all unqualified enthusiasm, and the result was that he felt he had been duller than the most cautious regular schoolman. He was lost for a while in the mass of his loosely connected notes. "I admire order and precision immensely," he wrote to one of his friends, "and it makes me angry not to achieve them in a subject about which I am so enthusiastic. Can one do these things without blushing?"

The truth was that educational reform did not concern him half as much as the spiritual realities about which he was also writing, but he said, "The reformer got such a terrific start in my youth over the artist that I'm afraid the latter is handicapped for life." Yet he worked over his reviews with a marked feeling for style, sometimes rewriting a sentence a dozen times before it satisfied him. While his prose had an effect of effortless ease, it caused him pain and anxiety, lucid and flexible as it always was. He had vowed never to read a book that did not interest and delight him and he found many

such books among the new writers. Some of these were problem novels about the younger generation, and he was especially drawn to authors who emphasized spiritual experiences
or, like *Jean-Christophe,* artistic aspirations. Among these
were *Pelle the Conqueror,* the Danish prose epic, the *Jacob
Stahl* trilogy, Gilbert Cannon, Gustave Frennsen and Archi-
bashev's *Sanine;* nor could one forget *O Pioneers!* "one of that
very small group of epics of youthful talent that grows great
with quest and desire." Of Willa Cather, Randolph said, "The
appearance of dramatic imagination in any form in this country is something to make us all drop our work and run to see."
He looked in literature for "a tang, a bitterness, an intellectual
fibre," for "the effort of reason and the adventure of beauty";
and his scorn for the pedantic and the conventional amounted
almost to an obsession. He had read, in Paris, Romain Rolland's *Vie de Tolstoy,* short but illuminating and written
with the verve and glow of a sane hero-worship; and he liked
The Tragic Comedians, "not sticky and fishy and pretentious
enough for the true Meredithian, I believe." Then, on a
steamer, he had read James's *The American,* absolutely
charmed by its smooth and golden art. He started novels by
Gissing and Masefield "and gave up the flabby things in sheer
revulsion"; but he read, in German translations, some stories
by Gorky and Andriev, and found them powerful and haunt-
ing with a tang of real life "that we Americans are afraid
of."

Randolph had been converted in college from the career of
a man of letters to a fiery zeal for artistic and literary propa-
ganda in the service of radical ideas, and he had then begun
to feel the vigour of literary form and the value of sincerity
and freshness of style. He read Nietzsche with a high fervour
and a sense of illumination, but novels especially appealed to

him and he found in Theodore Dreiser "our only novelist
who tries to plumb far below the conventional superstructure":
his hero was "the desire within us that pounds in manifold
guise against the iron walls of experience . . . He writes of
the erotic with an almost religious solemnity, and he seemed
strange and rowdy only because he made sex human, and
American tradition had never made it human. It had only
made it either sacred or vulgar, and when these categories
no longer worked we fell under the dubious and perverting
magic of the psychoanalysts." Dreiser, Randolph said, was
"a true hyphenate, a product of the conglomerate Americanism
that springs from other roots than the English tradition. Do
we realize how rare it is to find a talent that is thoroughly
American and wholly un-English? There stirs in Dreiser's
books a new American quality. It is not at all German. It is an
authentic attempt to make something artistic out of the chaotic
materials that lie around us in American life. Dreiser interests
because we can watch him grope and feel his clumsiness." In
The Art of Theodore Dreiser, he said, "You are seeing the
vacuous, wistful, spiritually rootless Middle Western life
through the eyes of a naive but very wise boy . . . He feels
a holy mission to slay the American literary superstition that
men and women are not sensual beings."

Preferring, like Constance Rourke, the life-giving elements
of literature, *bonae literae* rather than *belles lettres,* Randolph
praised Dostoievsky for jolting out of the American imagination its stiltedness and preconceived notions of human psychology. "We are adrift," he said, "on a far wider sea than our
forefathers. We are far more adventurous in personal relations,
far more aware of the bewildering variousness of human nature. If you have once warmed to Dostoievsky you can never
go back to the older classic fiction on which we were brought

up . . . When once you have felt the sinister, irrational turn of human thoughts, and the subtle interplay of impression and desire, and the crude impingement of circumstance, you find yourself,—unless you keep conscious watch,—feeling a shade of contempt for the Scott and Balzac and Dickens and Thackeray and Trollope who were the authoritative showmen of life for our middle-class relatives. [Dostoievsky] is healthy because he has no sense of any dividing line between the normal and the abnormal, or even between the sane and the insane . . . Dostoievsky has a strange, intimate power which breaks in your neat walls and shows how much more subtle and inconsequent your flowing life is than even your introspection has thought." Always with American writing in mind, he added, "If we are strong enough to hear him, this is the decisive force we need on our American creative outlook."

Meanwhile, on his return from Europe, Randolph had gone to live in one of the Phipps model tenements on East 31st Street. The windows overlooked the East River, and Carl Zigrosser lived with him. The kitchen was the largest and lightest room in the apartment: an Indian print table-cover and a row of books disguised the gas-range. There he experienced fully again the "golden glow of friendship," as he put it in one of his letters,—"The handicapped man arrives at a much richer and wider intimacy with his friends than do ordinary men with their light surface friendships, based on good fellowship or the convenience of the moment." There came Ellery Sedgwick, the editor who had published his earliest essays, and there came Ridgely Torrence, who said that Randolph's blue eyes seemed to shoot out flames when he was excited. One day Vachel Lindsay read aloud there from the manuscript of *General William Booth Enters into Heaven.* This was "great poetry—greater claptrap," Randolph said, for anything savouring of orthodox religion outraged him, and he resented the fact that, in spite of its Christian imagery, the poem stirred him profoundly. In *The New Republic,* he spoke of Lindsay's "powerful originality," but he also said that Lindsay's poems were "all tumbled in with an astonishing insensitiveness to what is banal and what is strong." He referred to "that Springfield which [Lindsay] idealizes with a certain pathetic unconvincingness."

To this apartment came some of the young women to whom Randolph was especially drawn,—for one, Alyse Gregory whom he described as "a splendid girl from Connecticut who is doing suffrage work, speaking at fairs and on street corners and organizing parades and pageants." Alyse Gregory was to become the managing editor of *The Dial* and the wife of Llewelyn Powys. To her he once wrote, "Everybody would be much worse off if you were not in New York. A whole society more or less depends on you for its social focus and would be lost and disintegrated without your presence, and I should be desolate indeed. I realize how little there would be left of me without my New York friends and the warmth of that Columbia and Greenwich Village atmosphere . . . I should like to hear more about your ideas on people. I am interested in nothing else, and all my studies are valueless except as they throw light on people's souls and personalities . . . What you say about men disburdening themselves of their disappointments and sufferings with women and women not having the same advantage with men is profoundly true. Men are habitual exploiters of the sympathy of women." When later Alyse Gregory wrote her novel, *Hester Craddock,* she made Randolph one of her chief characters. There, in Edwin Pallant, appeared the grotesque little dwarf, as the children saw him, with the thin spindle legs and the long black cape, always surrounded by young women who flew away at the first mention of love. He liked to explore every recess of their emotions, and, with his subtle divinations, interested in Dostoievsky, he seemed to throw light on everything his mind touched. One thing he could never bear was to be left without a companion, and Hester, repelled by his physical shape, was attracted and awed by his mind. A brilliant philosophic writer, with a congenital vein of malice, he seemed to hold her under a spell.

Another visitor was Beulah Amidon, who was to be connected with *The Survey* and who said that Randolph was "in a constant turmoil of emotional upheavals and frustration, devotion, disillusionment, anger, misunderstanding, anxiety." To her he spoke of the "closed rooms" in which everybody lived and the difficulty of opening doors or even windows to one's friends; and she said that he and she talked six or seven hours at a time, from dinner, on occasion, until four in the morning,—"and always there was more to say. My mind," Beulah Amidon said, "seemed full of exciting things when I was with him"; and he wrote to her, "When I drop a stone into your pool, I always get a ripple." Later she said, "There was no redeeming feature in his appearance,—even his eyes had no magnetism,—and his hands were clumsy and undistinguished. And yet when he talked one forgot the misshapen body, the scarred head and face, the awkward gestures. So many topics kindled him, not only the few things in which he passionately believed but the books he read, the people he met, flags on Fifth Avenue, a ferry-boat trip across the harbour, Greenwich Village history, the Greek dramatists,—there is no end to the list." She was eighteen and at Barnard when they first met. To another girl he wrote, "You will probably like me better if you don't see me. There have been one or two people to whom I gave much pain by appearing in my uninspiring reality after apparently a much nicer person had been created out of *The Atlantic*. So I warn you." But more than one who came to know him said that, after the first moment, one ceased to think of his deformity, and he himself had written in *A Philosophy of Handicap*, "as one gets older, the fact of one's disabilities fades dimmer and dimmer away from consciousness."

Still another Barnard girl said, "Randolph certainly had an unfailing instinct for feminine looks! And spirit!" To her he wrote, "Please don't get in the habit of calling experiences 'queer' that you don't think a Sunday-school teacher would consider exactly normal. Call them novel, picturesque, charming, interesting, vital, but not queer. That is a word which has been so often applied to my own ideas, character and actions that I shudder every time I hear it." And with a girl from Indiana whom he persuaded to come to Barnard but whom he never actually saw (for she had come when he was in Europe) he carried on a long correspondence. "I know the bewildering, cramping effect of not having anyone to talk to or understand," he wrote in one letter. "At college I met for the first time not only one person but many who thought as I did and formed an interesting social group in which the members constantly stimulated one another. Most of the professors were more or less in sympathy with you so that you found yourself no longer an alien, but one in thought with the people who are doing the thinking of the world."

Again, "Speaking of circles," he wrote, "there is a most delightful group of young women here who constitute a real 'salon.' Three or four of them live together in an old house down in the Greenwich section, while the rest have rooms in the neighbourhood and come to the house for meals. They are all social workers or magazine writers in a small way. They are decidedly emancipated and advanced (and so thoroughly healthy and zestful). They have an amazing combination of wisdom and youthfulness, of humour and ability and inno-cence and self-reliance, which absolutely belies everything you will read in the story-books or any other description of womankind. They are of course all self-supporting and inde-pendent, and they enjoy the adventure of life; the full, audacious way in which they go about makes you wonder if the new woman isn't to be a very splendid sort of person, and whether much of this talk about the hard road which a woman finds in the world, the dangers and difficulties and constraints, is really in the nature of things and not the re-flexion of her own timidities and constraints and conventions." But evidently Randolph had some doubts about this corre-spondence with a woman he never met, for to someone else he wrote, "I am very hard-hearted, but when a correspondence, begun on a highly intellectual plane of apparent understand-ing of my ideas and a very pleasing radiant sympathy with them, suddenly takes a swoop to the personal, it makes me very uncomfortable, and I see the dangers which sensible pru-dent people feel when they refuse to begin such a corre-spondence, or rather continue it at all. But my zest for the experimental life,—a life lived in conflict with my natural con-stitutional timidity, makes me unable to resist interesting episodes of all kinds, correspondence with unknown women among them."

No doubt one of these young women was the "Sophon-isba" he wrote about in a character-sketch and of whom he said, "I think the most delightful Bohemians are those who have been New England Puritans first." Probably younger than she had been at eleven, she had escaped from a town setting of elm-shaded streets, and she was engaged at various times in settlement work, writing and a position in a publishing house. Her allegiance had gone quickly to Freud, and once, in a summer flight to Jung in Zurich, she had sat for many hours absorbing his theories from a grave, ample, formidably abstract and unhumorous fräulein assistant. With her own blazing candour, she was a feminist to the core, and as you dropped in upon her to follow her work from week to week, you seemed to move in a maze of editorial conspiracy. She made the acceptance of an article an exciting event and her talk was all of the great causes that were just beginning, the great articles that were called off at the last minute, the delayed cheques and the magazines that had gone down with all on board. With her gay little blasphemies and bold feminine irreverences, she lived dizzily on a crust that might break at any moment and precipitate her on the intolerable ease of her dutifully loving family.

IV

When summer came round, Randolph wrote to another young woman, "Do you know of any attractive place in New England where one might go with the expectation of meeting somebody interesting?" It was Elizabeth Shepley Sergeant to whom he had written: he had met her through *The New Republic* for which she was writing literary criticism and especially articles on France. She told him about Dublin, New Hampshire, where she found a log cabin for him that belonged to one of her friends; and there with a friend of his own, whom he described as "Fergus," Randolph presently repaired. Fergus, who stayed for several weeks and of whom he wrote a literary portrait, spent much of his time in New York in the art museums, discovering tastes and delights he had not known were in him. Why had no one told him of the joy of sitting and reading Plato in these glorious rooms? His central interest was in music, and he had been a professional violin teacher; then, giving this up as uninspiring drudgery, he spent his time composing songs. But his main unconscious interest was the art of living.

For Randolph, a whole day was scarcely long enough for a real conversation, and he quoted Lady Gregory who said, "The lack of a conversable person is the abomination of misery." He complained of one or two girls who were unwilling to sit up all night talking with him. He had encountered "those funny prejudices about sitting up over the fire till morning, all speaking of a fussy sophistication and old-maidishness that I despise." But now in Dublin he found good masculine society, the "people of quick roving intelligence who carry their learning lightly" and whom he liked above all, people "who use their learning as fuel to warm them into sympathy with all sorts and conditions of men." The Raphael Pumpellys were there, and the Abbott Thayers who lived in a nest of studios and half-furnished rooms, serious, impractical, unworldly people,—Abbott Thayer seemed to Randolph "a winsome and Emersonian old person." George de Forest Brush used Randolph's barn as a studio.

At Peterboro, not far away, in the MacDowell Colony, Ridgely Torrence showed him MacDowell's grave and cabin, looking out over the pines towards the westering sun, with "all the atmosphere," Randolph wrote, "of a holy place, silent and undisturbed. In it was composed the noblest music yet thought in this country. Very noble too is the great rock in the little hedge-close that marks the grave. There is a high plateau with meadows that remind me of Switzerland and a background of forests with a great sweep of mountains." In Dublin also in the summer lived Amy Lowell, who "seemed to share with the Germans the faculty of letting off dynamite bombs in peaceful social groups, Amy Lowell, with her delightful zest for life, witty and keen and ready to spread out the contents of her mind before you." Randolph, reading Emerson and Nietzsche, wrote reviews for *The New Republic* in which he got down on paper the large vague feeling of a new time that all the young shared in those days. In one book he reviewed, by Mrs. Gerould, he found the same note one found in Galsworthy, that of people cultivated outside of the humanly animal sphere, yet in no genuinely new angelic sphere. "Much good art is wasted," he wrote to Elizabeth Sergeant, "in trying to touch you with the infinite pathos of such lives, when they are merely dull. The theme is usually the renunciation of individual desire in obedience to some higher immemorial social law which transcends the petty wilfulness of the one person. But such a law ought to transfigure those who obey it, and the hollowness of it all is shown by the fact that it never does, at least in English fiction and in the Puritan life I see around me." Of his own positive self, Randolph said, "I never feel so degraded as when I have renounced."

In Dublin, Randolph felt confident, strong and serene, and he wrote to Alyse Gregory, "I am becoming a kind of lotus-eater, very much reconciled to life, forgetting that I am poor, or that anybody is poor or ever has been. A society that is rich and also cultivated is a very demoralizing thing. I have never come across this kind of people. Perhaps they don't exist outside of New England. There are a few nouveaux from St. Louis and Baltimore, just enough to furnish the dark background, but the general atmosphere here is most charming.

Look around you as you will, you will not find a false or ugly note in the place, woods, houses, roads, lake. The occasional flashy houses are hidden in the trees. The mountain looms grandly from many points, and all my best friends seem to have appropriated the most charming houses and the best views . . . You get invited to dinners and teas, where you do not feel your lack of clothes, and you don't care whether you make a hit or not . . . There may be other American summer places with such a tone, but I have never seen them."

Again he wrote to Alyse Gregory, "We are getting all wrapped into the fortunes of an artist family which lives in the woods, in a romantic warren of studios and big low rough rooms, with great fireplaces, and windows that frame delicious pictures of pine trees and mountain and sunset. [These Abbott Thayers] are all such charming, simple, wistful, un-worldly people, with whom you can sit silently before the fire and know you understand them." Abbott Thayer was writing his book on protective colouration, which was so useful in the war, and he showed Randolph and Fergus his colour diagrams and demonstrations and told a great many stories. One night after supper they unearthed an antique piano that had been brought over from Germany about 1848, and Randolph and Fergus with his violin played Schubert songs for an hour out of an old Liederbuch. "Mr. Thayer's appreciation was almost embarrassingly ecstatic, and he proffered sketches and dinners and thanks if we would come two or three times a week and do it again. I liked his simple emotional ways and his telling us we had 'watered his soul'. He took us down to the road with the quaintest of lanterns and spoke constantly of the music." But later, Randolph wrote to Elizabeth Sergeant, "Mr. Thayer's head was so full of pie-bald warships and the conversion of college presidents to protective colouration that he couldn't any longer let his emotional nature be stirred by our Schubert and Bach"; and he continued, "Mr. Thayer finishes a portrait of his daughter Nancy, Titian-like, with rich draperies and classic calm. How amazing that so radical a mind should make his art so imitative! He seems completely untouched by the art-tendencies of the day, living only with the Italian masters and working devotedly after their principles."

One morning George de Forest Brush stopped, probably astonished to see them up so early, and talked long and charmingly on violins and violinists. He was full of socialistic ideas and the raciest tangiest talk. On another peculiarly heavenly morning, Mr. Thayer took them out in his boat, and, having got to the middle of the lake, discoursed on art and religion. Meanwhile, they went their own comfortable ways. One morning Randolph lay in bed and saw the most glorious orange dawn, deep orange springing from the deepest of the hills, with the picturesque village silhouetted against it. In the afternoon he went to his field again, warmer and even lovelier, and then to the Thayers. He had an hour watching the mountain turn purple in the sunset, and the golden clouds through the Western pines, and afterwards a talk by the fire about country houses and Dublin views: "supper and some Schubert on the piano and a walk under the belated moon along the lake wood-road, with mysterious shadows and sudden white forms of birches and queer luminous patches in the forest and the calm outline of the hills under the stars." One day he discovered a new road and walked along it, with tantalizing views through the trees, until he came to the fairest of meadows with a view like nothing so much as the view across the Roman Campagna from the Janiculum, the same valley, the same contours of hills, even jagged Mount

Soracte, called in New Hampshire Crotched Mountain. Only
the city and St. Peter's were absent. He lay in the warm grass
for hours, dreaming and hearing the foxes barking in the
woods behind him. But his conscience told him of some
retribution due for these stolen delights, books not read,
thought not achieved, articles not written.

One day there was a musicale at the Raphael Pumpellys',
with a Danish cellist, and tea later on a grassy terrace bounded
by a stone wall. It overlooked the mountain and the sunset,
and there were girls in bright Italian costumes, a most delightful picture. On another evening Randolph dined with
Amy Lowell when Edwin Arlington Robinson was there
and they both read poems. Randolph had gone to her house in
considerable trepidation, expecting to be overawed and pum-
melled, but instead he spent a wholly delightful evening.
Amy Lowell walked up to him as one of the oldest of friends
and they had a truly grand gossip. She was surprisingly fair-
minded and a lover of all sorts of queer and little people whom
she touched off inimitably; but later she told Louis Untermeyer
that she despised the "weakling." He had come to Sevenells
in Brookline and was terrified by her dogs, and she insisted
then that his deformity showed itself in his "twisted mentality
and tortured style." She said, "Everything he writes shows he
is a cripple." On another evening in Dublin, Randolph and
Fergus had a party for Mrs. E. H. James, who had been a
bright spot of Randolph's visit to Paris. Mrs. James's husband,
a nephew of Henry and William James, was a visionary international socialist, "founding red republics in various countries
when he was not libelling King George." Mrs. James was a
fine example of the best Boston idealism combined with cosmopolitan radicalism, of the bluest Boston blood, with serious
almost tragic feeling, with little of intelligent training to carry

it all off yet with a sheer nobility of emotion really doing it. She was a most distinguished and charming woman with great dramatic talent, which she displayed by reciting to little groups of friends plays of Synge or *L'Arlesienne* or Racine's *Attalie* or, on occasion, *The Trojan Women*. Later, in Boston, where Randolph often saw her, she started a socialistic salon to discuss the Industrial Relations report, and Randolph's relatively greater acquaintance with books and the placing of people made him, as he said, a fountain of light there.

When Fergus left, Randolph was joined in Dublin by the old Yankee artist Eastman Chase, who castigated George de Forest Brush and consigned him to limbo, even calling him a "fake" for his imitations. But he thought that Abbott Thayer would last as a real artist. A Bohemian New Englander, Eastman Chase had a studio in MacDougal Alley and came up to Dublin when he had no work in New York. He did the cooking and he and Randolph spent hours walking and talking poets and music and pictures before the fire. Seventy-four years old and quite untouched, he had once had a picture-gallery in Boston and he knew everybody and everything interesting, a rare old character, emphatically not, Randolph said, of the older generation. When work called him back to New York, he walked to Peterboro, eight miles, to get his train, and Randolph walked with him a couple of miles down the delightful Dublin hill with its little old houses and pleasant meadows. There were rounded hills in the distance that reminded him of Wales and here and there lovely old flower gardens, bright with purples and yellows.

Randolph and Fergus had amused themselves with thoughts of building a house in Dublin and coming back there always to live. But, as it turned out, they were not encouraged to return another summer. They were too exciting for Abbott

Thayer, and, as Randolph said, "I talk too much." But when Mr. Thayer's daughter Gladys came to New York, Randolph offered to find a studio for her. She had just marched in a suffrage parade in Boston, led by what she called "a hag-like lady in regal dress of gold brocade, riding on a black steed just in front of us (O.K. as far up as her neck)." She added, "Seeing the prim red-nosed antis with their unbearably *smug* and *pampered* demeanour I felt once and for all which was the *great* and *human* side and the lines of progress." Randolph, meanwhile, went to Boston to give a lecture and to visit Mrs. James. He wrote from Cambridge to Alyse Gregory, "Here I am seeing some of the *New Republic's* friends who terrify me when I see them in New York but who make me wholly buoyant here. Felix Frankfurter, for instance, who teaches law at Harvard, and Harold Laski, an Oxford Jew, now teaching history at Harvard, an incredibly brilliant specimen of the young English radical school. These two, with Walter Lippmann, make up a Jewish trinity which is the wonder of the world, or at least my world." He continued, "Boston seems so smiling and restful and yet modernly intelligent. I lose all that hectic, anxious note of New York. People here have much more time. One feels so much more of a person." Years later, Harold Laski wrote to Dorothy Teall, who was writing a biography of Randolph, "I thought of him then as the most incisively radical of all the people connected with the *New Republic*. He had not Croly's learning, nor Lippmann's magical style, but none of them felt wrong to be wrong as clearly as he did . . . He seemed to me the most *growing* mind, and also the most courageous, of all his group . . . His talk with me in Cambridge was a great day for me."

V

Randolph, who had lectured in Boston, was presently invited to lecture at the University of Wisconsin, and there he wrote, "I renounce Boston for Madison as my city of refuge. There was charm in four days of stimulating and exclusively masculine society, a rather rare experience for me." He met Max Eastman there and liked him,—"His tempo seems even slower than mine"; and, sitting around in Horace Kallen's room, he said, "I shouldn't have had my confidence always damped by thickly cynical Columbia and rapid, sure *New Republic*." He encountered on every hand the new vision of the coming generation, and it was there he met Karen, the Norwegian girl who "did not think but felt in slow sensuous outlines; you could feel her feelings cautiously putting out long streamers at you. If you were in the mood, a certain subterranean conversation was not impossible with her." She was as inscrutable in anger as she was in her friendliness, and, as she never went to her classes, he had long walks with her by the lake. She was twenty-five and wore picturesque peasant costumes, and she said things like this, "My mother keeps writing and asking if I know any young men, so she will know how much money to send me for clothes." Randolph, telling one of his friends about her, asked, "How do you like such little flashes of primitive sociology?"

Karen was one of those girls whom Willa Cather wrote about, who had grown up on farms in the Middle West, Scandinavians, Bohemians, Germans who showed her, as they showed Randolph, how the melting-pot failed to melt them. Among these young people, both men and women, he had found many of his true friends, acclimatized Austrians, acclimatized Italians, who kept up the cultural traditions of

their homelands, and he did not want these distinctive qualities to be washed out into a tasteless, colourless fluid of uniformity. All unawares, America had been building the first
international nation, it was destined to be a federation of
cultures, and nothing seemed more important than to shake
off the incubus of English traditions and ideas. English snobberies and literary styles, English ethics and superstitions had
been the cultural food that Americans had drunk in with their
mothers' milk, and the English today nagged and disliked
the Americans as people dislike their younger brothers. They
thought of Americans as cultural colonials still, and could a
transnational America put up with this?

Randolph had written to Carl Zigrosser that he liked the
English better than the Americans in Paris. Instead of staying at home, he said, and appreciating their own genius, the
Americans rushed to Europe and sat at the feet of old masters,
attended lectures by illiterates at the Bureau of University
Travel and expected culture to rub off on them somehow.
The French conserved their genius, listened to nothing but
French music, filled their galleries with French pictures,
created the most charming statues to every writer and artist,
and consequently had a rich and delightful culture that
saturated the nation. "We have, I am sure," he continued,
"at least one genius in every form of art that is as good, ex-
cepting Rodin, as any French genius living, but where are
our statues and our praise? Our uninspired millionaires are
paying millions for some Italian painting of the fifteenth
century, or presenting priceless sets of armour to some museum.
It is enough to make angels weep."

There was enough truth in this to make the point he had
in mind, that a certain cultural chauvinism was the most harmless of patriotisms and absolutely necessary for a true life of

civilization. "The Frenchman's attitude towards the things of culture is one of daily appreciation and intimacy, not the attitude of reverence with which we Americans approach alien art and which penalizes cultural heresy with us . . . Culture is not an acquired familiarity with things outside, but an inner and constantly operating taste, a fresh and responsive power of discrimination, and the insistent judging of everything that comes to our minds and senses . . . Our humility causes us to be taken at our own face value, and for all this patient fixity of gaze upon Europe, we get little reward except to be ignored, or to have our interest somewhat contemptuously dismissed as parasitic . . . This cultural humility of ours astonished and still astonishes Europe . . . Such grovelling humility can only have the effect of making us feeble imitators, instead of making us assert, with all the power at our command, the genius and individuality which we already possess in quantity, if we would only see it . . . Is it not a tragedy that the American artist feels the imperative need of foreign approval before he can be assured of his attainment? The only remedy for this deplorable situation is the cultivation of a new American nationalism. We need that keen introspection into the beauties and vitalities and sincerities of our own life and ideals that characterizes the French."

All this was written before the two world wars changed the relations between America and Europe, before the great burst of creative activity in the American twenties and before the wars had blighted the creative life in Europe. Randolph spoke truly when he said, "Our cultural humility before the civilizations of Europe is the chief obstacle which prevents us from producing any true indigenous culture of our own," and "By fixing our eyes humbly on the ages that are past, and on foreign countries, we effectively protect ourselves from that inner taste which is the only sincere 'culture' . . . We should turn our eyes upon our own art for a time, shut ourselves in with our own genius, and cultivate with an intense and partial pride what we have already achieved against the obstacles of our cultural humility. Only then can we take our rightful place among the cultures of the world, to which we are entitled if we would but recognize it." For "in the contemporary talent that Europe is exhibiting, or even in the genius of the last half-century, we will go far to find greater poets than our Walt Whitman, philosophers than William James, essayists than Emerson and Thoreau, composers than MacDowell, sculptors than Saint-Gaudens. Their works have expressed the American ideals and qualities, our pulsating democracy, the vigour and daring of our pioneer spirit, our sense of camaraderie, our dynamism, our hospitality to all the world." This "almost sounds as if I were practising for an essay," he wrote to Alyse Gregory in a letter in which he said, "Emerson, Thoreau, Whitman, William James could only have been written here; their spirit is really indigenous, utterly unlike that of any other country." Elsewhere he spoke of Whitman as "the glorious prophet of the true and perfect fusion of physical and spiritual camaraderie," and he shared Thoreau's belief that men have an infinite range of capacities, possibilities and choices. To another friend he wrote, "I am very fond of *Walden*. I see a thread running through Thoreau, Emerson, Whitman and William James, a sense of a background, mystical, inscrutable but healing and beneficent, my idea of religion."

Many of these ideas he expressed in his essay *Our Cultural Humility*, but he had also written in a letter from Paris, "I realized with a start the other day that in all my literary pantheon there was not a single English writer, except perhaps Hazlitt and Lamb,—Hazlitt, because of his artistic sensitiveness and superb psychology and undeviating radicalism (for while all that traitorous crew Wordsworth and Coleridge turned renegade, Hazlitt stood doggedly faithful to the French Revolution), and Lamb for his irony and exquisite charm. Of all the rest of the English classical canon, I don't think, outside of some poems of Keats and Browning, and some of the Elizabethans, that I ever read a page with real pleasure."

In the same letter Randolph wrote (to Alyse Gregory), "There is only one situation that I ever found really inspires me to write, and that is a shady garden with a sympathetic friend flitting about to make the atmosphere luminous with personality. I have only had it twice in my life." One of his sisters, meanwhile, had married the Rev. Lawrence Fenninger, later of the Union Theological Seminary, but at present the chaplain of the Hampton Institute, for coloured people, in Virginia. Randolph went down, in 1916, to visit his sister and brother-in-law, "the liveliest kind of modern chaplain," he wrote to Elizabeth Sergeant, "very modern in his theology and sociology." He found Hampton a most interesting school to look at and a Utopia of a place to live in, the only school he knew of where practically everything was worth the doing and all the energy went into living value. He took very kindly to the black man and was delighted when his sister invited the black commandant and his wife to dinner, and he said, "I think the Southern white man's policy of keeping down a race whose infectious personal qualities he never was really able to resist is the least defensible thing in the world. The thing is full of ghastly ironies, and I shall unburden myself of it some day." The teachers dropped in to see a mild celebrity, and one rather gay lady was much interested in what she conceived he hadn't said about the girl in *Mon Amie*. On this essay evidently rested much of his fame.

The South, he said, while the vast Northern development went on, still remained an English colony, stagnant and complacent, having progressed culturally scarcely beyond the early Victorian era. It was culturally sterile because it had had no advantage of cross-fertilization such as the Northern states had had. But meanwhile, travelling about the country, he had been struck again by the uncouthness of the general scene. What little he had observed of Connecticut town life from the train on his way to Danbury seemed almost too grotesquely squalid and frowsy to be true. He had learned to do what he supposed all Americans did, that is, pass through streets and cities without seeing anything or allowing anything at least to sink in. Whereas on the Continent he was always absorbing and assimilating, here he found himself constantly rejecting, denying the admission of the squalor and vulgarity that pressed upon him from every side. The only thing one could do was to sting people slowly into new tastes and new ideals, and meanwhile certainly not let one's own soul be poisoned by the hostile environment. When he thought of the German cities, beautiful and nobly planned, ours were more hideous than anyone cared or dared to say, a wilderness of dirty frame houses, gaunt factories and isolated tenements in all stages of decrepitude. To be sure, these were interspersed with trim rows of cottages and bright apartment-houses and here and there an imposing church or school. Our cities and isolated farms were mute witnesses that Americans had never learned how to live. Town-planning seemed to Randolph the most fascinating of current interests, and the study that packed into itself more historical and sociological stimulation than almost any other study he knew. For the rest, the cultural background of the well-to-do American household, with its "nice" people, its sentimental fiction and popular music, its amiable religiosity and vague moral optimism, was far more alien to the stern and secular realism of modern university teaching than most people were willing to admit. So he wrote in his essay *Our Unplanned Cities.*

VI

It was in 1915 that I first met Randolph. I was connected with the Century Company at that time, and the editor of the *Century Magazine* asked me to write to him suggesting an article that he wished to publish. The subject was the impossibility of dividing things into black and white, and Randolph wrote to me, "Only my usual shiftlessness has prevented me from following your suggestion. I had an idea of working in my favourite 'scientific curve of distribution,' and showing that from the modern point of view all classifications into black and white were inaccurate, because things shaded off into each other by degrees. I was then going to take up some of our social institutions and show how they were organized on the 'black and white' plan, and suggest how a popular appreciation of the new idea would put us into a receptive mood for social changes. If you think that this idea, worked out in a not too heavy way, would make a good paper, I will drive myself to it again." I don't think this article was ever written, but Randolph made his point in the essay on Dostoievsky in whom one was never conscious of a disparity between black and white. In this respect Dostoievsky was a parent of much contemporary novel-writing.

From that time on, I saw much of Randolph, and I delighted even in the sharp tongue for which he had a reputation.

There was a good deal of malice in his composition which I thoroughly enjoyed. His life up to 1915, as well as most of his older friends, were unknown to me, even by name, but he had a way of touching us all off that I heartily relished because his wit was unfailing. He was just as likely as not to give you a pleasant nip across the table, and, having a tender feeling for any good phrase, at anyone's expense, including my own, I liked this. Besides, it belonged to his mental constitution and was partly due to his physical state, a little like Alexander Pope's. At the time of *The Seven Arts* we were thrown closely together. James Oppenheim, Waldo Frank and I were the editors of this, and at a certain point we drew Randolph in, only to have his articles destroy the paper. For when in April, 1917, the United States entered the war, Randolph's contributions were all pacifistic, and the owner, who was the business manager, withdrew her subsidy, so that the magazine instantly foundered. In order to establish it, she had sold her great collection of Whistlers, and I could see how the wind blew when she caused the flag to be flown at half-mast in honour of the death of Joseph H. Choate. In politics she was an orthodox Republican who could not bear to oppose the war, although, when she lost her post, she lost her reason for being and drowned herself a few weeks later. Nor could I share the feeling of our editor-in-chief James Oppenheim or of my friend Randolph Bourne. I could not see why a magazine of art should destroy itself by opposing the war, and, for the rest, I asked myself, what would have become of us if Germany had dominated Europe? If it had not been for wars, we should never have had a country. But Randolph's rationality could not comprehend the irrationality of war. "Of the emotions that take the place of thought he had little grasp," Elsie Clews Parsons later wrote in *A Pacifist Patriot,* "nor of the emotional gratifications that are brought by war to the irrational. As an unmitigated intellectual, his understanding of irrational groups, wage-earner as well as millionaire, remained limited."

Randolph had read too well Gustave Le Bon's *The Crowd* and Trotter's *Instinct of the Herd,* books that absorbed us all in those days. He hated the "herd" as opposed to personality which all but disappeared in the universally-engulfing war-spirit. Yet *The Seven Arts* had been really worth preserving. As Romain Rolland wrote to us,—he whose *Jean-Christophe* was one of the Scriptures of that generation,—it was "the work of Americans who lived at the centre of the life of the world" and its purpose was "to achieve the fertile union of its great thoughts." It spoke for the young world of Randolph's own desire, a new international life, an interweaving of groups in all countries who shared the same culture and the same vision; and, although James Oppenheim wrote pacifist editorials and John Reed wrote *This Unpopular War,* it was really Randolph, ironically enough, who killed it. Robert Frost, who was on the staff of the magazine, expressed this fact in a jingle,

> In the Dawn of Creation that morning
> I remember I gave you fair warning
>   The arts are but six.
>   You add on Politics
> And the seven will all die a-Bourning.*

Elsie Clews Parsons, the daughter of Henry Clews, the banker, was an ethnologist who delighted in comparing the customs of primitive peoples with the customs of New York society. Randolph had met her through *The New Republic,* and, visiting her at Lenox, he said she had "ousted Miss Lowell from my bright foreground . . . After all, *I* am an ethnolo-

---

* Communicated to me by Louis Untermeyer, who was also one of the staff.

gist, and she is so clever and stimulating a one that she sets one's thoughts tumbling all over each other . . . such a fine adventurousness and command of life as she radiates. If you are interested in rare persons, there she is," he wrote to Elizabeth Shepley Sergeant. Elsie Clews Parsons spoke of the "tagging-on spouse problem" and told the story of a Barnard girl, thirsting for intellectual discussion, who accosted a young man in one of her classes with an opening, "Lovely weather we're having!" He replied, "Yes, *my wife* thinks it's charming," showing the non-existence of any conception of social freedom in graduate schools.

Meanwhile, *The New Republic* more or less closed its doors to Randolph, so that he was forced to do only translating and book-reviewing for *The Dial*. He had once looked upon translations, at least from the classics, as "implements of deadly sin that boys used to cheat with": his horror of them was "such as a saint might feel towards a parody of the Bible." *The New Republic* had never known just what to do with him and had been getting restive under the burden of paying him a hundred dollars a month for work they could not find space for, and now his anti-war position gave them an excuse for getting rid of him altogether. Feeling himself that war was what he once called an "upper-class sport," he ridiculed its programme of a "cosmically efficacious and well-bred war." He broke with John Dewey who had provided, he said, the theoretical basis for armed preparedness . . . "To those of us who have taken Dewey's philosophy almost as our American religion, it never occurred that values would be subordinated to technique . . . Surely that philosophy of Dewey's which we have been following so uncritically for so long breaks down almost noisily when it is used to grind out interpretation for the present crisis." Ellery Sedgwick wrote to Randolph that he could no

longer publish him after the hubbub of the *Seven Arts* articles; he even refused the superb essay on Cardinal Newman,
The Uses of Infallibility. Randolph argued that Newman put
dogma in a sort of storage-vault, while the interesting aspects
of life were left for discussion in the arena. Then *The Dial*
also refused to publish him, although, when Schofield Thayer
and Sibley Watson bought it, they planned, just before his
death, to make Randolph the political editor. Gilbert Seldes
later repeated a remark of Schofield Thayer that if Randolph
had lived he would have made him editor-in-chief. "The magazines I write for die violent deaths," Randolph said, "and all
my thoughts seem unprintable. If I start to write on public
matters I discover that my ideas are seditious, and if I start to
write a novel I discover that my outlook is immoral if not ob-
scene. What then is a literary man to do if he has to make his
living by his pen?" One might have said of him what Whitman said of Thomas Paine, "The tree with the best apples gets
the worst clubbing."

It was small consolation to Randolph that Jane Addams
wrote in praise of his article *The War and the Intellectuals*,
asking if the Women's Peace Party might make reprints of it,
for he thought of Jane Addams as a Lady Bountiful, con-
descending to her neighbours and exploiting their old-world
customs, crafts and music. Meanwhile, where was he living at
this time? "All my friends," he wrote to Alyse Gregory, "seem
to be living in the most charming apartments in a most admirably married way. I flit around from one to the other, a
homeless, helpless waif, eternally passing out into the cold
from their warm and confident firesides. It takes a strong soul
to handle one's own freedom." He lived for a while at 42 Bank
Street, in two small rooms, and he camped out for a few weeks
in Milligan Place in the half-furnished rooms of a friend who

was away. No doubt it was in one of these places that the young girl went to see him in Babette Deutsch's novel, *A Brittle Heaven.* There, as "Mark Gideon," he lived in his "narrow room, with its books, its huge desk, its sagging couch, its single piece of brilliant Indian embroidery to light the cracked wall." His retreat was "a sufficient cave for the anchoret that the war had made him . . . His articles, his serenely ironic, lucidly analytic articles, were being flung back at him even by his old friends, the liberals. He was blacklisted . . . He hated the war. It was destroying everything he cared about, the life of the mind, the contacts between races, the give and take of science, of art, the difficult business of rooting out the evils that stemmed from the old accepted economic system . . . He had a fiendish way of knowing what you were thinking and feeling even about yourself, even when you covered it up with the subtlest and most diverting camouflage. Mark [Randolph] took the leanest hint, the merest shadow of evidence, and worked backward from it, building, as he went, the whole fabric of your life. He would tell the books you had read, the books you had only tried and pretended to read. He knew the streets you walked most and the streets you'd never heard of." In some such way most of Randolph's friends, especially women, remembered him.

Randolph seemed to be nowhere wanted. He was generally barred out, and a Western business man named Bourne wrote to say that Randolph had disgraced the family name. He was excoriated and rejected. He had been classified, he wrote to his mother, as totally and permanently, mentally and physically, unfit for military service; but, facing the "state-obsessed herd" and "one hundred per cent Americanism," he continued to say that the duty of liberals was to remain apathetic to the war. Between the war and American promise one had to choose, for the effect of the war would be to impoverish American promise, and one should turn one's energies to promoting what was truly best in the country's life. The advocates of preparedness had been willing to spend millions on a universal military service that was neither universal nor educational nor productive, and could one not begin to organize a true national service that would help one to serve creatively toward the toning up of American life? For him, resentment against the war meant a vital consciousness of what we were seeking in life in America, and the spirit of William James, with its gay passion for ideas, had suggested a moral equivalent of war. Randolph asked, how can we all together serve America by really enhancing its life? William James, that inspiring prophet of the rising generation, had proposed a productive army of youth, warring against nature, and not against man, finding in drudgery, toil and danger the values that war and preparation for war had given. Randolph had in his mind a picture of a host of eager young people swarming over the land, spreading the knowledge of health, the knowledge of domestic science, gardening, tree planting, the care of roads. They might even come to the forcible rebuilding of slovenly farms and an imposition of cleanliness upon the American countryside.

Like Professor René Harding in Wyndham Lewis's *Self-Condemned*, Randolph had believed that the twentieth century was intended to be a new model. The liberal idealism of the nineteenth century would have eventuated in a twentieth-century rebirth, would have produced a new age of social justice, of tolerance, intelligence and decency, abolishing forever the evils of the bad old times, child labour, slavery, cruel sports, duelling and the ill treatment of animals. We had been standing, Randolph wrote, at the threshold of a better time.

The door was opening into promise, and now came this irrelevance of war. The monster had slammed the door, and it
might be a thousand years before it opened again; for men
stupid enough to resort to war were too stupid to make peace.
In this difficult time, when the fluid years were over, the light
that had been in liberals had become darkness, Randolph said,
and all sorts of sinister forces were still at work in what we
had supposed was an emancipating era. It seemed to him that
we were on a leaky boat, rudderless, captainless, pilotless, with
engines going at full speed. If the enterprise went on, the
work, so blithely undertaken for the defence of democracy,
would have crushed out the only genuinely precious thing in
the nation, the hope and ardent idealism of its youth.

"It is no fun being a free man in a slave-world," Randolph
wrote to one of his friends when Paul Rosenfeld was drafted
and he went to live in Irving Place in Paul's old rooms there.
Paul had introduced Randolph to Scriabine whose *Preludes*
and *Nocturnes* he was very fond of, and he said that Randolph "could manage the terrible stretches easily with his long
fingers." Randolph could get his mind off the war at times, he
could play duets with Waldo Frank, Waldo playing the cello
and Randolph the piano, and he wrote, a month before he
died, a fine criticism of George W. Cable in *The Dial*. But he
had begun to write a book about the State that he was to leave
unfinished. "Country," he said, "is a conception of peace, of
tolerance, of living and letting live. But State is essentially a
conception of power, of competition. It signifies a group in its
aggressive aspects . . . War is the health of the State. It automatically sets in motion throughout society those irresistible
forces for uniformity, for passionate coöperation with the government in coercing into obedience the minority groups and
individuals which lack the larger herd sense . . . In this great

herd-machinery, dissent is like sand in the bearings. The State ideal is primarily a sort of blind animal push towards military unity . . . All of which goes to show that the State represents all the automatic, arbitrary, coercive, belligerent forces within a social group. It is a sort of complexus of everything most distasteful to the modern free creative spirit, the feeling for life, liberty and the pursuit of happiness. War is the health of the State . . . It is the most noxious of all the evils that afflict man . . . Too many of the prophets [of war] are men who have lived rather briskly among the cruelties and thinnesses of American civilization and have shown no obvious horror and pity at the exploitations and the arid quality of the life lived here around us. Few of them had used their vision to create literature impelling us toward a more radiant American future . . . Their idealism is too new and bright to affect us, for it comes from men who never cared very particularly about great creative American ideas . . . Never having felt responsibility for labour wars and oppressed masses and excluded races at home, they had a large fund of idle emotional capital to invest in the oppressed nationalities and ravaged villages of Europe. Hearts that had felt only ugly contempt for democratic strivings at home beat in tune with the struggle for freedom abroad."

It was this book on the State that led John Dos Passos to write his poetical sketch of Randolph Bourne,—

> If any man has a ghost
> Bourne has a ghost,
> a tiny twisted unscared ghost in a black cloak
> hopping along the grimy old brick and brownstone streets
> still left in downtown New York,
> crying out in a shrill soundless giggle:
> *War is the health of the State.*

No doubt it was this book on the State that Emma Goldman had in mind when she said that Randolph "towered mountains high over the rest of the American young intelligentsia." Emma Goldman was writing in Berlin thirteen years after she had been deported from the United States.

Later, Theodore Dreiser paid tribute to Randolph. "In 1913 or 1914," Dreiser wrote, "there appeared a critic whose work interested me greatly. It was humanly sensitive as well as aesthetic. The view was large and the underlying natural understanding appeared to have been edged and clarified by experience. There was a gaiety, an optimism, a high sense of beauty and even a poetry of phrase;" and Dreiser described his meeting with Randolph: "It was an evening in late November or December or, possibly, January. I was in the vicinity of the old Night Court that stood at Tenth Street and Sixth Avenue. It was dark, and snow was falling, and, as I turned the corner at Sixth Avenue, I encountered as badly deformed and, at the moment, as I accepted it, as frightening a dwarf as I had ever seen. His body was so misshapen, the legs thin, the chest large, the arms long, the head deep sunk between the bony shoulders. More, the head was preternaturally large, with eyes the character of which I did not grasp at the moment. I did note, however, that the skull and even the mouth appeared to be a little askew; large ears flattened against the large skull, and, on top of that, a soft hat, of what colour I do not recall." Then there came "a knock on the door one late afternoon. There stood this same dwarf . . . He surveyed me now with what I saw to be large, clear and impressive blue eyes. He sat hunched in the chair I had given him, one knee crossed over the other, and continued to look at me with eyes which now were about all that I could see; and somehow the dwarfed body had by now as completely vanished as though it had never been and, in its place, was a mind, strong, tender, disarming, a mind that had suffered and had learned through suffering. It was truly a beautiful hour that he made for me . . . We passed into a warm, sympathetic understanding, and then, strangely enough, I saw before me, and even afterward, not a dwarf at all, but a tall, strong, powerful man whose body matched the fine mind that occupied it."

VII

Years before, Randolph had written in *Youth and Life,* "When we have acclimated ourselves to youth, suddenly death looms up as the greatest of dangers in our adventure of life. It puzzles and shocks and saddens by its irreversibility and mystery. That we should be taken out of this world to which we are so perfectly adapted, and which we enjoy and feel intimate with, is an incredible thing . . . The feeling of the precariousness of life gives the young man a sense of its preciousness; nothing shocks him quite so much as that it should be ruthlessly and instantly snatched away."

Randolph, who had always felt the rush of time past him, had gone to live a few days before his death at 18 West 8th Street, over the old City and Country School. There lived two young women, Agnes de Lima, engaged to be married, and Esther Cornell, with whom Randolph was in love. A Bryn Mawr girl, related to the founder of Cornell University, she had been on the stage in *Kismet* and *The Silent Voice.* She was extremely pretty, imaginative, gay, resilient, with eyes a greenish blue and copper-gold hair. She had an uncanny perception and insight into character, and Randolph had written to her from Hampton Institute, "I go on having delusions of grandeur that you could love me and be happy with me. All my life I have alternated delusions of greatness with the most cowering and abject feelings of worthlessness . . . Oh, what an adventure it would be to try to get the most out of life together!" Again he had written, "I loathe loggy knowledge, but your quality means light and air to me." In a fragment of another letter, written to some unknown person, he had written, "I did not spurn marriage without children. In that case, marriage seems, in the present state of public opinion, an exasperating but necessary evil, a sort of minimum socially-stamped ticket-of-leave to travel without annoyance. This is its use, and probably a valuable one." He had said, "I don't think my spirit is naturally roaming. But it has had to be restless because it does so awfully want an abiding place and has not found it. Or, if it did, it was torn and harried and treated more like a wayfarer taken in for the night than the friend found at last."

With Esther Cornell, he carried on his courtship largely through his music, Chopin's *Preludes,* Hugo Wolff's songs and MacDowell, and with her and Agnes de Lima he undertook to walk up to Martha's Vineyard in September, 1918. Esther had been taking lessons in "rhythmic dancing," and she was swaying and leaping about the rocks when they reached Cos Cob and saw a gunboat in the bay. There was a submarine scare at the time, and Randolph was afraid she might be supposed to be signalling; and indeed, the gunboat began to move along with them as they walked. At the end of two weeks they reached Martha's Vineyard, where they took rooms at the eastern end of the island, and, when Agnes de Lima was called back to New York, Esther and Randolph were left there alone. They were stopped in the street by a naval officer who cross-examined them and went to Boston with them in the train. But, lunching at the station, he telephoned his chief and reported that they were "just a couple of nuts." Randolph's letters had been opened by the censor and a trunk of his manuscripts had been lost between New York and Old Greenwich. Then he was challenged to explain a telegram which contained the mysterious word "Perfide." It looked like a code-word; there was nothing in English it could mean. But, nevertheless, he was not molested further.

About this time Randolph said to another girl that there were only eleven days' meals he could count on. He said this in irony but there were people who took his irony as matter of fact, and this was the secret of many of the fantastic stories that were told about him. He had, in fact, a philosophy of irony that, as he said, "forced his friends to move their rusty limbs and unhinge the creaking doors of their minds." Irony was thought to be synonymous with cynicism, and there were those who thought Randolph was cynical; whereas to him it had the free happy play of the Greek spirit, letting fresh air and light into the minds of others. "It was to the Greek," he said, "an incomparable method of intercourse, the rub of mind against mind by the simple use of simulated ignorance," and the ironist was always critically awake. Actually, driven to the wall as he was, he still had fairly large sums of money in two banks; and, when Esther Cornell all but promised to marry him, he was looking forward happily. But he was caught in the flu epidemic in December, 1918. He had said to Agnes de Lima, "One in every three persons gets it,—so one of us three will"; and, owing to his narrow chest, he died almost instantly. When he was dying he asked for an eggnog and exclaimed with pleasure over its gorgeous saffron colour.

Randolph was thirty-two years old. He was buried in Bloomfield from the Presbyterian church there. It was a dreary day, with a cold rain falling. The Abbott Thayers came to the funeral with others of his older friends; and Norman Thomas, at the time a clergyman, conducted the service. Lewis Mumford wrote, a little later, "Randolph Bourne was precious to us because of what he was rather than because of what he had actually written." In him one found "that mingling of passionate resolve and critical enquiry which was the very spirit of youth in America in 1914."

D